DATE DUE

THE DEVELOPMENT OF ROLE-TAKING AND
COMMUNICATION SKILLS IN CHILDREN

The Development of Role-Taking and Communication Skills in Children

John H. Flavell
University of Minnesota

IN COLLABORATION WITH

PATRICIA T. BOTKIN
University of California at Santa Barbara

CHARLES L. FRY, JR.
University of Virginia

AND

JOHN W. WRIGHT
University of Michigan

PAUL E. JARVIS
Mental Health Center, Fort Logan, Colorado

ROBERT E. KRIEGER PUBLISHING COMPANY
HUNTINGTON, NEW YORK
1975

Original Edition 1968
Reprint 1975

Printed and Published by
ROBERT E. KRIEGER PUBLISHING CO., INC.
645 NEW YORK AVENUE
HUNTINGTON, NEW YORK 11743

© Copyright 1968 by
JOHN WILEY & SONS, INC.
Reprinted by Arrangement

Printed in the United States of America

Library of Congress Cataloging in Publication Data

Flavell, John H
    The development of role-taking and communication
skills in children.

    Reprint of the ed. published by Wiley, New York.
    Bibliography: p.
    1. Social perception. 2. Communication--Psycholo-
gical aspects. 3. Child study. I. Title.
[BF723.S6F58 1975]   155.4'18   74-22477
ISBN 0-88275-238-3

Preface to the 1975 reprint edition of Flavell et al.,

The development of role-taking and communication skills in children

Two research topics are becoming increasingly popular in the fields of social and developmental psychology. One is the nature and development of social cognition, that is, the growth of the child's thinking and knowledge concerning human beings and their doings. The other is the relation, both during development and at maturity, between social cognition and actual social behavior. The subject matter of this book falls under both topics. Role-taking skills are social-cognitive skills, and the studies of their development described in this book are accordingly studies in the ontogenesis of social cognition. The book also reports research on the development of communication skills, with special emphasis on the contribution of the child's role-taking abilities to the construction of effective, listener-adapted communicative messages. But of course communication is as "social" as a behavior can be, and hence the pertinence of this research to the second topic.

The relevance of book to topics is not wholly coincidental. Some of the recent and current research on these topics is partly indebted to ideas, tasks, and findings contained within these covers, just as the latter built upon previous work by Piaget and others. Thus, we are immodest enough to believe that this book helped to create, beginning in 1968, the raison d'être of its own reprinting in 1975. We at least hope it still has a raison d'être in 1975, and are in any case very happy to see it back in print.

Preface

Adults normally spend a fair amount of their thinking time trying to make accurate guesses about the covert psychological properties of other people—about, for example, their abilities, knowledge, perceptions, attitudes, motives, and intentions with respect to this or that concrete situation. It is clearly adaptive for them to engage in this particular kind of guesswork (referred to as *role taking* in this book). Other human beings are our most important stimulus objects, after all, and making good inferences about what is going on inside these objects permits us some measure of understanding, prediction, and control in our daily interactions with them. It is apparent that this inclination and ability to delve beneath the surface attributes and actions of other individuals is a developmental product. The adult is clearly disposed and able to engage in this sort of social-cognitive activity; the infant manifestly is not; hence both disposition and ability must evolve during part or all of an intervening childhood.

The purpose of this book is to report and interpret an ensemble of research studies dealing with aspects of this evolution. Some of our investigations focus on the developmental acquisition of role-taking behavior considered primarily as a goal response, for instance, the child's growing ability to predict the visual experience of another person who views an object array from a perspective other than his own. In other investigations, the level of role-taking skill is inferred from behaviors that it presumably helps to mediate, in particular the construction of messages to other people; communications that are finely tuned to the informational needs of the listener normally presuppose an accurate prior reading of these needs on the part of the sender, that is, these communications comprise an end or goal response for which role taking serves as an important means. We have variously probed for these processes in the preschooler, the child of middle years, and the adolescent. And finally, we have looked into the possibility of hastening their development through systematic training procedures. In the course of our research in this area we believe we have clarified somewhat its developmental questions and problems, have accumulated a fair amount of preliminary but revealing factual evidence, and garnered some ideas about what one might do next.

We are most grateful to the various institutions and people who assisted us in carrying out these studies. We have acknowledged their specific contributions in the text and in footnotes. The bulk of our work was supported by two National Institute of Mental Health research grants: M-2268 to Flavell for the developmental studies; MH-07176 to Fry for one of the training studies. Much of this book was drafted by the senior author during a year's leave at the Laboratoire de Psychologie Génétique of the University of Paris. He expresses his gratitude to the University of Rochester and to the National Science Foundation for making the leave possible, and to Pierre Oléron, Alain Danset, and numerous others at the Laboratoire for making it so pleasant and memorable. We are also indebted to the following organizations for granting us permission to quote from their publications: Alfred A. Knopf, Inc., Holt, Rinehart, and Winston, Inc., and W. W. Norton and Company, Inc. of New York; The Journal Press, Provincetown, Mass.; University of California Press, Berkeley; Tavistock Publications, London; University of Chicago Press, Chicago; World Publishing Co., Cleveland; Stanford University Press, Stanford, Calif.; D. Van Nostrand Co., Inc., Princeton, N.J.; Massachusetts Institute of Technology Press, Cambridge; and American Psychological Association, Washington.

Contents

THE DEVELOPMENT OF ROLE-TAKING AND
COMMUNICATION SKILLS IN CHILDREN

CHAPTER ONE

Introduction

In a recent review of cognitive-developmental research, Wallach states:

In our examination of current research on the development of children's thinking, we obviously have concentrated on the child's knowledge of the physical world—i.e., on the traditional definition of thinking as reasoning, problem solving, and understanding, concerning the non-social environment. . . . The extent to which thinking about the social environment follows similar or different ontogenetic patterns must remain an open question at this point (1963, p. 270).

The research described in this book is concerned with the development of "thinking about the social environment," broadly defined, and was done to provide a tentative answer to the question which Wallach raises. Its major aim was to investigate the ontogenetic development of two important forms of social-cognitive behavior: (1) the general ability and disposition to "take the role" of another person in the cognitive sense, that is, to assess his response capacities and tendencies in a given situation; and (2) the more specific ability to use this understanding of the other person's role as a tool in communicating effectively with him. Piaget (Piaget, 1926; Flavell, 1963) and others have suggested that role-taking skills and communicative behaviors mediated by these skills do develop with age, but very little experimental work has been done to test their suggestions. Our principal effort has been to remedy this lack in part by undertaking a preliminary, broad-spectrum study of the problem.

THE RESEARCH STRATEGY

In any maiden research effort in a relatively unstudied area of inquiry, the investigator is very likely to find himself beset with decision problems. There are usually a variety of possible ways to begin and

1

the problem is to choose one. But which one? Once the first step is somehow decided upon and taken, which of the available second steps should then be followed? And so the decision making continues until the research program comes to its natural (or usually, unnatural) terminus. The decisions made at each choice point are obviously not randomly made. Rather, they derive, in part at least, from some superordinate research strategy or overall plan of action. And this strategy in turn emerges from a still more general context of beliefs and attitudes about what sorts of data are judged most important or interesting to obtain, and in what sequence they ought to be sought after during the course of the research program.

In the present case, there definitely was such a context and associated strategy, and the nature and sequence of our experiments derived from it in large measure. Since we doubt that our frame of reference is a commonly held one in contemporary child psychology, an attempt is made here to explain it. In general, our approach to the developmental study of role taking and communication was that of what might be termed a *developmental naturalist*. That is, we were above all interested in trying to glean from our research a detailed but essentially non-causal-analytic picture of a variety of developing subskills within the role-taking and communication domains. The aim was to get a perspective on what sorts of things develop at roughly what ages in the domain, an overview which would, however, be well-fleshed with a lot of concrete developmental data about responses to a wide range of domain-relevant tasks. We wanted to end up being able to answer the question of what develops here by saying: "Well, this subskill develops, and this, and this, and so on; moreover, X comes in quite early, Y a little later, and Z is a very late, middle-adolescence acquisition." In sum, we wanted above everything else to become as broadly and deeply knowledgeable as we could about the basic ontogenetic patterning in this area in all its qualitative diversity.

This research prospectus may sound like an all-encompassing one—even a trifle grandiose, perhaps—and it may be asked what is omitted from it. A great deal, actually. Above all, it leaves out the whole causal and correlational network in which these skills are undoubtedly embedded. The data from our studies, as will be shown, do not provide answers to questions of the following sort. What is the factor structure of role-taking and communication skills at any given age? What are the ontogenetic antecedents of individual differences in these skills, for example, social class background, parent-child relations, prior cognitive and linguistic learning experiences, and possible genetic-constitutional contributions? And analogously, what contemporaneous variables are associated with these individual differences, for example, general intelligence, academic achievement, and current social relations with peers and adults?

Answers to these and similar questions are obviously crucial to a full developmental and structural understanding of role-taking and communication abilities. Developmental psychologists of all orientations would agree on this point, the developmental naturalist no less than others. But there might well be differences of opinion—and ultimately therefore of research strategy and tactics—as regards the timetable according to which they are scheduled for investigation; here we return to the earlier point about the sequence of decisions in a time-limited research program. The strategy of the developmental naturalist is purposely to withhold questions of precise structural and, particularly, causal relationships until the developmental territory at large has been submitted to a searching, but nonetheless essentially descriptive, surveying-and-mapping operation. He prefers to defer a causal-analytic, *antecedent-consequent* as opposed to *developmental-descriptive* (Flavell, 1963, pp. 422-424) attack on the problem until the dependent variable, the "consequent" itself, has been at least roughly differentiated into some of its constituent subskills and the gross ontogenetic profile for each subskill plotted.

The developmental naturalist believes that the data from this extensive search-and-plot operation are intrinsically interesting and valuable. They can convey a vivid picture of the variety of different behaviors children are prone to engage in at different developmental levels, in an area where there had previously been no clear picture. In the field of child development particularly, it is usually rewarding to "see what" without yet "understanding how." These preliminary data may also provide grist for hypothesis testing of a developmental genre; it will be seen, for example, that we attempted to use certain of our data to check our theoretical expectations. But most important perhaps—and certainly most important from the point of view of the non-naturalist—such data provide just the kind of first-order purview of these burgeoning skills needed to plan intelligent studies of the causal-analytic, antecedent-consequent sort. Knowing one's way around the surface contours of a new psychological domain is a valuable if not indispensable requisite for more searching and analytic explorations.

Our research strategy, then, was to confine our efforts largely (but not quite exclusively, it turned out) to the preliminary business of contour tracing. The details of the strategy were as follows. The first step was to work out an overall conceptualization of the general skill area with particular emphasis, of course, on its developmental aspects. Drawing upon previous theory and research, we tried to construct a generalized picture of what role-taking and verbal-communication skills might entail, how they might be related to each other, and what sorts of developmental changes they might be expected to show. (Needless to say, this was not so much a step as a process, the analysis undergoing continual revisions and refinements as we went along.)

The second step consisted of differentiating a number of more specific subskills within the general role-taking and communication skill area. This amounted essentially to spelling out what appeared to be the implications of our initial conceptualization. For instance, our generalized picture of the nature of role taking would lead us to think that the ability to do X might be a role-taking subskill, and so might the rather different-looking capacity to do Y, or the ability to perform Z, and so on. The developmental-naturalistic orientation was particularly intrusive at this step in the strategy. For what we tried to do was to work downward from the abstract picture towards the specification of a whole range of diverse capacities, each one putatively a concrete instance or expression of role-taking or/and communication skills. It was in this sense that most of the research program could be thought of as a contour-tracing affair, as a preliminary search for interesting developable "consequents" in this area of social cognition.

The third step was to find tasks that looked as if they would be appropriate measures of these derivative skills. Since in most instances there were no already-existent tasks relevant to these skills, we found ourselves spending a good deal of time inventing and pretesting new measures. And finally, of course, we administered these tasks to children at different age levels and analyzed the developmental data so obtained.

The next section presents the outcome of step one: a general analysis of the nature and development of role-taking and communication skills. The concluding section offers some context and background for the schema by way of a review of the pertinent research and theoretical literature. And Chapters 2 to 6 deal with the subsequent steps, that is, they define the derivative skills, the tasks which purport to measure them, and the procedures and findings of the developmental investigations which made use of these tasks.

THE NATURE AND DEVELOPMENT OF ROLE-TAKING
AND COMMUNICATION SKILLS

As they grow and develop, children typically acquire a wide array of knowledges and skills with respect to the objects in their milieu, both human and nonhuman. An important subset of their acquisitions regarding human objects, that is, in the area of social learning, undoubtedly includes that complex of abilities which have been variously called *role taking, role perception, role playing, role enactment, empathy, person perception,* and the like. Piaget (1926) long ago argued that the child is at first an *egocentric* organism, unwittingly the prisoner of his own individual perspective and largely ignorant of and unconcerned with the differing perspectives of other people. One of the principal purposes of our research program was to examine in detail the developmental progression from this initial egocentrism toward the acquisition of various skills of the role-taking variety.

Just what are these "various skills of the role-taking variety" for which there appear to be so many confusing near-synonyms in the literature? Our own analysis closely follows that given in Sarbin's review of the area (1954), although diverging from it at certain points.[1] The basic and essential ingredient of any sort of skill sequence in this area appears to us to be that process in which the individual somehow cognizes, apprehends, grasps—whatever term you prefer—certain attributes of another individual. The attributes in question are primarily of the type that could be described as inferential rather than directly perceptible, for example, the other's needs, his intentions, his opinions and beliefs, and his emotional, perceptual or intellectual capacities and limitations. Tagiuri and Petrullo have in mind the same class of attributes in their definition of person perception:

> Indeed, when we speak of person perception or of knowledge of persons, we refer mostly to the observations we make about *intentions, attitudes, emotions, ideas, abilities, purposes, traits*—events that are, so to speak, inside the person (1958, p. x).

The role taker's estimate of these attributes is normally a synthesis of information from two sources: (a) his knowledge of people and their behavior in various situations (including, perhaps, some previous knowledge of this particular other and his habits); (b) perceptual input from the overt behavior of the other or from other cue sources in the immediate situation. Using Sarbin's terminology, we would say that the estimate is thus based on an integration of the subject's preexisting *role expectations* and his current *role perception* (1954). And finally, the estimate-taking process may be a deliberate and conscious action on the subject's part, but it need not and frequently will not be; likewise, the

[1]Sarbin's masterful survey also offers a detailed treatment of aspects of role theory which are not immediately relevant to our research and are therefore not included in the present analysis, for example, a discussion of social roles and an account of the development of the self.

process may be either very brief or considerably extended in time. This basic process of obtaining information about the other's internal events needs a title which will distinguish it from other processes in the role-taking domain. We prefer to call it the *discrimination of role attributes* in the other: *discrimination* is a suitably noncommittal name for the little-understood cognitive and perceptual activities through which the subject gains his information about the other, and *role attributes* is abstract enough to cover the host of inferrable properties of the other about which information may be sought.

We believe that the discrimination of role attributes is most profitably conceptualized as an act or process which forms a part, but *only* a part, of a larger context of motives and behavior. The context itself may vary considerably, however, and it is this variation which makes both for a proliferation of terms in this area (*role taking, role playing,* etc.) and for their all too frequent vagueness. The discrimination of role attributes is normally an initial instrumental act within the context, a first step in a chain of events directed toward some ulterior goal. Thus, we discriminate another's role attributes, not for its own sake, but for some reason, and what we do next with the information so obtained will depend upon what that reason was. An adequate overview of behavior in the general role-taking domain therefore requires an examination, not of role-attribute discrimination alone, but also of the variety of contexts in which it is observed.

Sarbin (p. 282) has made a good beginning classification of such contexts. He makes an important distinction between *role enactment* and *role taking*. In the former, the subject actually takes on the role attributes of the other and behaves overtly in accordance with them (for example, the child who plays the mother's role vis-à-vis her dolls, or the man who acts the part of an executive once he is promoted to this position). The latter refers to the more covert, more exclusively cognitive process of adopting the perspective or attitude of another, silently "putting yourself in his shoes" in a given situation. More generally, a distinction can be made between two major types of contexts in which role-attribute discrimination figures as an initial, instrumental response.

First, there are those cases (Sarbin's *role enactment*) where the discrimination process is followed by a literal and overt assumption of those attributes of the other which the process has uncovered; that is, one first determines the nature of the other's role (be it a socially defined, enduring role or some transistory one which the culture has not named), and then one proceeds to fulfill that role oneself. As Sarbin has shown (pp. 232-235), there is considerable variation among contexts of this type. They vary, for example, in the extent to which the whole self participates in the enactment of the role: there are casual roles (for example, customer in a supermarket) which one assumes with minimal organismic involvement; there are others in which the involvement is extremely intense and well-nigh complete (for example, states of ecstasy, or of taking the role of a moribund person in cases of Voodoo death); and there are numerous intermediate subtypes. There is also variation in the extent to which the role behavior one has adopted is carried out overtly. Sarbin points out, for example, that the empathic response, normally a more or less covert affair, *can* become overt (for example, one may shudder and grimace when another recounts a painful or terrifying experience he has had); cognitive behavior in the role-taking area will sometimes "spill over" into action, as he puts it (p. 232). As a further complication regarding the overtness-covertness dimension, Maccoby (1959) has suggested that many adult social roles (for example, that of "mother") are initially practiced covertly during childhood, preparatory to later, overt enactment.

The second major type includes all the remaining contexts and is the one most pertinent to our research. Here, the subject begins as usual by discriminating the other's role attributes and will frequently go beyond this to assume these attributes, but only briefly and covertly (Sarbin's *role taking*). However, this role assumption does not then progress very far toward overt role enactment and, above all, the *motives* for doing the discriminating and temporary assuming are something *other* than those which prompt full-fledged role enactment. That is, the goal behavior is not role enactment per se, with whatever rewards normally accrue to it (see Maccoby, 1959, for a discussion of some instigating conditions for role enactment). Rather, the subject seeks out the other's role attributes, not to *play out* his role, but to *understand* it—and understand it from his own, still active role position vis-à-vis the other.

In some cases this act of understanding is itself the only immediate objective, and does not serve as an instrumental response to other actions immediately following. For example, most of us sometimes play the part of observers of the human scene, simply curious about how person X sees the world, about "what makes him tick," with no thought of doing anything more useful with what we discover than satisfying our curiosity. The information-seeking motive is a powerful one in human beings, and it can be directed toward role attributes as well as toward other events in the milieu.

Often, however, the act of understanding does serve as a means to one's subsequent behavior, the latter generally being in some sense complementary to the behavior of the other. For example, the other is our opponent in some kind of a contest, perhaps a competitive game, and our understanding of his role attributes helps to govern our own strategy and tactics. Or the other is, on the contrary, our collaborator or fellow team member in some joint enterprise, and our knowledge of his role attributes and derivative behaviors will again maximize the effectiveness of our own actions in furthering the enterprise. Or the other is trying to convey a subtle, hard-to-characterize feeling he has experienced, and your ability to grasp how it felt to him will determine your next response and, perhaps, the whole course of the subsequent interchange between you (psychotherapy is a familiar prototype here).

There are obviously many everyday examples of this general type: in all cases, the essential process consists of discriminating the other's role attributes for the purpose of—a vague but inclusive expression is needed here—"behaving appropriately" toward him, within the confines of one's *own* role. One important subtype to which we have given considerable research attention in the present investigation is the case where role-attribute discrimination facilitates effective verbal communication directed toward the other. Piaget called attention to this apparent dependence of effective communication on role-taking skills in his early writings (1926), and also gave the relationship a developmental cast by arguing that the younger child's egocentrism seriously hampers his ability to communicate with others. Our analysis here is essentially an elaboration of his. To the extent that the child fails to discriminate those role attributes of the other which are relevant to the sort of message the child should send to the other, in the latter's role as listener, to that extent is the message likely to be ill-adapted to the other's informational needs and hence inadequately communicative. Conversely, to the extent that the child does take an accurate measure of the other's listener role attributes, and then actively uses this knowledge to shape and adapt his message accordingly, to that extent ought the communication be an effective, nonegocentric one. An important part of what is involved in effective communicating might be conceptualized as a coding-then-recoding process, in which the recoding component is "monitored," so to speak, by role-taking activity. An ineffective, egocentric communication, on the other hand, is essentially arrested at the initial, coding step of the process. The following is a schematization of the probable microdevelopment involved in each type of communication.

Egocentric Communication

1. *S* (speaker) cognizes X (data) and covertly codes them so that they are meaningful and "communicable" to himself.

2. *S* sends *L* (listener) a message about X. The message is in all important respects unrecoded, that is, it is essentially a simple externaliza-

tion without modification of his private coding and is hence an egocentric communication (see Figure 1).

Figure 1. Schema of egocentric communication.

Nonegocentric Communication

1. S cognizes X and covertly codes it for himself, just as in step 1 above.

2. Prior to and/or during his communication to L (step 3 below), S attempts to discriminate those role attributes of L which appear to be pertinent to L's ability to decode communicative input regarding X.

3. S recodes X and externalizes it as a message to L about X. This recoding-and-externalization process occurs under the aegis of two concurrent (and related) activities: (a) S uses the information gained in step 2 to shape and fashion the message in such a way as to maximize the likelihood that it will meet L's communicative needs; (b) S actively suppresses the insistent and recurring tendency to allow his message to drift or "regress" toward the initial coding of step 1 (the egocentric error), a tendency which exists by virtue of the fact that this initial coding is both continuously and intrusively present in S's consciousness and, by definition, is communicatively adequate for him, that is, communicatively satisfying from his point of view (see Figure 2).

The schematization just presented is of course a simplified one, and there are other important factors which qualify and complicate it. In the first place, the aim of a communicative message is not always simply

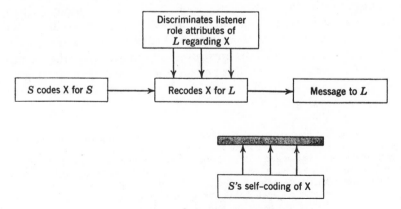

Figure 2. Schema of nonegocentric communication.

to *inform* the listener, as the preceding discussion would imply. For example, some communications are intended to be *persuasive*, that is, to move the listener toward some specified course of action. Although we did do one developmental investigation of persuasive communication (IIC),[2] most of our research dealt with the former, information-giving type of message. Likewise, our thinking and research has been almost exclusively focussed on *oral* communication. While the present schematization ought in principle to apply to *written* and *gestural* messages too, it might well require some emendations to fit these special cases.

Second, the sequences of events shown in Figures 1 and 2 and described above probably do no more than approximate what happens in real-life communicative acts. In the first place, it seems likely that the major components of nonegocentric, affective communication do not really occur in a single, fixed sequence, but rather alternate and interweave in diverse ways throughout the course of the entire communicative act. For instance, after a part of the message has already been sent, the speaker may return to the data, code some hitherto unnoticed aspect, recode it, perhaps reject that recoding on the basis of a further look at the listener's role attributes, recode again, externalize this recoding as a new addition to the message, return again to the data, etc., etc. Also, the basic distinction we have made between coding for self and recoding for other may itself not always be a clear one. Zajonc (1960) has shown, for example, that if the subject is aware that the information he is coding is to be communicated later, he will tend to code it in a particular way, presumably for easier recoding when it comes time to construct his message; under these conditions, the initial coding seems already to approach a recoding, is already a kind of "prerecoding." Our model of egocentric communication may likewise be too simple. In particular, it may well be that the child's private and covert coding must always differ *somewhat* from its externalized expression as a message to another person, no matter how incognizant he may be of the other's role attributes, *qua* listener.[3] If this be true, the situation given in Figure 1 is best regarded as an idealized one which egocentric communications approach, but never quite reach.

[2]Most of our studies (those described in Chapters 2 to 5) involved the administration of a battery of tasks, in a constant sequence, to a sample of children. For easier reference, each study will be labelled with a Roman numeral, and each task by a capital letter which gives its position in the sequence. Thus IIC refers to the third task of the series of five which were administered in Study II (described in Chapter 4).
[3]Vygotsky's (1962) interesting speculations about the differences between covert and overt coding are relevant to this point, and will be discussed in the next section of this chapter.

There is a final qualification which is especially important to keep in mind: although it is our view that role-attribute discrimination ordinarily lends a powerful assist to the communicative process, in the manner previously described, we do not regard it as a *sufficient* condition for the construction of an effective message nor, in certain special cases perhaps, even a *necessary* one. It cannot be a sufficient condition because there are other, what appear to be different, skills which also contribute. For example, the subject can scarcely communicate data X adequately if his perceptual and cognitive abilities are inadequate to code it properly for himself at the outset; that which cannot be discriminated can manifestly not be communicated. In the same way, an effective verbal message obviously presupposes a set of already-developed verbal skills, for example, an adequate vocabulary, and the ability to construct clear sentences and arrange them in a communicatively useful sequence. This is not to suggest that perceptual-cognitive skills, verbal skills, and the disposition and ability to discriminate role attributes comprise three distinct and noninteracting behavior domains. Just how difficult it is to set boundary lines here will be pointed out in the next section, in connection with Piaget's theory. Nonetheless, the reference to sufficient conditions here is still worth making, at least as a general principle. However frequent or rare its occurrence in reality, one can at least imagine the case where the speaker has probingly discriminated all relevant role attributes in the listener and nonetheless cannot communicate effectively because he lacks the requisite perceptual, cognitive, or verbal equipment.[4]

There is also a situation where role-attribute discrimination ought not even be necessary for effective communication, namely, where the listener role attributes of speaker and listener coincide; here, the speaker's externalized self-coding should in principle be as communicable to the listener as it is to himself. Although this situation may never quite be realized in everyday life, it certainly must be approached at times. The fact of its existence has an interesting methodological implication for research on the development of a functional liaison between role-attribute discrimination and communicative behavior. The implication is that one can *only* detect the workings of the former on the latter

---

[4]In order to keep things at a manageable level of complexity, we have been assuming a more or less constant input capacity on the listener's part. In reality, however, this capacity is, of course, another vital determinant of the success or failure of a given communication. In the example above, for instance, it may be the listener, rather than the speaker, who lacks the necessary tools to make the message successful; or conversely, his superior "communicative receptors" may yet save the day in the case of an unendowed speaker. See Piaget (1926, ch. 3) and Fry (1961) for a more extended discussion of the listener's role in the communicative interaction.

in experimental situations where the role attributes of speaker and listener are certain to *differ* in some substantial way. If they do so differ, one has the possibility of distinguishing, on the basis of what the communicative product looks like, those subjects who have been attending to the listener's attributes from those who, in egocentric fashion, have not. If the two sets of role attributes are similar, on the other hand, one can make no such distinction, since there will be no inferential basis for it in the communication protocols (that is, the one message is just as likely to be adapted to the listener's input needs as the other). As will be seen in subsequent chapters, we tried to heed this implication in the construction of our role-taking and communication tasks.

To recapitulate, it has been suggested that the common component of all behavior in the general role-taking area is the discrimination of the other's role attributes. This discriminative act functions as an instrumental response within two broad types of behavioral and motivational contexts, overt role enactment and a residual, hard-to-label category in which the discriminative act may serve a variety of interpersonal purposes. In the present research, our interest in these various phenomena has been primarily "developmental-naturalistic," that is, oriented toward a descriptive-level examination of their acquisition across the period of childhood. Furthermore, virtually all of our attention has been focussed on developmental happenings in the residual category, although we did include one small investigation of role-enactment skills (IID). And within the residual category, many of the studies dealt with the communication subcategory specifically, that is, where role-attribute discrimination is instrumental to something else (for example, IA, IIA). An attempt was made here to construct communication tasks which would highlight the contributions of role-attribute discrimination (as opposed to the other types of factors mentioned earlier) and which would permit us to infer its presence or absence in the child's communicative behavior. Other studies dealt with a variety of noncommunication subcategories, for example, where role-attribute discrimination is instrumental in playing a competitive game with another individual (IB), and instrumental in predicting his cognitve (ID) and perceptual (IC) response in a given situation. Finally, we departed from our developmental-naturalistic orientation in two studies which explored educational techniques for improving children's communication and role-taking abilities (Chapter 6).

PREVIOUS THEORY AND RESEARCH

A survey of all writings which are in one way or another "relevant" to this research area would be lengthy indeed, and the review which follows is by no means exhaustive. On the contrary, it is decidedly selective in its coverage. Major emphasis is given to theory and research dealing with the sort of role-taking and communication phenomena which have been of central concern in our own thinking and research. Thus, for instance, higher priority is assigned to communication theory and research which feature role-attribute discrimination as an important instrumentality; to writings on role taking of the residual versus role-enactment types; and to developmental versus nondevelopmental approaches. And finally, we have adopted the space-saving expedient of simply citing previous reviews, instead of trying to duplicate their coverage, especially in the case of bodies of theory and research judged to be of lesser relevance.

Theoretical Contributions

Our conceptualization of role-taking and communication behavior and development has a number of theoretical ancestors. Although research follow-up, especially of a developmental sort, has not been extensive, theoretical ideas similar to those presented in the preceding section have frequently been voiced over the past few decades. In several major instances, moreover, the theorist has, as we have done, singled out as especially important the case where role-attribute discrimination serves as an instrument of communication. Although choices here are a little arbitrary, there appear to be three individuals whose writings in this area are of particular importance: Mead, Piaget, and Vygotsky. We shall begin with these three, highlighting the essential contributions of each and trying to show how they complement each other in building an integrated conception of role taking and communication. Subsequently, evidence of the ubiquitousness of their ideas will be given by citing parallel views in the writings of others; and finally, there will be a brief account of other, recent theoretical developments in the field. There are several useful sources to which the reader can turn for aspects of the problem not dealt with here (Sarbin, 1954; Strunk, 1957; Taft, 1955; Tagiuri and Petrullo, 1958).

According to Mead, the fundamental human acquisition is the capacity to utilize what he calls *significant symbols* (Mead, 1947; Smith, 1946). The basic paradigm is a two-person, communicative interaction in which person *A* makes a gesture which *B* perceives (the term "gesture" is used in the broadest possible sense to include any observable behavior on *A*'s part, but with special attention given to verbal communication). This gesture is a significant symbol if it calls out the same response (or the covert analogue thereof) in *A* that it calls out in *B*, that is, if *A* shares *B*'s cognition—"takes his role"—with respect to that gesture. By this definition, a dog who growls menacingly at another dog is making a gesture which is not a significant symbol, since there is no reason to infer that the gesture is a stimulus for the same response in the first dog as it is for the second (for example, fear and withdrawal). Thus, meaningful human communication, entailing significant symbols:

> . . . involves not only communication in the sense in which birds and animals communicate with each other, but also an arousal in the individual himself of the response which he is calling out in the other individual, a taking of the role of the other, a tendency to act as the other person acts. (Mead, 1947, p. 183).

And again:

> Gestures become significant symbols when they implicitly arouse in an individual making them the same responses which they explicitly arouse, or are supposed to arouse, in other individuals, the individuals to whom they are addressed . . . (ibid., p. 180).

Mead appears to make this process of significant symbol formation the cornerstone of the development of all behavior which is uniquely human. Initially, the child only apprehends the attitude of particular others towards his own gestures, but gradually they coalesce for him into the attitudes which whole groups in the society possess in common, that is, into the attitudes of what Mead calls the *generalized other*:

> I have pointed out, then, that there are two general stages in the full development of the self. At the first of these stages, the individual's self is constituted simply by an organization of the particular attitudes of other individuals toward himself and toward one another in the specific social acts in which he participates with them. But at the second stage in the full development of the individual's self that self is constituted not only by an organization of these particular individual attitudes, but also by an organization of the social attitudes of the generalized other or the social group as a whole to which he belongs (ibid., p. 186).

As this passage suggests, the formation of the self system is one of the "uniquely human" acquisitions founded on this process. Another is effective social interaction of all types including, of course, verbal communication. Still another, but less obvious, derivation is that thinking itself is a kind of role-taking affair, involving the same basic process as other, more public and social activities. Mead describes thinking as an "internalized conversation of gestures" and suggests that the most "generalized" of generalized others, the reference group which includes the most members, is that defined by the "logical universe of discourse," consisting of the community of rational thinkers (ibid., p. 185).

The relevance of Mead's theory to our own conception is apparent.

In the first place, he has in his notion of the significant symbol provided a rough but useful definition of intentional, deliberate communication, as distinguished from the plethora of other situations—often loosely called "communicative"—where the behavior of one individual is the stimulus for a response by another. And second, it is obviously relevant because of the central place accorded to communication and role taking in the development of human behavior—the primitive situation in which the significant symbol arises, it will be recalled, is none other than a communicative one, and moreover, a communicative one in which something like role-attribute discrimination is deeply implicated. Mead's writings have thus made it difficult for all subsequent theorists, both to ignore the importance of communication processes in human development, and to ignore the importance of role taking in communicative processes.

However, one should not read more into Mead's theory than it actually asserts, and there are in fact several crucial things which one cannot readily draw from it in constructing an adequate picture of role taking and communication. It is hard to convey what the theory lacks in this respect without caricaturing it, that is, without making it appear more simplistic and oblivious to important problems than is really the case. However, the basic difficulty can be described as follows. Although the theory is, as we have shown, vitally concerned with role taking and communication, it curiously enough does *not* provide—*qua* theory—for role-taking and communication *difficulties* or *errors* in the individual performing these acts, and hence does not really deal with the developmental process by which the difficulties are gradually surmounted and the errors gradually diminished.

Although Mead, of course, acknowledges the fact of individual differences in adult attributes (1947, p. 189), his theoretical constructs (significant symbols and generalized others) are basically mechanisms for generating sameness, for creating interindividual homogeneity. Because of this, there are important interpersonal paradigms of which Mead the theorist cannot take due account. In particular, there is the situation where A and B have markedly different role attributes; here, any role taking and communication which A carries out vis-à-vis B must have a problem-solving character, if the former process is to be accurate and the latter process to be effective. That is, A must actively search out the crucial differences between his own orientation and B's and, if a communication to B is in order, use the fruits of this search in forging an informative, recoded message. By virtue of the ubiquitousness of adult differences in role attributes—momentary, situational ones as well as the more enduring, characterological ones—this kind of situation is the rule rather than the exception in adult human interactions. In consequence, accurate discrimination of role attributes and effective communication will still pose problems, will still require the utilization of certain skills, even after the incorporation of the generalized other has taken place. The question then remains, whence come these skills? Although Mead's theory has developmental aspects to it, they do not explicitly pertain to the development of *these* skills. The capacity to make use of significant symbols, for example, is indeed a developmental affair (Mead, 1947, pp. 179-182), but it appears to entail a development which is different from and prior to the one of which we speak, although obviously related to it. The two-year-old who looks at his mother, points to the household pet, and says "Doggie" has met at least the minimal requirements for Mead's acquisition. The ten-year-old who can picture to himself how an object in front of him appears to a friend standing on the opposite side of it, and who simplifies his message when explaining something to his three-year-old brother—he is well on the way to acquiring the kind of skills we have in mind. Mead defines a significant symbol as a gesture which arouses the same response in both A and B; what he does not deal with is how A acquires the ability to discern B's qualities as a responder generally, and in particular how he acquires the ability to select those gestures which will, in fact, arouse the same response in B.

It would be redundant to present an extended discussion of Piaget's views (for example, Piaget, 1926; Flavell, 1963), since they have in large measure already been expressed in the previous section's conceptualization of role taking and communication. It is enlightening, however, to contrast them on key points with those of Mead. First, Mead took the communication situation as his theoretical point of departure and derived from it, among other things, a conception of thinking (thought is an internalized conversation of gestures, etc.). Piaget, on the other hand, drew his notions about communication from a prior analysis of cognition. As indicated earlier, he asserted that a fundamental and pervasive quality of the young child's thought is its egocentrism, consisting of a general incognizance of the notion of "points of view," and hence a lack of awareness of how the child's own may differ from other people's. His cognitive field of vision includes the data thought about, but not the process of thinking itself. Insensitive to the very fact that the way he construes the data is only one construction among many possible (because the construing process itself never becomes an object of thought), it follows that he can scarcely check for cognitive bias in his own view of events, can scarcely inquire about the difference between this and other views, and so on. Thus, intellectual egocentrism is fundamentally an inability to take roles; it is an inability, in our terms, to search out the role attributes of others, compare them with one's own, and make effective use of the comparison in any of a variety of adaptations.

The variety of adaptations is indeed large: Piaget suggests that egocentrism taints the child's efforts in virtually all spheres of activity. For example, his primitive conceptions about the physical world (among which are animistic beliefs) are thought to be an egocentric product (Flavell, 1963, ch. 8). In the same way, egocentrism gives rise to curious attitudes about moral-ethical phenomena (ibid.). And finally, it casts its shadow over the spectrum of interpersonal activities which require role-taking ability including, of course, verbal communication:

There is no reason to believe that cognitive egocentrism, marked by unconscious preferential focusing, or by a lack of differentiation of viewpoints, has no application to the field of interpersonal relations, in particular those which are expressed in language. To take an example from adult life, every beginning instructor discovers sooner or later that his first lectures were incomprehensible because he was talking to himself, so to say, mindful only of his own point of view. He realizes only gradually and with difficulty that it is not easy to place oneself in the shoes of students who do not yet know what he knows about the subject matter of his course (Piaget, 1962, p. 5).

It is clear from the above that Piaget also differs from Mead in attending to the disparity in role attributes which may exist between individuals, and hence to the fact that role-taking and communication situations are frequently problem-solving situations requiring considerable skill for their solution. And from this it is but a short step to the view that such skills are slowly acquired during childhood, with corresponding developmental changes in role-taking and communication behavior. In contrast to Mead, Piaget expended both a great deal of thought and some ingenious experimentation (for example, Piaget, 1926; Piaget and Inhelder, 1956) on this developmental problem. His research evidence led him to believe that the inroads of egocentrism on communication and related interpersonal skills are especially pronounced up to the early school years:

How then are we to characterize the stage of understanding between children before the age of 7 or 8? It is no paradox to say that at this level, understanding between children occurs only in so far as there is contact between two identical mental schemas already existing in each child . . . [in other words, in those cases which demand no role taking on the speaker's part]. In all other cases the explainer talks to the empty air. He has not, like the adult, the art of seeking and finding in the other's mind some basis on which to build [in our terms, recode] anew (Piaget, 1926, p. 133).

After age 7–8, the child gradually rids himself of the egocentric illusion, and begins to use role-taking techniques to make his communications adaptive. The decline in egocentrism is believed to result from reinforcements—often negative ones, it appears—issuing from interactions with peers:

> . . . social interaction is the principal liberating factor, particularly social interaction with peers. In the course of his contacts (and especially, his conflicts and arguments) with other children, the child increasingly finds himself forced to reexamine his own percepts and concepts in the light of those of others, and by so doing, gradually rids himself of cognitive egocentrism (Flavell, 1963, p. 279).

We alluded earlier to the problem of distinguishing among the various factors which contribute to the quality of a communicative message— especially, role-taking skills versus perceptual, cognitive, and linguistic ones. Piaget's conceptualization sheds some light on this difficult problem. His analysis implies that the child's role-taking deficiencies (that is, his egocentrism), may contribute to the inadequacy of the final message in two ways. First, there is the straightforward effect we have been discussing all along, that is, these deficiencies prevent the child from assessing listener role attributes for the purpose of adapting the message to the listener's needs. Second, they are regarded as also influencing the perceptual, cognitive and linguistic factors themselves; this is the intellectual versus the social side of Piaget's egocentrism concept. According to Piaget, the fact that the child is continually a prisoner of his own point of view adversely affects his perceptual and cognitive discriminations, and also his comprehension and use of the language. Since these factors are, as we have said, of undoubted importance in shaping both the child's initial self-coding and his ability to recode, we have here a second, more indirect effect of role-taking deficiencies on the final communicative output. The causal structure here can be illustrated by a simple diagram. Figure 3 depicts the two "routes" by which the child's generalized egocentrism could affect this output. At the top, there is its

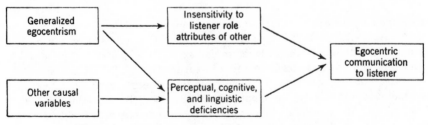

Figure 3. **Causal structure of egocentric communication.**

direct and concrete expression in the form of insensitivity to the listener's role attributes. The first diagonal arrow represents its contribution to deficiencies in the perceptual, cognitive and linguistic skills which, in addition to sensitivity to role attributes, are presumed necessary for the construction of an effective message (the two diagonal arrows on the right). It would be too extreme to suppose that egocentrism is the *only* factor which sets limits on these skills, hence the lower, left-hand box in the diagram. Since the origin of nonrole-taking factors in communication is not of central interest to us, we shall not try to speculate about these "other causal variables"; presumably, they would be of the genre of insufficient practice and experience in making discriminations, in linguistic coding and recoding, and the like.

If this formalization of Piaget's views is correct, it has an interesting implication for the interpretation of communication data. It makes one susceptible at once to an overestimation and an underestimation of the contributions of role-taking skills to any overt communicative product. Take the case of an inadequate communication which a child has produced in one of our task situations. These situations were deliberately constructed to highlight insensitivity to listener role attributes as a factor in such communications, and it usually seemed easy enough to infer its machinations. For example, one could often see that the child failed to say something which this particular listener needed to know, despite the fact that its inclusion in the message would *appear* not to have been beyond the child's perceptual-cognitive and linguistic capabilities. In other words, it *seemed,* at least, that he could and would have said it if *only* he had attended to the listener's informational needs, if *only* he had put himself in the listener's place. But appearances can be deceiving, and it may be that our data interpretations throughout this monograph can be justly criticized as allotting too large a causal role to this factor and too small a one to the others. We had an interpretative bias at the outset, after all, and it may have led us consistently to overestimate role-taking inadequacy as a cause of communicative inadequacy. On the other hand, there is the indirect effect of egocentrism to be reckoned with (that is, on the child's perceptual, cognitive, and linguistic capabilities), the neglect of which leads to a systematic underestimation of the potency and pervasiveness of role-taking deficiency as a causal agent here. For instance, Piaget makes a persuasive case for the view that a generalized egocentrism would have to play a vital part in the child's initial self-coding of the communication's raw materials. It would seem, then, that there are interpretative hazards on either side of the midline, and that "nothing but" arguments of both varieties—communication failure is due to "nothing but" inadequate perceptual-cognitive-verbal equipment, or to "nothing but" an inability to discriminate the other's listener role attributes—are bound to be off the mark.

Although Piaget assumed that the viewpoints of self and other regarding data X are apt to differ markedly (and that the egocentric child does not recognize this fact), he did not try to work out any general principles by which these differences in viewpoint could be described. In particular, he did not try to describe the typical characteristics of what we have called the communicator's initial self-coding of data X, as contrasted with its subsequent recoding in an overt, public message. Vygotsky (1962, especially ch. 7), however, did include an analysis of this problem as part of a general theoretical account of the development of language and cognition. His analysis is highly germane to our schema of communication and role taking, inasmuch as it asserts that one's private self-coding of events is a decidedly unedited, communicatively inadequate affair, and that an extensive recoding is usually necessary if it is to become an adequate, public communication. According to Vygotsky, speech in the early, preschool years is at once private and social, with no real differentiation between self-coding and coding for others. All of his speech is overt, and equally personal and public in orientation. With development, however, the two functions gradually diverge. Social, communicative speech remains overt and is presumed to become progressively elaborate and complex, as mastery of the language increases. Private speech becomes progressively covert and, as it does so, undergoes certain alterations in its formal characteristics.

It is these alterations in form which make *inner speech*, as Vygotsky calls it, an unfit vehicle for communication. In particular, it is said to become highly abbreviated and condensed, in comparison with social speech. This abbreviation and condensation is due primarily to the fact that sentence subjects tend to be discarded, leaving only predicates or pieces thereof. Thus, the inner-verbal expression of "I guess I'll go there tomorrow" might be "go tomorrow" or simply "tomorrow"; since the subject of the action is already understood, the whole meaning is "carried" by one or more parts of the predicate. As Vygotsky states it:

> This tendency (predication), never found in written speech and only sometimes in oral speech, arises in inner speech always. Predication is the natural form of inner speech; psychologically, it consists of predicates only. It is as much a law of inner speech to omit subjects as it is a law of written speech to contain both subjects and predicates (*ibid.*, p. 145).

Inner speech, then, appears to be a special type of verbal coding, largely made up of a few of what would be the "key words" in a public utterance; it seems to be an efficient and optimally nonredundant language for communicating data to and for oneself, via a kind of "minimal-cueing" or prompting technique. If this is really the language of self-coding, it is clear how great a linguistic metamorphosis must occur behind the scenes in a full and effective public communication. And it is also obvious why an egocentric externalization without recoding (see again Figure 1), or anything approximating it, is so unlikely to meet the listener's informational requirements. Vygotsky's conceptions, perhaps even more than Piaget's, point up the wide gulf which is liable to exist between speaker and listener, with the corollary that the everyday business of bridging this gulf in adult communication entails no mean skill:

A single word (in inner speech) is so saturated with sense that many words would be required to explain it in external speech. No wonder that egocentric speech is incomprehensible to others. . . . It is evident that the transition from inner to external speech is not a simple translation from one language into another. It cannot be achieved by merely vocalizing silent speech. It is a complex, dynamic process involving the transformation of the predicative, idiomatic structure of inner speech into syntactically articulated speech intelligible to others (Vygotsky, 1962, p. 148).

It is easy to find echoes of Mead, Piaget, and Vygotsky in more recent writings. A few quotations will illustrate this. In a textbook on social psychology which heavily emphasizes communication and role-taking processes, we find, for example, this passage:

In one sense, the very process of translating thought into speech implies the use of "the image of the other," since it involves the recognition of a difference between autistic or private symbols and common symbols. In finding words to convey meaning we acknowledge a recognition of differences between ourselves and other people; otherwise words would not be necessary. We implicitly acknowledge that we cannot expect to have others understand us by a "thought reading" process. Young children, on the other hand, do expect this to occur. They frequently cannot understand how people with whom they are in close contact, such as parents or nurses, do not know what they want or what they object to without having to be told in words. . . . This comes about because their differentiation between self and "not-self" is incomplete (Hartley and Hartley, 1955, p. 107).

Similarly, Ruesch and Bateson (1951) define a *determinative group* as one in which each participant is attuned to the perceptions of the other participants:

Operationally, to determine whether a group is of this higher order, it would be necessary at least to observe whether each participant modifies his emission of signals in a self-corrective manner according to his knowledge of whether the signals are likely to be audible, visible, or intelligible to the other participants. Among animals, such self-correction is certainly unusual. Among men it is desirable but not always present (pp. 208-209).

Gough (1948) conceives of role-taking skills as serving a variety of adaptive ends:

This role-taking ability provides a technique for self-understanding and self-control. Learned prohibitions . . . may be observed by "telling one's self" not to behave in a certain way. Or speech may be editorially "reviewed" as it is emitted, and the inadmissible deleted. Role-playing, or putting one's self in another's position, enables a person to predict the other's behavior. Finally, role-playing ability makes one sensitive in advance to the reactions of others; such prescience may then deter or modify the unexpressed action (p. 363).

Cameron's (1954) writings on communication development recall Mead's definition of the significant symbol:

Social communication depends upon the development of an ability to take the role of other persons, to be able to reproduce their attitudes in one's own response, and so learn how to react to one's own behavior as others are reacting to it . . . (p. 60).

Finally, several theorists have applied communication and role-taking conceptions of this genre to various psychopathological conditions in adulthood. Thus, Cameron (1954) and Sullivan (1954) have attributed the schizophrenic's cognitive and linguistic disorders to role-taking deficiencies, and others have done the same for the psychopath's deviant thinking and behavior (Gough, 1948; Sarbin, 1954). A brief quotation from Cameron (1954) will give the flavor of this kind of theorizing:

It is our view that disorganized schizophrenics are persons who never have developed very adequate role-taking skills and have, therefore, not been able to establish themselves firmly in their cultural pattern (1954, p. 62; the italics are Cameron's).

There are other important theoretical writings in the general area, but they appear to be less relevant to the specific kind of role-taking and communication phenomena under consideration here. Examples would include Newcomb's theory of communication acts (1953), Taft's review of research and theory on interpersonal judgments (1955), methodological articles by Cronbach and Gage (Cronbach, 1955, 1958; Gage and Cronbach, 1955; Gage, Leavitt, and Stone, 1956), and several chapters in Tagiuri and Petrullo (1958). A recent theoretical paper by Maccoby (1959) deserves something more than a passing citation, however. Although primarily concerned with role taking in the enactment-of-social-roles sense, it contains ideas which might profitably be generalized to the phenomena we have been discussing. She poses the question of how

children acquire adult role behavior, for example, the caretaking behavior of a mother towards her child, and suggests that this acquisition
might take place partly through covert imitative actions, actions which
may be repeatedly rehearsed, often internally, in the absence of the
model. The following passage elaborates this idea and also summarizes
the rest of the theory:

> In summary, we have proposed that a child acquires a repertoire of actions
> by practicing covertly the actions characteristic of the adults with whom he
> interacts most frequently and who control the resources that he needs. Certain
> of the response-tendencies thus acquired may not manifest themselves overtly
> until a much later time. Specifically, actions which are part of adult-role be-
> havior (e.g., to discipline a child) will remain latent until a situation arises in
> which the individual can appropriately play the adult role, sometimes even
> until the child himself becomes a parent. We have suggested that not all
> features of parental behavior are equally well learned by the child through
> covert-role practice; he should learn verbal behavior more efficiently than
> motor skills by this means, and may learn the responses of others while failing
> to learn the cues which guided the responses. And finally, we have suggested
> that covert-role-playing is a means of learning not only adult-like social actions
> directed toward others, but of learning reactions toward the self (Maccoby,
> 1959, pp. 251-252).

It is Maccoby's notion of rehearsal which is of particular interest to us.
As mentioned earlier, Piaget had suggested that the child sharpens his
role-taking and communicative skills through actual exchanges with
others, especially peers. But it may be that they are also sharpened
through covert (or overt, as in solitary play) activities when the child
is by himself, in between social exchanges. He may not only practice
adult social roles, later to be enacted overtly, but also role-taking activities of the residual variety, for example, those involved in competitive
or cooperative social enterprises, or in communication. That is, he may
rehearse past or anticipated interchanges with others, mentally recoding
when an imagined interlocutor fails to understand or to be persuaded,
covertly readjusting his actions in the face of new behavior by an
imagined other occupying some complementary role, etc. As with Maccoby's adult social roles, there are models of effective role-taking and
communicative behavior available in the milieu for the child to imitate,
and it may be that these, too, instigate repeated imitative behavior of
the covert and solitary variety.

Adult Role Taking

A great deal of research has now accumulated on adult role taking.
By way of illustration, Taft's (1955) review of the literature contains 81

references and Strunk's (1957) contains 110, with neither one being exhaustive. This section will not duplicate their efforts with a detailed, study-by-study coverage; instead, it will try to convey the general tone and structure of the research, as well as some of its problems. It turns out to be a curious research corpus, all in all, and rather less helpful to our efforts than one would have expected.

The paradigmatic task for virtually all investigations in this area is one in which S is required to make inferences of some sort about one or more Os. Taft (1955) and Gage and Cronbach (1955) have tried to classify the structural varieties which have or could occur within this paradigm. According to Taft's analysis, there is first of all a dimension concerning the type of inference which S makes about O: it may tend toward a global, overall judgment, or it may be of the more analytic and differentiated, trait-by-trait variety. Also, the test situations which researchers have used vary considerably as regards what S is required to do: (a) interpretation of emotional expressions in photographs, drawings, models, and movies; (b) rating and ranking of traits; (c) personality descriptions; (d) personality matchings (for example, correctly match a series of Os with a series of personality descriptions); (e) prediction of behavior or life-history data; (f) miscellaneous other techniques. And finally, he makes an important distinction within tasks of type (e) above. There are *empathy* tests, which require S to make predictions about *specific* Os with whom he is actually acquainted or about whom concrete data is supplied, and there are *mass empathy* tests, where S predicts the combined or mean responses of a whole *group* of people. The rest of Taft's review is substantive, consisting of an examination of the existing literature as it bears on two broad questions: is there a general ability to judge others, and what are the characteristics of good judges?

Gage and Cronbach's (1955) structural analysis proceeds in a somewhat different way. They begin by describing the four basic components of a judging task: (a) S; (b) O; (c) the *input*, or information about O which is available to S; (d) the *outtake*, or statements about O which S makes on the basis of this information. The relationship between S and O can vary as regards S's *degree of acquaintance* with O. The relationship between input and outtake can vary as regards the *degree of extrapolation*, or the amount of inference required between input and outtake. These four components and these two relationships between pairs of components give rise to four different patterns of judging situations: (a) much acquaintance between S and O and little extrapolation between input and outtake; (b) little acquaintance, little extrapolation; (c) much acquaintance, much extrapolation; (d) little acquaintance, much extrapolation (see Gage and Cronbach, 1955, p. 414). To illustrate, an example of pattern (c) would be a task in which S is required to predict the personality test responses of his wife. The degree of acquaintance is great, but so is the inferential gap between what he knows about her and any predictions of this ilk. The authors also take account of variations in the type of O, but make finer differentiations than Taft (1955) did in his distinction between empathy and mass empathy. Depending upon the nature of the study, S may have to predict:

(a) How *persons in general* will behave.

(b) How *a particular category of persons* deviates from the behavior of persons in general.

(c) How *a particular group* deviates from the typical behavior of the particular category it belongs to.

(d) How *an individual* deviates from the typical behavior of the particular group he belongs to.

(e) How *an individual on a particular occasion* will deviate from his typical behavior (Gage and Cronbach, 1955, p. 413).

The combination of these five with the four patterns just mentioned yields a total of 20 rather different "operational definitions" of judging ability. Since the cells of this 5×4 matrix are rough categories only, and since there are undoubtedly other important dimensions which the matrix does not take into account, we may be sure that the figure of 20 is a conservative estimate of the range and diversity of behaviors which can be distinguished under rubrics like *role taking, person perception, and empathy.* We would hope, of course, that this diversity is of a logical-definitional rather than an empirical order, that is, that in reality these various behaviors are highly correlated. Although certain other problems in this research literature (see below) keep the question open, the evidence so far gives little promise that the structure of abilities in this area will turn out to be a simple one, for example, that these rubrics define one, or at most a few, judgmental skills (Taft, 1955; Gage and Cronbach, 1955).

In any case, however, all present attempts to analyze ability structure here are frustrated by serious methodological shortcomings which have been found to exist in most of the existing studies (Cronbach, 1955, 1958; Gage and Cronbach, 1955; Gage, Leavitt, and Stone, 1956). The problem is essentially the following. In the modal research design in this area, the investigator obtains data (a) and (b) below, and sometimes (c) as well: (a) O's self-description, for example, on a personality inventory; (b) S's prediction of O's self-description; (c) S's own self-description, on the same test. Let us suppose, for example, that descriptions (a) and (b) agree closely, that is, that S has been highly accurate in his prediction

of O's behavior. The problem is then to know how to *interpret* this accuracy. Common sense would suggest that it bespeaks role-taking or
empathic abilities on S's part, and this is in fact how most researchers
have interpreted the accuracy score. However, Cronbach and Gage have
persuasively argued that this score is made up of a number of components, most of which have little to do with accurate role taking in the
ordinary sense (Cronbach, 1955). There is, for example, a component
deriving from the way S interprets and uses the response scale, and
another from his ability to predict the profile of item means across a
group of Os. Furthermore, there is the problem of "assumed similarity":
if S has the general response set of assuming that others are like himself,
and if the Os he judges do happen to be similar to S, a high accuracy
score of doubtful significance automatically results. Cronbach summarizes
the whole interpretative issue as follows:

> Studies of perception may be concerned either with constant processes or
> with variable processes. When social perception is regarded . . . as a process
> of interpreting the expressive cues O presents, or of empathizing with him,
> the search is clearly for a variable process. The concept of an "intuitive" per-
> ception of Os which underlies much of the relevant research implies that J
> [that is, S in our terminology] is reacting to the particular O as a stimulus,
> and ignores the fact that the perceptual response also depends on stereotypes in
> J's mind. . . . We have seen that the measures currently used are affected by both
> constant and reactive processes, and therefore cannot serve well to investigate
> either. . . . An argument can be presented for concentrating attention on con-
> stant processes, taking up interactions between J and O only after the constant
> processes characteristic of J are dependably measured (1955, p. 190).

There appear to be two general conclusions which emerge from the
critical writings of Cronbach and Gage. First, the whole area of role-
taking skills has been "only hazily conceptualized" (Gage and Cronbach,
1955, p. 411) by previous researchers, with little attempt at analyzing
the basic variables in play and their interactions (for example, Gage and
Cronbach's 4 $\times$ 5 matrix described above). And second, most existing
measures of inferential accuracy are impure, making it well-nigh impossible to interpret the results of the majority of studies. Moreover, it is
no simple matter to separate the role-taking component from the unwanted components with which it is confounded in the accuracy score.
All in all, it appears that task situations of the traditional type (that is,
S predicts O's self-ratings and E compares these with O's actual self-
ratings) have an unpromising future as valid measures of individual
differences in adult role-taking abilities.

Should this state of affairs make us pessimistic about the developmental study of role-taking abilities? We think not, because there exist

other methodological approaches which escape most of the measurement quandaries Cronbach and Gage have described. Although these approaches may also have some promise for the investigation of adult individual differences as well, they seem to be especially well-tailored to the study of the basic formation of these skills in childhood. As one approach, we can avoid the problems inherent in accuracy scores by shifting our measurement orientation away from role-taking *accuracy* and toward role-taking *activity* per se. During childhood, when these skills are still in the very process of formation, accuracy may be a distinctly secondary issue; the primary issues may instead be whether the child shows any role-taking activity at all, and if he does, how complex and searching an inquiry into the other he makes (regardless of whether or not this inquiry yields an accurate assessment of O). In other words, we can bear witness to an important developmental process, of a genuinely role-taking sort, without getting entangled in the difficult problem of veridicality, namely, the development of a propensity to seek out the other's point of view and, along with this, an increasing subtlety and complexity of the viewpoint imputed. These activities are obviously not sufficient conditions for accuracy of interpersonal perception, but they must be necessary ones (excluding "accidental accuracies" of the sort Cronbach and Gage have talked about). The traditional, S-predicts-O's-self-ratings method is clearly an adult-centered method. It assumes both that S understands the basic concept of *viewpoint* (that is, that O *may* differ from S) and that S is disposed to try to read O's characteristics (indeed, he is explicitly instructed to do so); the amount and complexity of interpersonal inference which S may make is not measured, and the only research question is the accuracy of the final output. Moreover, as we have just seen, this method has serious methodological shortcomings, even when used with the age group to which it is suited. We would therefore suggest an approach which is at once more suitable for child subjects and apparently free of at least these particular shortcomings.

A nonaccuracy or activity approach is not our only option when studying role-taking development, however. We could also work effectively with accuracy estimates provided that the task situation is designed to include a particular feature which the traditional method does not possess. That is, it is essential to make sure that those role attributes of O which S is supposed to discover are quite *different* from S's own. For instance, the task can be structured so that O's role is the complement or opposite of S's in some sense, with respect to some body of data. In the traditional design, E provides S with the relevant dimensions (that is, the scales which O will use for his self-ratings); these dimensions apply to both S and O (for example, they refer to personality attributes on which all individuals are potentially ratable); and the extent to which S and O differ with respect to their scale positions on these dimensions is left to chance. In the approach we are proposing, S is left to discover for himself what the crucial dimensions are that he must attend to (that is, the crucial ones for this specific task), and then go on to discover just how he differs from O on these dimensions (the design of the task situation having insured that he *will* differ). If S achieves veridical estimates under these circumstances, they seem unlikely to be artifactual in the ways Cronbach and Gage have described. For example, S obviously cannot achieve a high accuracy score through an egocentric, "assumed similarity" set, because S and O are not similar; likewise, contamination by the other unwanted components these authors have discussed seems equally improbable.

We have described two approaches to the developmental study of role-taking skills which we believe to be methodologically superior to previous ones, one which works with accuracy estimates and one which does not. An example of the latter is the task used in Study IB, described in detail in Chapter 2. The child subject is about to play a game of strategy with an adult (one of the Es). His task is to predict E's next response and to explain why he thinks E would decide on that particular response. We predicted, and found, developmental change in the direction of more complex and subtle reasoning imputed to E by the child, that is, more deep and searching inferences about his inner state. The situation was such that the *veridicality* of these inferences never came into question (and indeed, could not really have been measured); we were simply interested in developmental trends toward a more and more vigorous and searching role-taking activity on S's part.

Study ID (Chapter 2) illustrates the other approach. The child is given a series of seven pictures and instructed to tell the story which the pictures illustrate (an easy task for all subjects). Three of the seven pictures are then removed, an E enters the room, and the child is instructed to tell the story which E would tell from looking at the remaining four pictures alone (because of the way the series was constructed, the four-picture sequence suggests a radically *different* story from the original, seven-picture one). The child's problem is to suppress his previous (seven-picture) perspective and look at the four pictures naïvely, as if seeing them for the first time. Veridicality can be measured here, because there *is* a rather compelling, "correct" four-picture story, and it became our major criterion of role-taking activity. To achieve it, however, the child had to bridge a gap—a gap deliberately engineered by us—between two quite different perspectives. Had the gap been left to vary randomly across S–O pairs, as in the traditional method, veridicality would have been beset with all the uncertainties of meaning which Cronbach and Gage have attributed to traditional accuracy scores.

The methodological proposals just made are not wholly new; for example, Gollin (1958) and Dymond, Hughes, and Raabe (1952) have also been aware of the distinction between accuracy and activity orientations in role-taking research. Similarly, the adult literature already includes a few investigations with designs similar to those just discussed. The most interesting examples (Feffer, 1959; Gollin, 1954, Milgram, 1960), however, have eventuated in developmental studies (Feffer and Gourevitch, 1960; Gollin, 1958; Milgram and Goodglass, 1961) and will be described in the next section.

Role-Taking Development

While there are nowhere near as many developmental as nondevelopmental studies of role taking, there is a similar diversity of methods and aims. Some have dealt with S's ability to predict O's cognitive responses, others with his perceptual responses, that is, how O "views" something in the literal-perceptual rather than figurative-intellectual sense. Some studies have been preoccupied with role-taking activity per se, while others have tried to work with accuracy criteria. And of the latter, some appear to have surmounted the more serious measurement problems while others manifestly have not.

The earliest developmental studies appear to be those of Gates (1923) and Walton (1936). Both found that the ability to identify correctly the intended emotional expressions in a series of posed pictures increases with age. While these early studies appear to have some relevance to the ontogenesis of social perception in general, they are of uncertain pertinence to the specific genre of skills we are concerned with.

There are two investigations which report developmental trends in the ability to predict one's own sociometric status accurately (Ausubel, Schiff, and Gasser, 1952; Dymond, Hughes, and Raabe, 1952). The accuracy measure in both studies was of the traditional type involving a comparison between S's prediction of Os' attitudes toward S and their actual (reported) attitudes toward S. While we are also of the belief that sensitivity to the other's attitude toward the self is a developmental affair, the results of these two studies cannot be taken as research support for it because of the Gage-Cronbach type problems which attend that kind of accuracy measure. Indeed, Gage and Cronbach (1955) actually cited the Dymond et al. study to illustrate these problems.

There is an accuracy-oriented study by Milgram and Goodglass (1961), however, which seems to avoid such difficulties by building into the design a clear-cut hiatus between S's and O's role. Children of second through eighth grade were presented with two equivalent forms of a multiple-choice word association test. The first form was given under an instructional set to respond as a *young child* would, that is, "choose the word that younger children in the first and second grade think of." The other form was then administered to the same children, this time with the instruction to associate as an *adult* would. The test was also given to a comparable group without special role-taking instructions, to provide baseline data on spontaneous associative preferences at the various ages. It was found that the younger Ss (especially the second and third graders) made essentially the same associative choices under all three instructional sets. The older ones, on the other hand, were able to shift preferential styles both up and down the ontogenetic scale. That is, when operating under the young-child set, their associations approximated the actual young-child norms. And conversely, when associating with an adult set, their preferences accorded closely with those obtained from adult Ss in a previous study (Milgram, 1960). Milgram and Goodglass give evidence which suggests that this developmental finding is not an artifact, for example, of such variables as word frequency and reading ability. Their data suggest that children of 11–12 years and older have made fairly accurate discriminations between childish and adult associative tendencies, "habits of thought," or whatever, and can mimic both of them if called upon to do so.

There are several interesting studies which emphasize role-taking activity rather than role-taking accuracy. Dymond, Hughes, and Raabe (1952) gave their Ss (second- and sixth-grade children) a second test which, unlike the first, was of this type. S was presented with a series of pictures showing children with and without adults in a variety of situations and E read a simple story about each picture. The child was then asked a standard series of questions designed to elicit the thoughts and feelings of the story characters. S's score was a function of the amount of prodding (that is, of questioning) required to elicit such inferences about each character. As predicted, the older Ss needed significantly less prompting in this regard. The authors discuss this finding as follows:

Do the scores mean that empathic ability increases significantly over this age period, or can the difference be explained on other grounds? It seems possible that the increase was due to the development of verbal facility, but a careful analysis of the individual records established that this was not the case. Some records of second graders actually contained a greater amount of verbalization than those of sixth graders, but these records were more concerned with a description of external details than with the internal thoughts and feelings. A definite qualitative difference is apparent in the records of the two groups; the sixth graders have obviously become more aware of, or at least more articulate about, the inner world of thoughts and feelings of others (*ibid.*, pp. 203-204).

Feffer has devised a more complex inferential task of the same general sort (Feffer, 1959) which has also been applied to the study of role-taking development (Feffer and Gourevitch, 1960). The materials of his Role Taking Task (RTT) are taken from Schneidman's MAPS Test and consist of background scenes, for example, a living room, or street corner, plus a variety of little cardboard men, women and children which may be placed in various positions against these backgrounds. *S*'s initial task is to tell a story for each of three scenes, using at least three of the cardboard figures in each story. Following this, he is to retell each story from the point of view of each actor in turn ("Now you are the mother here. How do you as the mother feel, how do you size up the situation, etc.?"). The scoring procedure is difficult to summarize, but in general the child's score is a measure of the extent to which he does two things: (a) changes his characterization of each actor as a function of changes in the actor through whose mouth he is speaking; (b) makes these changes in a consistent and balanced fashion, for example, so that how *A behaves* according to *B*'s observation is not inconsistent with how *A feels* according to *A*'s self-report. Thus, it appears that the RTT not only measures the ability to take on (cognitively) a series of different roles, shifting readily from one role to the next, but also the ability to keep the whole series constantly in mind so as to insure a measure of interrole and intrarole consistency and balance for the social situation as a whole. The *S*s were 68 children distributed across age groups 6–7, 8–9, 10–11, and 12–13 years. The results can be summarized as follows. Older children perform significantly better than younger children on the RTT, the most striking rise in performance apparently taking place between 8–9 years and 10–11 years. Verbal productivity and RTT scores showed a negligible correlation, reminiscent of Dymond et al. And finally, RTT scores are significantly correlated with WISC Vocabulary scores, and with performance on certain of Piaget's intellectual tasks (with Vocabulary scores partialled out).

Gollin (1954, 1958) has also created a role-taking like task which tests *S*'s ability to maintain consistency in the face of change, but the achievement of consistency here seems to demand more subtle and searching inferences than is the case with the RTT. *S* is shown a five-scene silent film. The first scene simply introduces the central character, a boy (*O*) of about 11 years of age. The next four show *O* engaged in inconsistent behavior: "bad" behavior in two of the scenes (for example, taking a ball away from two younger boys playing catch) and "good" behavior in the other two (for example, helping a small boy who has fallen off his tricycle). After the showing of the film, *S* was told to give a full description of what he had seen, including his own thoughts and opinions about *O* and *O*'s behavior. The child's narrative was scored for the presence of two characteristics. The first, called *inference,* is analogous to Dymond et al.'s measure and includes statements which go beyond simple behavioral description, for example, ascribing motives to *O*. The second, *concept,* recalls Feffer's scoring criteria in that it refers to attempts—whether successful or unsuccessful—to account for the apparent inconsistency of *O*'s actions across the four scenes. The test was group-administered to about 700 children of ages 10, 13, and 16 years. Both *inference* and *concept* showed striking increases with age within this range. Approximately 20, 60, and 90 percent of the *S*s made use of *inference* at ages 10, 13, and 16, respectively. The corresponding rough figures for *concept,* on the other hand, were 2, 15, and 50 percent. Gollin's data suggest that these skills may also be dependent on intelligence, social class, and sex (with girls tending to perform better than boys).

Wolfe (1963) administered Gollin's test and a group form of Feffer's RTT to 136 boys in grades 6–12, inclusive. He too found a significant association between age and performance on Gollin's test. Although the correlation between age and RTT scores was also positive, it was not statistically reliable. This may simply indicate that the performance curve for the RTT begins to level off in late middle childhood: Feffer and Gourevitch (1960) found increases in RTT scores up to 10–11 years but no further increases in their 12- to 13-year group, and Wolfe's *S*s were roughly of this age. Wolfe also found that the two measures were significantly correlated with each other but unfortunately did not ascertain whether this was entirely due to their common association with age. One other finding suggests that there may be something beyond common age variance in this relationship, however. Both RTT and Gollin test scores were found to be significantly related, age *and* intelligence held constant, to a third measure. This last, originated by Harvey, Hunt, and Schroder (1961), involves levels of conceptual systems and itself has some *prima facie* role-taking components to it (Wolfe's study was actually primarily concerned with the construct validation of their measure, rather than with the replication of Feffer's and Gollin's work). It may be that such tests as these three do in fact tap some sort of general role-taking-activity factor, although further research is certainly needed to be sure.

Piaget has made several important investigations of role-taking development. In two of these (1928), he used a research strategy quite different from those described so far. This strategy consists of making inferences about the child's developmental progress in role-taking skills from an assessment of his level of understanding of certain relational concepts, that is, concepts whose very meaning seems to imply the notion of differing viewpoints. Elkind (1961, 1962) has carefully replicated both of these early Piaget studies. Since his findings agree closely with those of Piaget, we shall report his work only. Elkind's Ss in both studies were 5- to 11-year-old children, 30 at each year level. The first study (1961) dealt with the relational concepts "left" and "right." On the basis of responses to a series of tasks Elkind, like Piaget before him, was able to distinguish three rough stages in the understanding of these concepts. In the first (age 7–8), the child can accurately identify his own right and left arms and legs but not those of E facing him. Similarly, he seems to regard these concepts as applicable to bodily appendages but not to other objects (for example, a penny is "to the left of" a pencil). There is marked progress during the second stage (7–8 to 10–11), and the child gradually masters problems of the above type. However, he is not yet wholly free of the younger child's belief that right and left are somehow inherent properties of objects, rather than pure relations which only hold between objects from some particular point of view. Thus, he has difficulty recognizing that, if objects A, B, and C are arranged in a row, B is at once to the *left* of C *and* to the right of A. Finally, around age 10–11, the child attains a completely differentiated and abstract conception of these particular relational terms. Like Piaget, Elkind found his data readily interpretable in terms of an underlying development from egocentrism to role-taking disposition and skill:

> When judging two and three objects while facing E . . . a good number of the oldest children made errors because they *spontaneously took E's point of view*. When asked about this they said "I thought you meant from where you (E) were sitting." This tendency to judge things spontaneously from E's point of view never appeared before the age of nine but became increasingly frequent thereafter. . . . There was thus a noticeable correspondence between the tendency to spontaneously take E's point of view and success with relational judgments in agreement with Piaget's interpretation (Elkind, 1961, pp. 274-275).

The second study (Elkind, 1962) dealt with the concepts "brother" and "sister." On the basis of his findings Elkind departed somewhat from Piaget in suggesting that there are two different but related developments here. One concerns the *class* meaning of these terms, for example, "brother" as a class concept referring to males who possess one or more siblings. The other, of more interest to us, has to do with their *relational* meaning, for example, the relation "is brother to" which may hold be-

tween individuals. Elkind again used a three-stage format in discussing
the child's growing understanding of this relational meaning. In the first
stage (5–7 years), the child is unable to coordinate his own point of view
with that of his siblings. For instance, although aware that he is a
brother and that he has a brother, he is in egocentric fashion prone to
deny that his brother also has a brother (that is, himself). In the second
stage (7–9), he achieves an intuitive-level symmetrical conception of the
relation between having and being a brother, but cannot readily construct one from the other. Thus, problems of the following type still
pose difficulties: if A has three brothers B, C, and D, how many brothers
does C have, and how many brothers are there in the family? From age
10–11 on, conceptions of "brother" and "sister" tend to become wholly
symmetrical and abstract, and such problems are readily solved.

In a later series of studies, Piaget turned his attention to role taking
of a somewhat different type from those considered so far in this section
(Piaget and Inhelder, 1956). In the usual role-taking task, S tries to determine O's "viewpoint" in the figurative rather than literal sense of the
term, that is, how he "sees" data X cognitively rather than perceptually.
In the research to be described, on the other hand, S's task was precisely
that of discovering how X "looks," literally, to an O who sees it from a
different perspective. In the most interesting of these studies (ibid., ch.
8), 100 children of 4–11 years of age were shown a scale model of three
mountains and tested in various ways for their ability to predict the
appearance of the mountains from positions other than their own. In
one of the procedures, for instance, the child was seated on one side of
the model and had to select from a series of photographs the one which
showed what it would look like to a doll placed on the opposite side.
Thus, if mountain A were to the left-rear of mountain B from where
the child sat, it would be right-front as the doll saw it. Piaget and Inhelder found that the ability to identify O's image of the mountain was
clearly age-dependent across middle childhood. The younger Ss showed
a variety of behavior patterns which attested to shortcomings in their
perspective-taking abilities. Some, for example, kept selecting the same
photograph again and again, regardless of where the doll was placed,
namely, the photograph which represented their own view of the mountains; the authors felt that this kind of response epitomized childish
egocentrism. Others acted as though a number of different perspectives
could all be correct for the doll. With development, however, the
children became increasingly aware that only one photograph could be
correct for any given perspective and that perspectives change regularly
with changes in the position of the observer vis-à-vis the mountains.
Moreover, they became increasingly successful in predicting in detail O's

image from any given position, that is, just where each mountain ought to appear to be relative to the other two. There were several other studies of the same general type from which similar developmental conclusions could be drawn (Piaget and Inhelder, 1956, chs. 6, 7, 9, and 10). In one, for example (ch. 6), the child had to cope with a single object only, for example, a needle which the doll views from different positions. As would be expected, this task was easier than the multiobject mountain problem. However, children of preschool age still had considerable difficulty with it, as Lovell (1959) also found in replicating this study with 3- to 6-year-old children.

The Piaget and Inhelder experiments dealt with S's sensitivity to O's *visual* percepts. An interesting recent study by Moore (1958) concerns S's sensitivity to O's *auditory* input. Teams of children were given a problem whose solution would be facilitated by each team's members constructing a private code, one which would permit them to communicate aloud to one another without at the same time informing the members of the opposing team. Only 3 out of 16 teams made up of 9- to 11-year-old children thought of trying to construct such codes, whereas 11 out of 14 teams of 12- to 14-year-olds attempted to do so. Moore discussed these developmental findings in role-taking terms:

> In general, these young teams (i.e., the 9–11-year-olds) interrupted each other frequently and behaved as if the messages of the opposing team were simply an obstruction to intrateam discussion. It was obviously difficult for them to take the role of the other player . . . (the) development of codes presupposes that, to a considerable degree, each team saw its own actions in dual perspective, i.e., from its own standpoint as well as from that of its opponent (p. 148).

With the exception of the Piaget and Inhelder (1956) study and its replication by Lovell (1959) just mentioned, all of the research described so far concerns the growth of role-taking abilities during middle childhood and early adolescence. Evidence about developmental changes prior to this, during the preschool period, is extremely meagre. Murphy's (1937) classic study of the development of sympathy behavior dealt with this age group, but the ability to express sympathy to a playmate appears far from synonymous with role-taking ability as we have been describing it. A study by Burns and Cavey (1957) seems at first glance to be more relevant, but unfortunately there are problems in the interpretation of its results. The test materials consisted of pairs of pictures, with one member of each pair containing an incongruity. For example, one picture of a pair shows a birthday party scene with cake and presents (call it picture A). The other picture (B) is identical except that it includes a boy with a *frown* (incongruity) on his face. The Ss, 39 children of 3–6 years, were shown the series of pictures one after another (with sequence properly counterbalanced). When shown pictures of type A, S was asked to predict his *own* reactions in that situation, for example, "How would you feel if this were your birthday party?" When shown pictures of type B, however, he was asked to guess the boy's actual feelings, for example, "Here is a boy at his birthday party—how does he feel?" An "empathic response" on S's part was thus defined as an *accurate* (nonegocentric, nonprojective) estimation of the other's feelings, for example, that *this* boy is apparently unhappy (picture B) even though I *myself* would be happy in this situation (picture A). Burns and Cavey found a striking increase in accurate identifications across this age range, interpreted as a decline in egocentrism. It is questionable, however, whether these results are most parsimoniously explained in terms of the growth of empathic or role-taking abilities. For example, it may be that the younger children simply do not notice the boy's frown (especially those Ss who have seen the A picture before the B picture), or, noticing it, either misinterpret it or ignore it in the face of its dissonant context (a happy birthday scene). Their technique may have measured role-taking growth, or it may instead have measured only growth in perceptual discrimination or something of the sort. Just what sorts of beginning role-taking skills (or precursors thereof) may develop during early childhood is still a question for which no previous research provides an answer.

Adult Communication

The studies of interest to us here are those which have some sort of role-taking undertone, that is, those in which S's communicative behavior is shown to be affected by his knowledge about the listener. There are two papers which report effects of an audience on the initial self-coding component of communicative activity. It was mentioned earlier that Zajonc's (1960) study demonstrated that adult Ss tend to code information in a particular way if they know a communication is to ensue later. Similarly, Zimmerman and Bauer (1956) tested and confirmed the hypothesis that what one retains of new information is more likely to be that which one's audience (in a subsequent communication) is likely to accept and agree with; in other words, material congruent with the attitudes of the prospective listener is remembered better than material which is incongruent with these attitudes.

Most investigations, however, have dealt with the effects of audience characteristics on the message itself, that is, the recoding part of the communicative sequence. Kaplan (1952; Werner and Kaplan, 1963) attempted to assess the communicative consequences of having versus not having an external O as listener. Following Vygotsky's theory, she looked for differences between written communications intended for the self alone and those directed towards another person. College students were presented with a series of stimuli and instructed to write two one-sentence descriptions of each: one description was solely for S's benefit, that is, to help him recognize the stimulus later; the other description was intended to help an O identify it. Kaplan found that messages for O tended to be longer than those for S, and contained more adjectives and other qualifiers. Also, the private codings contained more personal-affective and "physiognomic" characterizations of the stimulus. One amusing example: a girl wrote a long, obsessively elaborated description of a stimulus (an odor) to O, but simply the word "Ernie" for herself! These differences between the two kinds of communication were heightened when the stimulus was perceptually articulated versus diffuse, for example, abstract line drawings as contrasted with watercolor blots. In discussing these results, Kaplan hypothesized that children and disturbed adults (for example, schizophrenics) would likely show considerably less differentiation between the two message types than her adult Ss did.

There are three studies which focus instead on variations among listeners, especially how S's knowledge of O's informational needs affects his communicative behavior. In one (Ratner, Darling, and Jackman, 1957), S has the task of telephoning instructions to a mechanic about how to get from the latter's garage to S's car, broken down at position X on a map which S has before him. There were three groups of college student Ss. Just prior to the communication, the mechanic tells one group that he does not "know much" about the area in question, another group that he knows it "fairly well," and the third group that he knows it "very well." Ss in the first group produced messages which were clearly different from those given by the other two (with no significant differences between the latter). Their messages contained more words, more repeated words, and were more likely to be "complete," as defined by describing the entire route from garage to car.

Leavitt and Mueller (1951) studied the effects of variations in feedback from O to S on both speaker and listener. S (a teacher) described a complex visual figure to a group of Os (his class) and the latter tried to draw it on the basis of this description. There were four levels of feedback: (a) S can neither see nor hear the Os while he communicates; (b) S sees his audience but they cannot speak to him during his communication; (c) the Os are allowed only to say "yes" or "no" in response to S's questions, that is, his attempts to get feedback about the effectiveness of his message; (d) free interchange between speaker and audience during the communication. Increasing feedback was found to produce longer communication time, more effective communication (as measured by the accuracy of Os' drawings), and greater confidence on the part of both S and Os in the success of the message. A second study gave the same results and also showed that the effectiveness of S's message improved over successive communicative attempts under the *zero* feedback condition. The authors interpret this interesting finding as follows:

> This improvement can perhaps be thought of as a kind of personal feedback in which the instructor's own words are utilized to help him to increase his own effectiveness in the future. Much of it is no doubt empathetic, the instructor imagining himself in the receiver's place and correcting his sending as a consequence (p. 409).

The authors point out that absence of feedback appears to be distressing to both speaker and listener alike in this kind of communicative situation. So far as S is concerned, both this distress and the above-mentioned improvement across nonfeedback trials seem to attest to the basically nonegocentric, listener-oriented approach which adults are likely to bring to communicative tasks.

An experiment by Maclay and Newman (1960) has elements in common with both of the preceding two studies. College students were to describe a picture to a listener (one of the Es) seated behind a screen so that the latter could identify it from among a number of pictures he has before him. Ss' communicative behavior in a series of such tasks was studied as a function of two independent variables. First, there were three types of *feedback*: (a) *negative,* where S was told that O had made a wrong choice on the basis of S's previous communication; (b) *positive,* where S was told that O had just made a correct choice; (c) *zero,* where S was told nothing about the accuracy of O's choice. And second, there were two levels of *discriminability* among O's set of pictures: (a) a *homogeneous* range, where S was given the impression that O's pictures were all similar and therefore difficult to distinguish; (b) a *heterogeneous* range, where he was led to believe that the pictures were clearly distinguishable. The measure of communicative performance most sensitive to the action of these variables turned out to be the total number of morphemes which the message contained, that is, the message length. Thus, successive negative feedback resulted in longer and longer messages over a series of trials. Both zero and positive feedback, on the other hand, resulted in progressively shorter communications, with zero feedback yielding the longer messages at each trial. Similarly, the homogeneous range condition produced more detailed communications than the heterogeneous one under all conditions of feedback. The three studies taken together give strong evidence that normal adult communicators are likely to show a fair amount of sensitivity to the listener's apparent input needs, augmenting their messages whenever they have information, such as negative feedback, which suggests that these needs are high.

Communication Development

There is very little existing research on the developmental growth of communicative skills taken as a function of emerging role-taking activity. There are of course many studies in the general area of language development (for example, McCarthy, 1954; Ervin and Miller, 1963). However, even the most interesting of these tend to deal with aspects of linguistic growth which are of uncertain relevance to role-taking development, for example, studies of the acquisition of morphological and syntactic rules. An important exception is the research reported in Piaget's earliest book (Piaget, 1926; Flavell, 1963, pp. 271-273). Some of his studies were of the purely observational variety. For example, Piaget recorded the spontaneous verbalizations of a number of 4- to 7-year-old children in a preschool setting. He found that a considerable percentage of their utterances could be classified as *egocentric*: utterances which, whether emitted when alone or in the company of others, seem to lack a genuinely *communicative* aim, in the sense of being intentionally adapted to another's input needs through the offices of some sort of role-taking activity. He also noted the character of verbal interactions among children in this age range. Initially, these interactions frequently take the form of *collective monologues,* with each child talking "at" rather than "to" the other, attentive neither to the other's messages nor to the effect of his own message on the other. Subsequently, the interchanges become genuinely social: where there is agreement between children, we see a bona fide collaboration of thought on a common topic; where there is disagreement, we see the beginnings of real argumentation, with each interlocutor attempting to justify his position to the other.

Piaget also conducted an interesting experiment on this developmental problem (1926, ch. 3). The Ss were 50 children: 20 of age 6–7 years and 30 of age 7–8 years. S was given a body of information (for example, a story) and told to relate it to a second child of the same age group. The latter was then to communicate what he had understood of the story back to E. Piaget's analysis of the children's verbal protocols was rather involved and complex, but his general conclusions were straightforward enough. Children in this age range (especially the younger ones) tend not to communicate very effectively, principally because they fail to take account of the listener's viewpoint. Likewise, as listeners they often fail to grasp information which has in fact been adequately imparted (although they usually *think* they have grasped everything), again because of egocentric factors. As in most of Piaget's studies, his verbatim protocols here give a vivid picture of the child's communicative inadequacies. One of the stories told to S was the following:

> Once upon a time, there was a lady who was called Niobe, and who had 12 sons and 12 daughters. She met a fairy who had only one son and no daughter. Then the lady laughed at the fairy because the fairy only had one boy. Then the fairy was very angry and fastened the lady to a rock. The lady cried for ten years. In the end she turned into a rock, and her tears made a stream which still runs to-day (1926, p. 82).

Here is one child's account of the story, together with Piaget's commentary in brackets:

> Gio (8 years old) tells the story of Niobe in the role of the explainer: *"Once upon a time there was a lady who had twelve boys and twelve girls, and then a fairy a boy and a girl. And then Niobe wanted to have some more sons* (than the fairy. Gio means by this that Niobe competed with the fairy, as was told in the text. But it will be seen how elliptical is his way of expressing it). *Then she* (who ?) *was angry. She* (who ?) *fastened her* (whom ?) *to a stone. He* (who ?) *turned into a rock, and then his tears* (whose ?) *made a stream which is still running today"* (p. 102).

The ellipses and indefinite pronouns in this message are taken as evidence of a basic failure on Gio's part to keep the listener's role in mind while communicating to him, that is, a failure to anticipate what he will and will not understand, what will and will not confuse him, and the like. Piaget obtained a number of messages of this ilk from his Ss, and concluded that it is not until age 7–8 years or later that budding role-taking skills make possible any substantial amount of genuinely social, nonegocentric communicative behavior. As Piaget puts it, the younger child:

> . . . always gave us the impression of talking to himself, without bothering about the other child. Very rarely did he succeed in placing himself at the listener's point of view (p. 115).

Recent studies by Krauss and Glucksberg (1965) appear to confirm Piaget's observations. Their research technique was similar to that used by Maclay and Newman (1960). Pairs of children were seated on opposite sides of a table with a screen interposed between them. One member of the pair (the speaker) was to describe a novel or "nonsense" graphic design to the other member (the listener) in such a way that the latter could identify it from among a set of designs he had in front of him. Listener and speaker could intercommunicate prior to the listener's final identification of the intended design; for example, the listener was free to ask for a more precise and discriminative message before making his selection. The results were as follows. Four-year-old children were apparently able to understand the general requirements of the task (whereas three-year-olds were not), but were nonetheless wholly unable to perform effectively on it. Speakers tended to give idiosyncratic, nondescriptive characterizations of the figures (for example, "Mommy's hat") which the listeners quite naturally could not use for identification purposes. The listeners, in turn, generally failed to seek further clarification from the speaker in these instances, tending instead to attempt identifications on the basis of the meagre and cryptic information available (adults tested on similar problems almost always sought additional information under these circumstances). On the rare occasions when the listener did provide some kind of negative feedback, the speaker simply repeated his initial message instead of trying to improve it.

Krauss and Glucksberg were able to show that preschool listeners could identify the designs moderately well if they received more effective messages, that is, characterizations which adult speakers had used successfully in communicating with adult listeners. More interesting, they also found that the idiosyncratic and egocentric messages which the young speaker was prone to construct did have communicative value for the speaker himself; that is, these messages were fairly effective in permitting him to identify the correct designs when he received them in the role of the listener—even with a lapse of six weeks between his initial production of them and their playback as messages to him from another speaker (E). The pertinence of this finding to our previous analysis of egocentric communication (see Figure 1) is apparent. And finally, the authors report a substantial developmental improvement in communicative performance on this task from kindergarten through ninth grade.

CHAPTER TWO

Role Taking in Middle Childhood and Adolescence

This chapter and the next describe the first and most extensive of our studies. Five tasks were individually administered in a fixed sequence to 160 children. The middle three in the sequence (Tasks IB, IC, and ID) were designed to measure role-taking skills and are described below. The first and last (Tasks IA and IE) were communicative tasks and are taken up in Chapter 3. The following paragraphs provide general information about the study as a whole concerning the subject sample, the procedure, and the method of data analysis.

Subjects. The sample was drawn from a suburban public school system in upstate New York.[1] Although no systematic data on socioeconomic status was obtained, the great majority of these Ss were probably of middle-class background. As Table 1 shows, there were 10 Ss of each sex at each of grades 2, 3, 4, 5, 6, 7, 8, and 11. All grade groups, as well as the male-female subgroups within each grade, were closely matched on whatever recently obtained group intelligence test data were available in the school records. The tests in question were: California Short-Form Test of Mental Maturity (1957 Edition) in the case of grades 2–7; Otis Quick-Scoring Mental Ability Test (Beta Test) for grade 8; and the Henman-Nelson Tests of Mental Ability (Revised Edition) for grade. 11.

The particular grade range 2–8 was chosen for intensive, grade-by-grade investigation because previous research and our own pilot work led us to guess that most of the developmental changes on these five tasks would take place somewhere within the middle childhood and early adolescent period. The group of eleventh graders was added primarily to check this guess, that is, to find out if there would be any appreciable

[1]The authors are greatly indebted to District Principal John W. Parker and other members of his staff in the Rush-Henrietta, N.Y. school system for their splendid co-operation in providing subjects and facilities for our studies.

Table 1
IQ Means and Standard Deviations (SD) of
Subjects in Study I (N = 160)

Grade	Boys			Girls		
	N	Mean	SD	N	Mean	SD
2	10	108.2	6.3	10	107.6	7.6
3	10	108.0	7.7	10	107.6	7.3
4	10	107.4	8.1	10	108.8	7.1
5	10	105.0	7.1	10	106.9	6.8
6	10	108.8	6.8	10	107.8	6.4
7	10	108.3	6.9	10	108.5	6.5
8	10	108.2	6.8	10	108.3	6.7
11	10	108.3	6.6	10	108.2	6.5

changes after age 14 or so. It will be noted in Table 1 that all the standard deviations are quite small; actually, the IQ range in each group was approximately 95–120. We had decided at the outset to keep the IQ range fairly restricted, hoping thereby to obtain a clearer picture of age changes, in accordance with our developmental-naturalistic orientation (Chapter 1). It may not have been a wise decision, however: as will be shown, we did test for IQ effects on task performance after all, as an incidental analysis, and of course this restriction in variance may well have led to an underestimation of these effects.

Procedure. The five tasks were administered in a single testing session which took place in a small, improvised experimental room within the child's school building. En route from classroom to experimental room, E attempted to reassure S about the nature and purpose of the study and to arouse his interest in the tasks he was about to perform. The method of doing this varied somewhat with the age of the S, but generally included the following three points: (a) we were interested in developing new games and tasks which would appeal to children of different ages and we were in S's school to try some of them out; (b) the selection of S as a participant was a random one, unconnected with S's characteristics as an individual; (c) likewise, S's performance was our private concern only, and would not be reported back to the school. We also told the older Ss that some of the tasks might strike them as a little childish, since they were also being administered to younger children; they were nevertheless harder than they looked, we said, and S was encouraged to take them seriously and put forward his best efforts. It was our impression that these preliminaries, together with whatever inherent appeal the tasks themselves may have had, did succeed in eliciting sustained interest and motivated performance for the great majority of Ss. What exceptions there may have been probably occurred mostly in the eleventh-grade group, where we occasionally thought we detected an attitude of tolerant amusement bordering on outright disinterest regarding our "games."

The typical task in this study required the intervention of two experimenters. One of the two (E_1) had an executive role, that is, setting up the task materials, instructing S, etc. The second (E_2) functioned as an "other" vis-à-vis the child, that is, as a listener in the communicative tasks and as an O whose behavior was to be predicted in the role-taking tasks. John W. Wright served as E_1 in Tasks IA and IB, with Charles L. Fry as E_2. The roles were then reversed for the next three tasks (with the exception of IE, which required no "live" O). As will be explained in the next chapter, a second E_2 was needed for certain Ss in Task IA; John H. Flavell performed this function.

Since the child's verbal behavior was the major datum in these tasks, his responses were tape recorded on a small portable machine (Stenorette) and later converted into typescript for analysis purposes. For the younger Ss especially, we also used the tape recorder as a "warm-up" device when the child first entered the experimental room. We explained what it was and that we were using it to help us remember better what was said during the session and then let S record and play back his own voice to show how it worked. So far as we could tell, the recording procedure did not bother or distract the children; on the contrary, they seemed to forget the machine was there once engaged in the tasks.

Analysis of Data. Almost all the scores which entered our statistical analyses in this study were derived from ratings made by a judge. That is, each child's behavior protocol on a given task was judged in terms of a category system described in a small "manual" of rating instructions. A single judge (Patricia T. Botkin) carefully rated the 160 protocols for each of the five tasks and her scoring was taken as "final," that is, all statistical analyses were carried out using these scores as raw data. A second judge (Rita Iker), unconnected with the research project, also scored all the protocols of 40 of the 160 Ss for reliability purposes. These 40 were selected randomly, save that they were made to spread more or less evenly across the age range. The major judge was familiar with the purposes of the study; the reliability judge was not. All ratings were made without knowledge of the identity of the protocols' owners. Thus, the reports of interjudge reliability given in this and the next chapter invariably refer to the level of agreement achieved between these two judges on the 40 protocols which they rated in common.

TASK IB

As mentioned in Chapter 1, this task was designed to assess developmental changes in role-taking *activity* rather than in role-taking *accuracy*.

S is engaged in a game of strategy vis-à-vis an opponent (E_2) and is asked to predict E_2's game behavior and then to give a rationale for his prediction. The structure of the game was such that inferences about S's role-taking prowess could be drawn from the prediction and rationale he gave. It was hypothesized that there would be an age-dependent increase in the subtlety and complexity of the game strategy which S would impute to his opponent, presumably reflecting an underlying development in his propensity and ability to discriminate the role attributes of another.

Procedure

S sees before him two plastic cups, turned face down on a felt board. One has a nickel glued to its bottom (upturned) side and the other similarly displays two nickels. Both Es are initially present in the room with the child and E_2 instructs him as follows:

"Now here is another game, a different kind of game. You see these two cups? One has *one* nickel stuck to the top and the other one has *two* nickels stuck to the top (points). Now the money stuck to the top tells you how much money is inside. You see (lifts cups), *one* nickel under here and *two* nickels under here. I'll show you how the game works. First, I'll close my eyes and Mr. Fry here (E_2) will take the money out of *one* of the cups but I don't know which because my eyes are closed (E_2 then silently removes the money from the two-nickel cup). Now I'll open my eyes and choose one of the cups. Now if I choose the one with money still under it, I'll get that much money to keep. If I pick the one with *no* money under it, I wouldn't get *any* money to keep. Say I pick this one (picks up one-nickel cup). It has a nickel under it, so I'd get to keep a nickel. What would I get to keep if I'd picked the other one? (If S responds incorrectly, E_1 shows him.) Now say I close my eyes again and say he took away the money from the one-nickel cup (E_2 does this) and then, say, I choose the one-nickel cup, what would I get? And what would I get if I picked the two-nickel cup this time? You see how to play the game? Fine.

"Now Mr. Fry, please leave the room (E_2 leaves). Now you and I are going to play this game with Mr. Fry. We'll take the money out of either the two-nickel cup or the one-nickel cup. Then he'll come back in and choose, and if he chooses right, he'll get some money to keep, either one nickel or two nickels, and if he chooses wrong, he won't get any money. Now we'll try to *fool* him—we'll try to *guess* which cup he'll choose and take the money out of *that* one. Now you think *hard* for a minute and see if you can *guess* which one he'll choose. Now of course he *knows* we'll try to fool him, he *knows* we're going to try to figure out which one he'll choose. Which one do *you* think he'll choose—think hard! (*S* indicates one of the cups.) Tell me *why* you think he might pick that one."[2]

At this point E_1 encourages the child to introspect and give reasons but tries to avoid all leading or suggestive questions. The only questions to be asked are those which E_2 deems necessary to clarify, for the tape record, which choice *S* made and its stated rationale. Once this is accomplished, Task IB is completed from our standpoint: the choice and rationale made on this single, nonfeedback "trial" comprised the only experimental datum analyzed in this study. The procedure was of course allowed to run its natural course for the child's sake, however. That is, the money is then duly removed from the cup *S* selected, E_2 returns to make his "choice" (actually made according to a preset pattern across *S*s), and either "wins" or "loses."

Results

A logical analysis of this two-person game suggested a workable means of ordering *S*s' choices and rationales in terms of the depth and complexity of interpersonal inference which they seemed to reflect. Accordingly, the judge was given the task of assigning each *S*'s response protocol to one of four categories. Each category describes a game strategy imputed to E_2, a strategy which leads him to select one cup rather than the other. The categories are entitled O, A, B, C, in order of increasing strategic complexity.

Strategy A. S asserts that E_2 will choose a particular cup for one of two reasons: *monetary* and *other*. The former simply attributes a straightforward, greatest-financial-gain motive to E_2 and always predicts the choice of the two-nickel cup (that is, E_2 will choose that cup because it potentially yields the most money). The latter, as its name implies, covers all other strategies of the same general level; for example, E_2 is said to recall that cup X paid off frequently during the demonstration trials and thinks it is likely to continue to pay off now. The essence of Strategy A, whether *monetary* or *other*, is that it seems to attribute to E_2 nothing beyond cognitions and motives which bear on the game materials them-

2In this as in other studies reported in this volume, there was the continual problem of adapting a single task to children of different maturity levels. We attempted to cope with this problem by making small, nonessential changes in the instructions and procedures wherever they seemed appropriate, for example, when the standard ones risked boring the child or, worse, appeared to insult his intelligence. In the present task, for example, E_1 was left free to abbreviate slightly the preliminary explanation of how the game was played when dealing with older *S*s who seemed to grasp it quickly.

selves, that is, it does not take into account any cognitions which E_2 might have about S's behavior in the role of E_2's opponent. The following is a protocol scored as Strategy A (*monetary* type):

"Do you want me to tell you?" (Umhum. Which one do you think he'll choose?) "The dime." (You think he'll choose the dime cup. Why do you think he might choose that one?) "He'll get more money—if the money is under there."

Strategy B. S begins with a prediction about E_2's motives and response dispositions (either *monetary* or *other*), just as the Strategy A child does. But unlike the latter, he then goes on to attribute additional cognitions to E_2: the recognition that S may have predicted precisely these intentions and that he, E_2, had therefore better change his choice, for example, from the two-nickel cup to the less remunerative, but perhaps surer one-nickel cup. Here is an example:

(*S* chooses the one-nickel cup.) (Why do you think he'll take the one-nickel cup?) "Well, I figured that, uh, if it was me I'd take this one (two-nickel cup) because of the money I'd get to keep. But he's gonna know we're gonna fool him—or try to fool him—and so he might think that we're gonna take the most money out so I took the small one (the one-nickel cup), I'd go for the small one."

Strategy C. This category includes all imputed E_2 strategies which are analogous to Strategy B, but are carried one or more steps further. Having first reasoned according to Strategy B, for instance, S might make the further inference that E_2 will predict *this* reasoning, *too*, and will consequently shift back again to his initial choice in order to combat it (for example, pick the two-nickel cup after all). The judge felt that this interesting protocol deserved a Category C scoring (*other* type):

"Uh, when we were, he chose the dime cup the first time . . . and uh . . . well, let's see . . . I think uh that he would, I think that he would think that we would choose the opposite cup." (Opposite cup from what?) "From the, in other words this cup, the nickel cup, but then might, he might, he might feel that we, that we know that he thinks that we're going to pick this cup so therefore I think we should pick the dime cup, because I think he thinks, he thinks that we're going to pick the nickel cup, but then I think he knows that we, that we'll assume that he knows that, so we should pick the opposite cup." (Okay, so we should pick the dime cup?) "Yes."

Strategy O. This category includes all S protocols which cannot be assigned to any of the three preceding categories. Almost all of these protocols were of either one of two types: (a) S cannot or will not impute a choice to E_2, despite E_1's urging; (b) S attributes a choice to E_2 but is unable to offer any rationale for it.

Since Strategies A, B, and C could each be subclassified as either *monetary* or *other,* the judge was confronted with 7 possible scoring alternatives in rating the 160 protocols (these 6 plus Strategy O). She and the reliability judge made identical ratings for 29 of the 40 protocols rated in common, and showed only minor disagreements on most of the remainder. There is a final comment to be made about the category system before turning to the statistical data. While the presence of Strategy B or C behavior strongly suggests that S may have substantial role-taking abilities, the absence of this behavior does not necessarily imply the lack of such abilities. In the first place, the task was a one-trial affair, scarcely a fair test of absolute capacity. Moreover, it is quite possible that an S who possesses considerable role-taking skill might nonetheless, for one reason or another, attribute to E_2 a straight-forward monetary-gain motive (Strategy A) or even a random choice (Strategy O). Despite instructions which hint otherwise, a given S might for example assume that E_2 is not clever enough to warrant Strategy B or C treatment, that is, S *might* actually have considered such strategies and then deliberately rejected them. Thus Task IB, perhaps more than most tests administered to children, probably underestimates the skills it was designed to tap. Fortunately, there is no compelling reason to suppose that this underestimation would give rise to a variable rather than systematic error across age groups, and the developmental results actually obtained suggest that it probably did not.

Table 2 shows the number of children at each grade scored at each of the four strategic levels, with the *monetary* and *other* subcategories of A,

Table 2
Number of Subjects per Grade Scored for Each Strategy in Task IB

Strategy	Grade							
	2	3	4	5	6	7	8	11
O	2	4	4	6	4	3	6	6
A	17	14	13	10	8	8	4	7
B	1	2	3	4	6	9	10	5
C	0	0	0	0	2	0	0	2

B, and C pooled. Of the 125 A, B, and C scores represented in the table, only 20 fell into the *other* subcategory, and thus no separate analyses of the two subcategories seemed indicated. An examination of the table shows that Strategies A and B exhibit the most clear-cut developmental changes. Strategy A is strongly dominant in the younger groups and diminishes more or less regularly with age. Strategy B, on the contrary, is very infrequent in the early grades but eventually equals or surpasses A, as though tending to replace it as the strategy of choice with increasing age. Strategy C, as might be expected, is everywhere a rare event, occurring only twice each in grades 6 and 11. The residual strategy, O, is more frequent but shows no impressive age variance, accounting for an average of about one-fifth of the responses at each grade level. An eight-cell chi square table was constructed from Table 1 by combining adjacent grades and adjacent strategies; for example, one such cell would include the second and third graders who show either Strategy O or A. This procedure yielded a chi square of 18.18 ($df = 3$), $p < .01$, substantiating the impression of developmental change given by the table. Chi square tables were also constructed for sex and IQ (dichotomized as above versus below the median), again combining adjacent strategies (O-A versus B-C). There was a tendency ($p < .10$) for the boys to perform better than the girls, most clearly apparent in the upper grades. There were no significant IQ differences, a negative finding of doubtful meaning in view of the narrow IQ range.

Discussion

These data suggest that some sort of developmental change in role-taking activity may be in progress over the period of middle childhood and early adolescence. To understand the nature of this change, a careful analysis must be made of the processes underlying Strategies A and B, since it is these two which largely account for the significant age trend found. In this connection, we have found it useful to conceptualize them as two particular instances among a whole family of possible role-taking operations of differing quality and complexity. Figure 4 gives a diagram of the sort of operations we have in mind.

In this diagram, S represents the subject and O the particular other individual whose role attributes he is trying to discriminate. X stands for any (nonhuman) object or set of objects and O_1 for any person or persons other than S and O. The arrows designate any sort of experience which a person may have vis-à-vis another person or an object, and thus the exact meaning of any given arrow varies from case to case. The diagram depicts three levels of role-taking complexity, but it is obvious that additional levels could readily be generated in the same fashion. These probably occur only rarely in interpersonal cognition, however, and are in any case unnecessary for the present analysis.

The operations at Level 1 can be translated as: S thinks (knows, predicts, or whatever) that O has such-and-such belief (attitude, feeling, etc.) about something (X), about S himself, about O himself, or about some other individual or group (O_1). We believe that the operations at

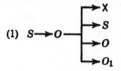

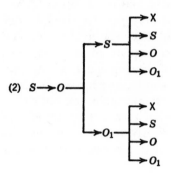

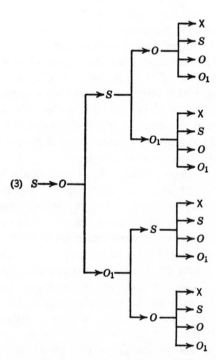

Figure 4. Family of possible role-taking activities at three levels of complexity.

this and the other two levels can and do occur in real-life human inter-actions, and that we can readily find conversational statements, made by S to O, which indicate that they have occurred. An example at Level 1 would simply be: "I know how you feel (about something or someone)." At Level 2, the translation would be: S thinks that O is aware of (un-aware of, dislikes, etc.) S's or O_1's thoughts (feelings, perceptions, etc.) regarding X, S, O, or O_1. A conversational example would be: "I'm sure you know what I think about Bill." There are more steps and branching operations in Level 3: S knows that O is aware (a) that S knows O's or O_1's attitudes toward X, etc., or (b) that O_1 knows S's or O's attitudes toward X, etc. We can find conversational paradigms here too, although they admittedly have a precious, ultraintrospective quality, for example, "I think you must feel that I can't understand your attitude about Bill."

We assume that there is a rough correlation within this family of operations between level of complexity and difficulty or developmental level. That is, operations at Level 2 ought generally to be more difficult to engage in, and ought to appear later in ontogenesis, than those at Level 1, and so on. However, the difficulty of any given operation will surely also depend on various other factors, that is, the precise kind of "experiencing" involved (the definition of the arrows) and who or what the "experiencing" concerns (what the arrows point to). Thus, the de-velopmental transitivity postulated for these three levels must be regarded as having an "all other things being equal" character, a situation which holds for developmental transitivities generally, we think (Flavell, 1963, pp. 442-446). If a limited ordering can be predicated for the three levels as a whole, what about the relations among operations within a level? Our suspicion is that, at any given level, operations in which S or S's experiences figure as an object of thought have a higher maturity status than the others. At Level 1, therefore, it is assumed that $S \rightarrow O \rightarrow S$ is likely to be a later genetic achievement than the other three. Similarly, the upper branch at Level 2 ($S \rightarrow O \rightarrow S \rightarrow \ldots$) should be more demand-ing than the lower one, and so on. X, O, and O_1 have an external, "out there" quality as conceptual objects (for S) which S himself does not possess, and Piaget has in his various writings elaborated the difficulty which children have in including themselves and their own experential acts within their own cognitive field, let alone anyone else's.[3] It can only be guessed whether this sort of difficulty is sufficient to make for

[3]Moore's experiment (1958), described in the previous chapter, gives evidence for the relative genetic maturity of the operation $S \rightarrow O \rightarrow S$. Only his older (12-14 years) Ss showed much apparent awareness of the fact that their own verbalizations were probably being monitored with profit by the opposing team.

more drastic ruptures in the hierarchy posited, for example, whether $S \rightarrow O \rightarrow S$ is not only more demanding than $S \rightarrow O \rightarrow X$, but also more demanding than $S \rightarrow O \rightarrow O_1 \rightarrow X$.

We believe that Strategies A and B can readily be located in this family of operations: the former is an example of $S \rightarrow O \rightarrow X$ and the latter of $S \rightarrow O \rightarrow S \rightarrow O \rightarrow X$. Consider Strategy A first. Most protocols so scored contained rationales phrased like: "he wants more money," "he wants the money," "he'd get more money, if the money's there," and "it's more money." In some of these cases (for example, "it's more money"), it is of course possible that no role-taking activity at all took place. The child may, for instance, have simply looked at the two cups and chosen the more remunerative one under some momentary self-instruction to indicate his *own* preference, forgetting all about the interpersonal-game character of the task. In most cases, however, the child's general demeanor, his use of the pronoun "he," etc., led us to infer that a genuine if elementary form of role attribute discrimination really had occurred. This form consists simply of attributing to E_2 (O) a certain "experience" ($\rightarrow$) vis-à-vis the two cups (X) which leads to a choice of one of them: thus, a case of $S \rightarrow O \rightarrow X$.

Such an operation can be regarded from two points of view. First, we can focus on its simplicity and shortcomings in comparison with the more complex and elaborate Strategy B operation. We shall do this presently. However, it also makes sense to look at it in a positive way, as a putative instance of a certain measure of developmental achievement. As Table 2 shows, most of our youngest Ss (age 7–8 years) carried out Strategy A reasoning in response to Task IB. Although of course we have no direct evidence on the question, other of our investigations (Chapter 5) make us wonder how many 4- to 6-year-olds could have reasoned at that level. Most of the role-taking studies reviewed in the preceding chapter seem to have dealt with one or another type of Level 1 operations (in a variety of task settings and, consequently, at a variety of difficulty levels). And most of these studies have shown that such operations, despite their apparent simplicity, are in fact quite difficult for young children and are only gradually mastered across the middle childhood period and beyond. In sum, then, it appears that even our youngest Ss already show a certain measure of role-taking competence in this particular task setting. The fundamental definition of role taking is after all the attribution of cognitions, in the broad sense, to another individual, and Strategy A appears to satisfy this definition.

In Strategy B, S reasons that E_2 will recognize that S would probably have divined E_2's rationale and preference vis-à-vis the game materials, and hence predicts that E_2 will revise his initial cup selection. This is a formidable bit of reasoning and does not seem to be describable by any operational expression simpler than $S \to O \to S \to O \to X$ (Level 3). As such, Strategy B appears to be not simply more advanced than Strategy A from the standpoint of inferential complexity, but considerably—two levels—more advanced. It is interesting to speculate how, by what developmental route, the child might get from the simple and straightforward Strategy A to the complicated, "wheels-within-wheels" inferential process represented by Strategy B. Task IB seems not to be structured in such a way as to reveal any intermediary, transitional processes—at least we were unable to identify any. However, Figure 4 provides a conceptual vehicle for some guesswork here. Our guess is that there are two principal transitional steps, two major way stations in the developmental progression from the one type of role-taking operation to the other.

The first step would be the awareness that O can have cognitions, not only about objects external to S (X, O, and O_1), but also regarding S himself. Nothing remotely like Strategy B can occur until S has achieved the basic recognition that he himself can be a cognitive object for O, since the essence of that strategy is that O's cognitive field is extended to include S as well as X. As mentioned earlier, there is reason to suppose that $S \to O \to S$ may be a later achievement than the other Level 1 operations, and it is our suspicion that its acquisition is a most essential first step toward the attainment of higher reaches of role-taking activity.

The second step is an elaboration of the first. It consists of S's recognition that O may not only experience S as object, but also as subject. That is, having grasped that fact that *he*, like X, O, and O_1, can be an object within O's cognitive field (first step), S then proceeds to realize that *his cognitions* about objects can also be included in that field (second step). It may be that, once childish egocentrism is sufficiently reduced to make possible the first step (if this is indeed what makes it possible), the second step is an easy one. Whether easy or hard, however, it is a crucial advance logically, because it completes the necessary minimum for generating all additional, more complicated operations of the same type. So long as S can do no more than admit that O cognizes him *qua* object, as one more X, the chain of reasoning can proceed no further. On the other hand, once admit the possibility that O can have the knowledge ($S \to \ldots$), and an infinite series of reciprocal inferences of the form $S \to O \to S \to O \to S$ presents itself.[4] One of the initial members of this series is, of

---

[4]In this connection, one wonders at what point in his role-taking development the child does in fact first become aware of this "infinite regress" property of such role-taking activity ("I think that he thinks that I think," etc.); its achievement strikes one, intuitively, as an important milestone in the ontogenesis of social cognition. Our analysis suggests that the point in question might be the attainment of operations at the second level of complexity, notably of the branch $S \to O \to S \to \ldots$

course, $S \rightarrow O \rightarrow S \rightarrow O \rightarrow X$, and hence the terminus of the hypothesized two-stage transition from Strategy A to Strategy B.

There remains the question of how and where these various role-taking activities might figure in the larger context of the child's everyday social life. It seems reasonable to suppose that the acquisition of a given type of inferential activity would make possible forms of social behavior hitherto inaccessible to the child. That is, the attainment of a certain role-taking skill should permit and foster types of social activity difficult or impossible to carry out prior to its attainment. Both Sullivan (1953) and Piaget (Flavell, 1963, ch. 8 and elsewhere) have suggested certain important social activities which first appear in strength during the middle childhood period, namely, genuine interactions with peers, marked by efforts at cooperation, compromise, real argument, and other characteristics which reflect some awareness of the other's point of view. The nascent role-taking activity necessary to support and facilitate these sorts of social commerce is probably of the genre of Strategy A. Activity at that level ought to be sufficient to allow, for example, S and O to coordinate their efforts in some joint enterprise (perhaps a cooperative game), each keeping in mind, at least in a general way, the other's viewpoint or position vis-à-vis whatever X constitutes the external focus of their joint endeavors. Likewise, real discussion and argument presupposes, as Piaget (1926) has pointed out, some capacity to divine the attitudes and beliefs of the other toward the subject matter. Our study, together with others cited previously, gives evidence that this elementary form of role-attribute discrimination is within the reach of middle childhood subjects, and it is probably an important factor in the social behavior we identify as typical of that period.

Sullivan (1953) has suggested that preadolescence usually brings in its train social interactions of a new and higher order. The child is now prone to develop intimate interpersonal relationships with a same-sex chum, relationships in which meticulous attention is given to the careful gauging of the thoughts and feelings of the other (especially toward oneself), of comparing and contrasting his perceptions of the world with one's own, and the like. And this sort of thing certainly continues with a vengeance during adolescence, to the child's profit and pain, with reference to others of both sexes: "Does she think I'm good looking?" "How will they take it if I do such-and-such?" etc., could scarcely be called atypical cognitions for this age group. The role-taking acquisitions necessary for this new plane of social interchange seem to be the operation $S \rightarrow O \rightarrow S$ at minimum, and often enough $S \rightarrow O \rightarrow S \rightarrow \ldots$ or even higher forms. Once again, the data from Task IB and from Moore's study (1958) suggest that these more advanced activities begin to make their appearance during the preadolescent and early adolescent era, and it seems most probable that they help to give the adolescent's social behavior its distinctive coloring.

TASK IC

This task was designed to measure "perceptual" role-taking skill, that is, S's ability to predict the appearance of a stimulus display from positions or perspectives other than his own. As such, the task was modelled after those of Piaget and Inhelder (1956), described in the previous chapter. The Ss were shown a series of four stimulus displays and were to reconstruct each one as it would look to E_2, seated at different vantage points vis-à-vis the display. That is, S's task was to reproduce the displays, not as they appeared to him, but as they would appear to another who saw them from a differential spatial perspective.

Procedure

Figure 5 is a diagram of the experimental setup, as seen from above. The four stimulus displays were presented to the Ss one at a time, always in the sequence 1–2–3–4. Similarly, for each display E_2 always sat first in the right-side position and then in the opposite position. The elements of each display were fastened to a small board to keep their spatial interrelationships constant. At each display presentation, S was given a duplicate set of elements (unattached) with which he could reproduce the display from any given perspective. Board and display, that is, the model, were placed in the center of Table A, with the elements arranged and oriented as depicted in Figure 5. S was seated in the position indicated, looked at the model on Table A, and attempted to reconstruct E_2's view of it on Table B. That is, he was told to arrange the duplicate elements on Table B so that they looked to him just like the model on Table A looked to E_2 from where E_2 was sitting. The arranging of the elements was done on a blank sheet of paper so that E_1 could make an exact tracing of S's construction. The elements of each display are described as follows:

Display 1 comprised a single blue-colored block of wood 6 in. long and 1 in. thick. It was 6 in. high at one end and 4 in. high at the other, and thus its upper edge was diagonal rather than parallel to the ground. As Figure 5 shows, it was always placed so that its higher side (H) was on S's right and its lower side (L) on his left, as he faced the model.

Display 2 consisted of three identical blue wooden cylinders, 4 in. high and 1 in. in diameter, standing on end in the spatial arrangement shown in Figure 5.

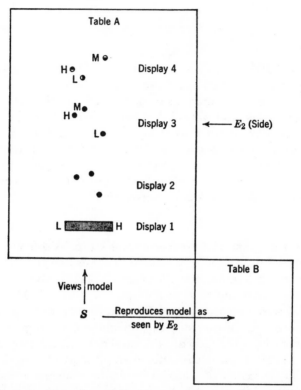

Figure 5. Task IC—experimental situation (viewed from above).

Display 3 also consisted of three blue wooden cylinders of 1 in. diameter. Their heights, however, were 6 in. (H), 4 in. (M), and 2 in. (L).

Display 4 included three cylinders identical in size to those of Display 3. However, each was painted red for half its circumference (including top and bottom cross sections—see Figure 5), and white for the other half.

These four displays form an ordered series in terms of apparent difficulty. That is, each succeeding display places an additional demand on *S*, by adding a new feature that must be taken into account in trying to reproduce E_2's perspective. Display 1 involves one object whose appearance varies with the position from which it is observed. *S*'s task is simply to rotate his duplicate of that single object until his perception of it matches E_2's perception of the model. Display 2, on the other hand, effectively fragments a single object, en bloc, into three separate parts, each of which must be placed in the proper position and at the correct distance relative to the others. Any cylinder can of course occupy any position in the configuration, however, since they are all identical; the configuration itself is the only invariant. This is not the case with Display 3; here, S must insure that each individual cylinder occupies one particular position in the configuration and no other. And finally Display 4 includes all preceding constraints and adds another: each cylinder must be placed, *within* its alloted position, in such a way that it has one specific appearance in terms of color; for instance, when E_2 is seated in the opposite position, the tallest block (H) must be made to show its red side, the middle one (M) its white side, and the shortest (L) a white right half and a red left half (see Figure 5).

The exact instructions and procedure were as follows.

E_2 is seated initially at the side position. E_1 places Display 1 in its proper orientation on Table A and lays its duplicate down flat on Table B. "Now he's going to sit there and look at the block very carefully. Now I'm going to give you some instructions about what to do with your block and I'd like you to listen carefully. And then, when I've finished, I'd like you to say them back to me in your own words—before you actually play the game. Now you take *your* block and put it on the paper here (on Table B) so that it looks to *you, here,* just like *that* block looks to *him, there*—so that *you* see on *your* block just what *he* sees on *his* block." If the child seems not to understand at this point, the instructions are repeated. If he then makes an incorrect response, he is told to walk over to E_2's position and "see what he sees from over there." If, upon returning, he still fails to orient the block correctly, E_1 does it for him, explaining why it is correct. E_2 then moves to the opposite position. "Now he's sitting in a different place and he's looking at his block from that seat. Put *your* block on the paper so it looks to *you* just like the *other* block looks to *him.*" If the child made a correct *first* try in the side condition but now fails when E_2 sits opposite, he is sent over to E_2's position and given a second chance, as described above. Thus any S who failed either the side or the opposite condition of Display 1 was given this second chance, in whichever condition the failure first occurred. Only one such second chance was given, however, and only in the case of Display 1. After Display 1 (Opposite), S was presented with Display 2 (Side), then Display 2 (Opposite), etc. At each new presentation, E_1 repeated the formula "Put *your* block so that it looks to *you* just like . . . , etc.," except in cases when it was perfectly obvious that the child was not going to forget what he was supposed to do. If it appeared to E_1 that S's responses to *both* subtasks of a given display were not even *approximately* correct, the next display was not presented, and the task was terminated at that point; we had discovered in pilot work that doggedly presenting Displays 2, 3, and 4 to Ss who could not manage Display 1 was a most trying experience for both E and S.

Results

The raw data available to the judge consisted of the sheets of paper on which the Ss had arranged their duplicate sets of display elements. As soon as S had finished a given arrangement, E_1 quickly traced around each element and made other necessary notations regarding position, height, and color (as in Figure 5). These annotated tracings could then be compared against a standard: a thin, translucent sheet of paper with the exact arrangement of elements traced on it, a kind of template. By superimposing this sheet over S's record and rotating it in 90° steps, the judge could make a variety of estimates concerning the record. The general judgmental strategy followed was of the "best fit" variety, and can most easily be conveyed through example. Suppose the judge wants to know if a given S's arrangement of Display 2 cylinders is a "correct" representation of what E_2 sees in the opposite position. The "best fit" strategy instructs her to place the standard sheet over S's sheet from all four perspectives (S, Side, Opposite, and the other, never-used side) and to score "correct" if S's arrangement resembles the opposite-perspective arrangement *more* than it resembles the other three. Thus S's arrangement need not be an absolutely faithful replica of what E_2 sees in order to be judged correct (and indeed, it seldom was); it simply needed to replicate E_2's perspective *more* closely that it replicated any of the other three.

The same general strategy could be applied to other scoring purposes. For instance, it could of course tell the judge not only that a given arrangement of Display 2 did not reproduce E_2's perspective, but also just which other perspective it *did* match by the "best fit" criterion. Both Displays 1 and 2 deal only with what might be called *configurational* aspects: the orientation of one object in the first case and the spatial pattern and orientation of three identical objects in the second. Displays 3 and 4 add a *height* aspect, and Display 4 a *height* and *color* aspect. It is obvious, for example, that a Display 3 (or 4) protocol may have a "correct" configuration, as defined above, but one or more cylinders may be occupying the wrong positions in this configuration, for example, H where L ought to be and vice versa. We can then apply the "best fit" strategy to this kind of problem by seeing if the front-to-back or right-to-left (or both) order of cylinders in any given record matches that which obtains from E_2's perspective. As for the *color* aspect, the same strategy would apply to each separate cylinder. We could thus establish, for example, that S had oriented two of the cylinders so that the proper color(s) show, but had not correctly oriented the third.

This strategy was followed in all scoring operations performed upon the Task IC data. The major analysis of this data was carried out by means of a scoring system devised to assess Ss' achievement level on the task as a whole. This scoring system embodied several assumptions. First, it was assumed that an adequate performance on a more complex and demanding display subtask should be weighted more heavily than success on a less complex and demanding one. Accordingly, the maximum scores for each subtask were 3, 4, 5, and 6 for Displays 1, 2, 3, and 4, respectively (and thus the highest possible total score was 36). It was also assumed that different levels or degrees of success within each subtask could be defined on an at least semilogical basis. For instance, it was supposed that an "egocentric" arrangement, one reproducing S's own point of view, constituted a prima facie less adequate performance than any other incorrect arrangement, that is, showed less evidence of role-taking activity. Other assumptions can be readily inferred from the following summary of the scoring system.

Display 1

Side position

3 configuration correct on first attempt
2 incorrect on first attempt, but correct on second attempt (that is, after going over to look from E_2's position)
0 incorrect on first attempt, and the second arrangement is the egocentric, S-perspective one
1 incorrect on first attempt, and the second arrangement is any other incorrect one

Opposite position

where S had "used up" his second attempt in the previous subtask:

3   correct
1 miscellaneous (that is, incorrect but nonegocentric)
0 egocentric

where S still had a second attempt available to him:

3 correct on first attempt
2 correct on second attempt
1 miscellaneous on second attempt
0 egocentric on second attempt

Display 2 (both subtasks)

- 4   configuration correct
- 1   miscellaneous
- 0   egocentric

Display 3 (both subtasks)

- 5   both configuration and height correct
- 4   configuration correct, L cylinder properly placed, but M and H cylinders incorrectly placed, relative to each other, on either the right-left or the front-back (or both) dimensions
- 3   configuration correct but height "more incorrect" than in 4
- 2   configuration incorrect but height correct or partly correct (that is, correct ordering of cylinders on either right-left or front-back dimensions, but not both)
- 1   miscellaneous
- 0   egocentric (both in configuration and in height)

Display 4 (both subtasks)

- 6   configuration and color correct, and height at least partly correct
- 5   configuration correct, height at least partly correct, but color only partly correct (i.e., only two of the three cylinders properly oriented as regards color)
- 4   configuration correct, and either height or color (not both) at least partly correct
- 3   either of the following: (a) configuration correct but neither height nor color even partly correct, (b) configuration incorrect but both height and color at least partly correct
- 2   configuration incorrect, but either height or color (not both) at least partly correct
- 1   miscellaneous
- 0   egocentric (in configuration, height, and color)

The term "correct" as used above was of course defined for the judge in terms of the "best fit" strategy. It became apparent that this criterion was a very liberal one, especially as regards configurational aspects on Displays 2, 3, and 4. That is, an S could arrange the cylinders in a pattern which was really not much like the one E_2 sees, but simply (and barely) *more* like it than what one would see from the other three positions. An attempt was therefore made to make the scoring system more responsive to this kind of variation. Whenever, on these three displays, an S's arrangement was judged only *minimally* correct as regards configuration,

1 point was subtracted from whatever score would otherwise have been given him on that subtask.

Despite its apparent complexity, the scoring system turned out to be fairly easy to use after a little practice, and its interjudge reliability was highly satisfactory: the product-moment correlation between the two sets of total scores was .98, with 91 percent of the Ss actually being assigned the same score by both judges.

Table 3 presents the total-score means and standard deviations for each grade group. It can be seen that the mean scores show an almost completely regular increase with age, and this developmental trend was found to be highly reliable statistically. An 8 × 2 × 2 factorial analysis

Table 3

Means and Standard Deviations of Task IC Total Scores

Measure	Grade							
	2	3	4	5	6	7	8	11
Mean	6.35	8.40	11.65	13.70	18.00	21.30	19.45	26.35
SD	3.07	3.41	4.67	8.16	8.40	9.09	11.54	7.84

of variance was carried out on these total scores. The three independent variables were: grade, sex, and IQ (above versus below the median for each grade-by-sex subgroup). The most important outcome of this analysis, from our point of view, was a significant ($p < .001$) main effect for grade. Additionally, the main effect for IQ was significant ($p < .05$), but so was the IQ-grade interaction ($p < .01$). A plot of this interaction showed that the superiority of the brighter Ss was more apparent in the upper grades (especially grades 7 and 8) than in the lower ones. And finally, there was a nonsignificant ($p < .10$) trend for boys to perform better than girls; this difference, too, was more apparent in the older groups.

Table 4 gives a more detailed picture of how each grade group performed on each subtask. Since it turned out that a fair number of otherwise correct responses were reduced 1 point for minimally adequate configuration in the case of Displays 2–4, the table also includes such responses in its definition of "maximum score." Thus, for example, the Display 3 entries include both those Ss who scored 5 and those Ss whose original score of 5 had been reduced to 4 for configurational reasons (but does *not*, of course, include those Ss whose *original* score was 4). The data in Table 4 suggest that the four displays do form an ordered series in terms of difficulty level, as we had supposed: thus, each display was mastered by roughly twice as many Ss as was its successor in the series. It is clear that the youngest Ss found even Display 1 difficult, despite the fact that it required the correct orientation of only a single object. Likewise, only a minority of even the oldest Ss could cope with Display 4 successfully, entailing as it did the joint management of configuration, height, and color with respect to an ensemble of three objects.

Table 4

Number of Subjects per Grade Achieving Maximum Scores on Each Subtask of Task IC

| | Subtask | | | | | | | |
| | Display 1 | | Display 2 | | Display 3 | | Display 4 | |
Grade	Side	Oppo-site	Side	Oppo-site	Side	Oppo-site	Side	Oppo-site
2	10	6	5	1	0	0	0	0
3	15	7	6	10	0	0	0	0
4	19	8	7	8	4	0	1	0
5	19	14	11	7	3	4	1	1
6	20	12	13	10	7	5	2	0
7	20	11	12	13	9	8	4	4
8	19	17	11	10	7	9	5	6
11	20	16	15	16	12	14	8	8
Σ	142	91	80	75	42	30	21	19

Note. The entries here also include those Ss for whom 1 point was subtracted for a "minimally correct" configuration (see text).

The column sums in Table 4 give the impression that the Opposite subtask was substantially more difficult than its Side counterpart in the case of Display 1, but not appreciably so in the case of the other three displays. Table 5 presents data which confirm this impression. This table enumerates the Ss, within each display, who achieved a "maximum score" (including the "minimum configuration" cases, as in Table 4) on one subtask only, that is, either Side but not Opposite (Pattern A) or Opposite but not Side (Pattern B). The A-B comparisons for Displays 2, 3, and 4 do not approach statistical significance, whereas that for Display 1 is obviously highly significant: 58 of 65 Ss perform better on Side than on Opposite here. It is difficult to find any plausible explanation for this curious finding. We might have supposed, a priori, that Opposite subtasks would tend to be more difficult than Side ones *in general.* For instance, it could be hypothesized that it is always harder to place oneself, imagistically, in the former perspective, since it involves a 180° versus 90° "turn" from one's own point of view. However, we found no *general* trend of this sort, as Table 5 plainly shows. We might refine the hypothesis a bit by making it interactional: the Opposite position poses more of a problem than the Side position for *younger* Ss only, that is, for individuals who are just beginning to acquire role-taking skills, who perhaps rely heavily on visual imagery for such tasks, or whatever. But again, a glance at the first two columns of Table 5 shows that the A-B ratio does not vary appreciably as a function of age: the

Table 5
Number of Subjects Showing Each Pass-Fail
Pattern on Each Task IC Display

| | Pass-Fail Pattern | | | | | | | |
| | Display 1 | | Display 2 | | Display 3 | | Display 4 | |
Grade	A	B	A	B	A	B	A	B
2	7	3	4	0	0	0	0	0
3	10	2	1	5	0	0	0	0
4	11	0	3	4	2	0	1	0
5	6	1	5	0	1	2	1	1
6	8	0	6	3	4	2	2	0
7	9	0	4	5	5	4	3	3
8	3	1	4	3	0	2	1	2
11	4	0	2	3	3	5	2	2
Σ	58	7	29	23	15	15	10	8

Note. Pattern A indicates that S achieved a "maximum score" (as defined in Table 4) for the Side subtask but not for the Opposite subtask of a given display. Pattern B indicates the converse.

older Ss also found Opposite more difficult than Side in the case of Display 1.[5]

As mentioned earlier, Task IC was patterned after one of Piaget and Inhelder's (1956) experiments on spatial representation. It is of interest therefore to analyze our data further in the light of their findings and interpretations. In their study, 100 children of 4–11 years of age were shown a scale model of three mountains and given the task of predicting the appearance of these mountains from various points of view. The "other," whose perspective the child was to identify, consisted of a doll which was placed at different positions around the mountains. Three different methods were used to evaluate the child's role-taking skill: (a) S was given three pieces of cardboard shaped like the mountains and

[5]Piaget and Inhelder (1956) make no reference to this question of differential difficulty as a function of the other's position, and presumably did not test for it in their studies of perceptual role taking.

told to arrange them so as to reproduce the doll's viewpoint (a method similar to our own); (b) S was shown a series of pictures representing various viewpoints and told to select the one which was correct for a given position of the doll; (c) conversely, S was shown a particular picture and was told to put the doll in the appropriate position. As is customary in Piagetian investigations, the results of the study were described in qualitative rather than quantitative terms. Specifically, the authors suggested a four-stage developmental sequence for this task, each stage roughly (only roughly, probably) associated with a certain age range. In the following summary of these stages, we shall dwell mostly on those assertions for which our own data may provide relevant evidence.

Stage IIA (4-6 Years). The child is wholly unable to free himself of the egocentric illusion, although he appears to make efforts to do so. In consequence, all his attempts at reproducing the doll's viewpoint end in a reproduction of his own. That is, no matter where the doll is placed, the viewpoint assigned to it (via arrangement of the cardboard replicas or via the selection of a picture) turns out to be the child's own viewpoint.

Stage IIB (6-7 Years). This stage witnesses a beginning but minimal movement away from egocentricity toward role taking and the notion of relativity of viewpoints. Aware that the doll sees *something* which is different from what he himself sees, he responds in any of several different ways. For example, he may reproduce his own viewpoint with the cardboard pieces and then slide them towards the doll, turn them so they face the doll, or some other global attempt to accommodate to the latter's viewpoint. Or he may focus attention on a single striking feature, orient it properly in terms of the doll's perspective, and neglect all the others. Whatever specific form his behavior may take, it is thought to reflect a first genuine effort at adapting to the other's point of view, but a very global, undifferentiated kind of adaptation in which the mountains are treated as a single, immutable whole.

Stage IIIA (7-9 Years). The child now recognizes that the intermountain relationships vary with the observer's position, but makes only partially successful efforts at coordinating these relationships. The mountains are no longer seen as a single, rigid whole, but the difficult problem of managing them as three related entities is only partly within his grasp. For instance, the child may arrange the pieces correctly in the front-back dimension while failing to reproduce the right-left ordering correctly, or vice versa [Piaget and Inhelder (p. 235) assert that right-left relationships generally tended to be more difficult for their Ss to manage than front-back ones].

Stage IIIB (9-10 Years or Later). This stage is completely continuous with the preceding one, and consists of the successful coordination of all the relationships in play for a given perspective. The child is now completely aware that for any perspective there is one and only one corresponding position, and vice versa, and he is able to represent with considerable accuracy the unique arrangement of mountains which determines each perspective.

The above summary omits much of the richness and subtlety of Piaget and Inhelder's account of this species of role-taking development, but it does provide certain important points of comparison with our data. First, if the age ranges set for each of their stages have any meaning at all, even our youngest Ss ought to be beyond Stage IIA. That is, it would be expected that most of our 7-9-year-old children should have some elementary concept of the relativity of roles coupled with an at least rudimentary ability to accommodate their block arrangements to the other's perspective. We would predict, therefore, that the blatant and incorrigible egocentrism of Stage IIA, concretely expressed by a predominance of egocentric versus other erroneous arrangements, should not be evident in our subject sample. The following analysis was carried out to test this prediction. The judge sorted each S's response to each subtask into one of five categories as regards configuration, using a variation of the "best fit" strategy described earlier. Four of these categories referred to the four basic positions defined by the sides of the large table shown in Figure 5. Thus, any given configuration could be Correct for wherever E_2 was sitting; it could be Egocentric; it could be either Side or Opposite (that is, Side if E_2 sat opposite or Opposite if E_2 sat at the right side); or it could be X, indicating the left-hand, "never-used" side of the table. If the judge deemed that the arrangement *clearly* deviated from what would be seen from *any* of these perspectives, she assigned it to a residual, Other category. If Stage IIA behavior were in fact strongly present in our data, we reasoned, then the Egocentric configurational error ought to be especially frequent, as measured against a baseline provided by the two "control" errors, that is, X and Side or Opposite.

Table 6 gives the number of Ss on each subtask showing each kind of configurational error, that is, omitting Correct configurations; in the case of Display 1 subtasks, data are given for both first and second attempts. It is clear that the column distributions for Displays 2–4 do not support the hypothesis of a systematic bias towards Egocentric errors. However, it is the distributions for Display 1 which should provide the most pertinent evidence, since it is the younger Ss—those most likely to show Stage IIA behavior—who account for the majority of errors here. And these distributions are quite puzzling at first glance. The Egocentric arrangement is strongly favored in the Opposite subtask, supporting the hypothesis, whereas the X arrangement predominates in the Side subtask. We think we have a plausible explanation for these data, an explanation which supports the original prediction that most of our younger Ss are in stages more advanced than IIA. The explanation states that most errors on Display 1 resulted from a correct orientation of the block as regards one, perhaps more salient aspect together with an incorrect orientation as regards another, perhaps less salient aspect. The

Table 6
*Number of Subjects per Subtask of Task IC
Showing Each Type of Configurational Error*

	Subtask							
	Side				Opposite			
	Type of Error				Type of Error			
Display	Egocentric	X	Opposite	Other	Egocentric	X	Side	Other
1 (first)	0	14	0	3	61	6	1	0
1 (second)	0	5	0	1	17	3	0	1
2	25	22	21	3	16	22	30	3
3	12	21	6	6	15	9	17	11
4	12	4	5	7	7	4	9	11

former aspect concerns the full-face as opposed to end-on dimension, that is, whether E_2 sees the block with its broad side or with its narrow side (end) facing him. The latter aspect has to do with whether, when seen full-face, its high side is to E_2's right or to his left and whether, when seen end-on, its high side is on the near end or the far end. If the Ss who made errors tended to make them because they paid attention to the former aspect (and correctly oriented the block with respect to it) while neglecting the latter, the distribution of Display 1 errors would approximate that actually obtained. Thus, in the Side subtask, an erroneous arrangement would tend to be X rather than Opposite or Egocentric, and in the Opposite subtask, an erroneous arrangement would tend to be Egocentric rather than X or Side. We could not say of an Egocentric arrangement in the Side subtask that it was "partly right" with respect to either of the two aspects mentioned. It is simply and purely "egocentric"—and it rarely occurred in our sample. But an Egocentric arrangement in the Opposite subtask is a different matter. Whereas it *might* of course have resulted from a complete absence of role-taking activity, it also happens to be partly correct (like its counterpart X in the Side subtask), that is, it correctly represents the fact that E_2 sees the block in broadside from his position—and it was a very frequent error.[6]

If Piaget and Inhelder's Stage IIA behavior cannot be identified in our data (a backhanded confirmation of their assertions about its developmental status, we think), what of their more advanced, transitional forms? It is difficult to go beyond banalities here. Development across Stages IIB and IIIA seems to be largely describable as a step-by-step, semicontinuous process of adapting first one, then another, then another, etc., aspect of the display to the other's perspective, of interrelating these

Table 7
Number of Younger (Grades 2–5) versus Older (Grades 6–11)
Subjects Achieving Minimally Correct (3) versus Correct (4)
Configuration Scores on Task IC Display 2

Subtask	Grade Group	Score		Significance Level
		3	4	
Side	2–5	26	3	$p < .001$
	6–11	23	28	
Opposite	2–5	23	3	$p < .01$
	6–11	23	26	

various aspects with increasing exactitude in terms of that perspective, and so on, with S's success in these activities no doubt dependent upon task complexity as well as his level of skill. Thus, the Display 1 errors just described could perhaps be classified as Stage IIB behavior, involving a global rather than differentiated accommodation to E_2's perspective. Likewise, our data on the other subtasks of course contain many instances of the more differentiated but still incomplete coordinations of Stage IIIA, for example, responses scored 4 on Display 3 and those scored 4 and 5 on Display 4.

There is also evidence which suggests an age-dependent progression towards greater precision and exactitude of configuration. It turned out that the judge scored the majority of the correct Display 2 constructions as "minimally correct" (score of 3 rather than 4), whereas such scores were quite rare in Displays 3 and 4. Although it is not clear why this was the case, the fact that it happened makes possible the developmental

[6]An analogous method of analysis was tried for the height and color dimensions of Displays 3 and 4 in order to find out if errors on these dimensions tended to be egocentric. This analysis also gave a negative answer, although the problem of defining error types on these dimensions was admittedly more difficult than in the case of configuration.

comparison given in Table 7. The table shows that, whereas minimally adequate configurations were common at all age levels, more accurate block placements are much rarer in the lower grade groups than in the upper ones (both chi squares were highly significant, as the table shows).

Finally, Piaget and Inhelder reported an impression in connection with Stage IIIA which is readily testable in our data: that the right-left dimension is more difficult to cope with than the front-back dimension in trying to reproduce the other's view of a set of objects. Data on height errors of these two types had been gathered automatically in the course

Table 8
*Number of Subjects per Subtask of Task IC
Showing Each Pattern of Height Error*

| | Subtask | | | |
| | Display 3 | | Display 4 | |
Error Pattern	Side	Opposite	Side	Opposite
FB correct, RL incorrect	9	17	15	14
RL correct, FB incorrect	8	4	5	6
Significance level	NS	$p < .01$	$p < .05$	$p < .10$

of the main scoring operation. Table 8 gives the number of Ss showing each of two types of error pattern on Displays 3 and 4: (a) correct alignment of the blocks in the front-back (FB) dimension but incorrect right-to-left placement (RL); and (b) the converse. It can be seen that the distributions generally support Piaget and Inhelder's impression.

Discussion

Our discussion of developmental changes on Task IB had a distinctly qualitative cast. That is, we found it easy to identify two, quite different response strategies (A and B) and could readily speculate that they might represent two distinct steps or levels in the ontogenesis of a particular species of role-taking activity. The data obtained in that study just seemed tailor-made for a qualitative, developmental-stage sort of interpretation, one which talks in terms of sequential changes in approach or strategy. In contrast, the data of Task IC have from the outset struck us as much less amenable to this sort of interpretation, and thus we have been describing them largely in quantitative terms, as though development here were primarily a question of gradual and progressive refinement of some unitary approach or skill. Although successful negotiation of these subtasks in the *quantitative* sense certainly proved to be age dependent, as predicted, we were not able to do much in the way of identifying corresponding age dependencies regarding *qualitative* differences in performance.

It was seen, however, that Piaget and Inhelder (1956) offered a thoroughgoing developmental-stage interpretation in a similar study, and there arises the question of why they felt they could while we feel we cannot. Interexperimental differences of this genre are never easy to explain. One thinks first of methodological differences: the Piagetian informal and quasiclinical procedure as opposed to our more standardized and less probing one, the fact that they used three different approaches within a single task whereas we used one approach and an ordered series of tasks, etc. It may have been that they found a qualitative diversity in this behavioral area which we, with our particular procedural and analytical techniques, could not discern; or again it may have been that their threshold for stage-developmental interpretations for a given body of data was lower than ours.

There is, however, one difference between the two studies, discussed earlier, which may be of crucial importance here: the difference in age between their and our youngest Ss. Arguments have already been presented to the effect that most of our youngest Ss had advanced beyond the primitive, highly egocentric task behavior which Piaget and Inhelder reported for their youngest Ss (younger than ours). Moreover, a close scrutiny of Piaget and Inhelder's developmental-stage account suggests that it is precisely these more primitive behaviors which appear most clearly separable, *qua* stages or levels, from the rest. A simplifying but not wholly distorting paraphrase of their account would divide the developmental sequence into two rather than four periods. At first, the child is wholly or almost wholly unaware of the basic fact that the other does not see the display as he does. The result is either a repeatedly egocentric response or at best one which represents a woefully inadequate accommodation to the other's viewpoint. Subsequently, he becomes clearly aware of this basic fact and makes progressively more and more adequate accommodations. The operative term here is *progressively*, because although wide individual variation in degree of success is encompassed within this second "stage," this variation is liable to be very difficult to partition further in terms of qualitative differences, in terms of "substages." Indeed, the difference between Piaget and Inhelder's later stages, particularly between IIIA and IIIB, seems to be of an essentially quantitative rather than qualitative sort.

If, as we suspect, most of our Ss fell somewhere in the second rather than the first of these two "stages," it is not to be wondered at that we were more impressed with differences of degree than of kind. We think that these children were in fact largely aware of what the task demanded (and knew that simply copying the model display from their own perspective was not the implicit requirement). However, this awareness being a necessary but hardly sufficient factor, they differed widely in their ability to cope with these demands—differed as a function of age, task, and doubtless many other variables. There is a faint parallel here with their performance on Task IB. There too, most of these Ss appeared to grasp the basic role-taking requirements of the game, but differed markedly—and in a more unequivocally qualitative way—in their response to these requirements.

TASK ID

A preview of this task was given in Chapter 1. E_1 displays a series of seven pictures and asks S to tell the story which they illustrate. Three specific pictures are then removed, E_2 enters the room, and S is requested to predict the story which E_2 would probably tell from the remaining four pictures above (E_2 had supposedly never seen the whole series of seven). The pictures are so constructed that the entire series suggests a certain story while the series of four suggests another, quite different story. This task constitutes a role-taking problem under the following interpretation. During the second part of the task, S presumably views the four-picture sequence from a cognitive perspective different from that of E_2. E_2 is supposed to see them in isolation, as it were, and "read" them for the dominant story line which they alone suggest. The child, on the other hand, apprehends them simply as elements taken from a previous whole, that is, the seven-picture sequence, and construes them in terms of their meaning within that whole. Whereas E_2 sees them naïvely and afresh, S can scarcely help but see them through the lens of his just-previous experience. S's role-taking task, therefore, is believed to consist in suppressing his own perspective in favor of participating in E_2's, so as to interpret the data as E_2 might interpret them.

There are several points of similarity and difference between Task ID and its two predecessors. Like IC and unlike IB, the criterion here is role-taking *accuracy* rather than *activity*, since there is in fact a putatively "correct" four-picture story with which the child's story can be compared; however, as will be seen, the data did offer a little more insight into the underlying processes involved than was the case with IC. And while the visual appearance of things plays a larger role here than in IB, it is not really a "perceptual" role-taking task in the sense that IC is: that is, it is not the bare visual input from the four pictures to E_2 which must be predicted, but rather the inferences he would draw from it in linking the four pictures into a coherent story. Actually, like IB but unlike IC, the visual input in the "retinal image" sense is obviously the same for both S and E_2 in this task.

Procedure

The stimulus materials consisted of seven pasteboard cards, some square and some rectangular, with an average surface area of about 20 square inches. On each card was painted in color a scene in which a boy is the central figure. The pictures were the following.

Card 1. The boy is walking along the sidewalk, whistling and waving a stick.

Card 2. The boy looks frightened and drops his stick as he sees a rather ugly looking dog running towards him.

Card 3. The boy runs, looking anxiously over his shoulder at the dog, who is in hot pursuit.

Card 4. The boy is shown running with arms outstretched toward an apple tree laden with fruit. The dog is not shown in the picture and the boy's face (showing fear in the two previous pictures) is hidden by a branch of the tree.

Card 5. The boy scrambles up the tree, with the dog nipping at his heels.

Card 6. The boy is shown standing up in the tree. The dog can be seen across the street, trotting away (he looks smaller in this picture, and with no visible evidence of ferocity). Although the boy's head is partly turned in the dog's direction, it shows no particular emotional expression.

Card 7. The boy is seated in the tree, munching an apple, with the dog nowhere in evidence.

It was intended, of course, that this sequence of seven pictures would elicit stories something like the following: a vicious dog chases a terrified boy who finds refuge by climbing a handy tree; once secure there, and with the dog abandoning the chase, he takes advantage of the kind of tree he happens to be in and eats an apple. The four-picture sequence was constructed by simply deleting cards 2, 3, and 5 (the only cards which depict a *threatening* dog), leaving cards 1, 4, 6, and 7, in that order. This set of pictures was designed to elicit a very different story, of which the following might be the prototype: a boy spies a tree laden with apples, climbs up to get one, and sits there eating it; the dog shown in the third picture in the sequence (card 6) is simply part of the background and of no relevance to the story.

The instructions and procedure were the following.

"He (E_2) has left the room and he won't be able to see what we are going to do, will he? Here is a series of seven pictures which tell a story, just like the comics in the newspaper." The cards are then placed in proper sequence on the table. "You tell me what's going on. Begin here at the beginning." If the child failed to indicate these things in his narration, he was asked why the boy climbed the three and what he was doing in the last picture. (It turned out that virtually all the Ss quickly seized the essentials of the seven-picture story and could express them without difficulty, either spontaneously or upon minimal inquiry). "That's fine. Now Mr. Wright hasn't seen any of these pictures. I'm going to call him back into the room and show him *just* these four pictures (cards 1, 4, 6 and 7). I want you to *pretend* you are he and tell the story that you think *he* would tell. Okay (calls in E_2). Now (speaking to E_2) these pictures tell a story." E_2 then addresses S and says: "What story do these pictures tell me?" Again, if S failed to clarify these matters spontaneously in the course of his story, he has asked: "Why does *he* (point to E_2) think the boy climbed the tree?" Or: "What does *he* think about that dog there (card 6), what does *he* think the dog is there for?"

Results

As in IB, each S's response to this task was assigned to one of four categories, with an interjudge agreement of 85 percent.

Category 1. When asked to predict the story E_2 would tell, S gives a more or less straightforward presentation of the "correct" four-picture story, that is, the boy is said to climb the tree in response to some non-fear motive (almost always to get an apple) and the dog is said not to be a motive for climbing (is said to be irrelevant to the story, "just walking along," etc.). If these crucial points had not been mentioned spontaneously during the narration proper, they were readily given during the brief inquiry afterwards. Here is an example:

"Apparently the boy is just walking down the sidewalk and, uh, he sees the apples on the tree in this case and he goes to climb 'em. And the dog in this case would be just, uh, a passerby and he's just eating the apples. He just climbed the tree to eat the apples."

Category 4. S gives a more less straightforward presentation of the seven-picture story rather than the four-picture one. That is, the dog is clearly established as the motive for climbing the tree during the narration proper, prior to inquiry. For example:

"Well, he's walking along with a stick. I mean should I say what—um—um?" (You would say—you want to say just what Mr. Wright would say, don't you?) "He's walking along with a stick, and the dog's gonna chase him so he runs—

he goes up the tree with his stick. The dog's walking away and while he was there he's eating an apple."

Category 3. Although the fear-of-dog motive is not explicitly mentioned during the narration, it is readily supplied during the inquiry. In most cases so scored, the narration is a bare account of the boy's action, devoid of motivational statements of any kind. But when E_1 subsequently asks why E_2 thinks the boy climbed the tree, the usual response is the flatly given, "because the dog chased him." Although categorized separately, we would not try to defend the position that these responses really represent a higher performance level than the preceding ones. The absence of a spontaneously given fear-of-dog motive here seemed in most cases to be due to an indisposition to make spontaneous motivational inferences in general. Here is an example of a Category 3 response:

"He's singing and, then he runs, he sees a tree. He climbs up it and he's eating an apple." (Fine. Why does Mr. Wright think that the boy wanted to climb the tree?). "So the dog don't get him—bite him."

Category 2. All responses not scorable for the previous three categories were assigned to this one. It was not simply a "wastebasket" category, however. In most cases, it subsumed stories in which (in narrative or in inquiry) some sort of fear motive is introduced, as in Categories 3 and 4, but the child also says *something* which bespeaks some recognition by the child that E_2 is operating from the four-picture sequence only, that is, something which suggests at least a modicum of sensitivity to the role-taking aspects of the task. He might, for instance, include expressions like, "he could tell from these pictures that. . . ." Or S might attempt to rationalize the fear motive on the basis of what E_2 might infer, for example, "he's running to the tree and there's a dog here, so he was probably afraid of the dog." As a third example, he might even substitute some other fear stimulus for the dog ("he's afraid of a ghost or something"), perhaps as a kind of "compromise" between his and E_2's perspective. Although some responses of uncertain maturity level surely found their way into this residual category, the modal response here appeared to us to show evidence of more role-taking activity than those scored for Categories 3 and 4.

Table 9 presents the distribution of Ss at each grade level across the four scoring categories. As in Task IB an eight-cell chi square table was constructed from Table 9 by combining adjacent grades and adjacent categories (that is, Categories 1 and 2 versus Categories 3 and 4). The resulting chi square was 22.10 ($df = 3$), statistically reliable at $p < .01$. Analogous chi squares for sex and IQ as independent variables were not significant (although IQ showed a weak trend in the expected direction). A glance at Table 9 shows the major sources of the significant age trend. Category 1 appears to increase with age, Category 3 to decrease with age, and Categories 2 and 4 to maintain a fairly constant minority status at all grade levels. Moreover, most of the frequency change for Categories 1 and 3 occurs between third and fourth grade; the chi square would certainly not have even approached statistical significance had the two youngest groups not been included in the sample.

Table 9
Number of Subjects per Grade Scored for Each Category in Task ID

Category	Grade							
	2	3	4	5	6	7	8	11
1	8	8	12	12	13	18	12	14
2	0	1	4	2	2	1	2	4
3	8	8	1	4	2	0	3	0
4	4	3	3	2	3	1	3	2

Another, incidental analysis was performed on the data of Task ID. In his early studies (Piaget, 1928; Flavell, 1963, pp. 275-276), Piaget found that the tendency to link statements by means of causal and logical connectives ("because," "therefore," "although," etc.) develops with age. Older children have a better grasp of causal and logical relationships than younger ones, and this is reflected in their spontaneous language usage. Since the action sequences represented in both the seven- and four-picture series involve relationships of this genre (for example, the boy climbed the tree *because* . . .), we decided to see if we could corroborate Piaget's developmental observations. Accordingly, the judge was instructed to make two counts on the spontaneous portion of each S's entire verbal protocol, that is, excluding his responses to any inquiry E_2 may have made to either story. She first took a count of *total connectives*: all utterances linking two clauses together, such as "and," "so," "and then," "because," etc. Following this, she counted the subset of this total judged to be *causal connectives*, that is, those which appear to relate two assertions in some sort of cause and effect rather than merely juxtapositive or serial fashion. "Because" was a clear and frequent instance. "So" was also frequent, but was regarded as *causal* only when it substituted for "thus," "hence," "therefore," etc., rather than for "and then." For instance, the "so" in this sentence was scored as *causal*: "The dog chased him *so* he climbed up the tree." It was not scored *causal*, however, when it occurred in settings like the following: "The boy is walking down the street whistling, *so* he sees a tree, *so* there's this dog

chasing him, etc." The ratio of *causal* to *total connectives* was then computed for each *S*. The correlation between the ratios given by the two
judges was .94.

The prediction was of course that the magnitude of the ratio should
increase with age, reflecting a developmental trend toward the use of
causal connectives (or, in the case of words like *so*, toward the causal use
of ambiguous connectives). The ratios were divided at the median and
adjacent grade groups were combined, yielding an eight-cell chi square
table. The chi square value was 12.63 ($df = 3$; $p < .01$), with the trend
in the predicted direction; similar analyses of IQ and sex effects yielded
nonsignificant chi squares. There is undoubtedly a direct connection between this developmental finding and the relatively high prevalence of
Category 3 scores among the younger children: as mentioned earlier,
the *S*s so categorized tended to give stories largely devoid of motivational
inference, that is, devoid of statements joined by "because." The child's
tendency or lack of tendency to include motivational inferences in his
story may of course also be taken as a rough index of his general dispositions to engage in role-taking activity, and thus of his level of role-
taking development (Dymond, Hughes, and Raabe, 1952; Gollin, 1954,
1958).

Discussion

The data shown in Table 9 suggest the presence of some developmental change with respect to Task ID. So far as our measures indicate, this change is fairly modest, quantitatively, and seems to be largely
completed by age 9–10.[7] A conceptual analysis of the task requirements,
buttressed by an examination of the *S*'s actual responses, suggests some
ideas about the character of this change.

Viewed from a certain perspective, it is difficult to see why *any S* in
this age group should have trouble predicting E_2's story. All he has to do,
it would seem, is to let himself be the passive and compliant servant
of the perceptual evidence directly before him. This evidence, that is, the
four cards taken above, has a dominant inferential "pull" toward a
particular story. Since this story is in fact the "correct" one, that is,
that which E_2 would presumably tell, all *S* need do to perform success-

---

[7]It seems doubtful that the role-taking skills relevant to this task have really achieved
their maximum development by age 9–10. A more reasonable hypothesis is that there
are developmental changes beyond this age which Task ID (and/or the category system
used to measure responses to it) is insufficiently sensitive to reveal. In the paragraphs
which follow, we shall therefore emphasize what we believe our *S*s' responses suggest
about the cognitive processes elicited by this kind of role-taking problem, rather than
making conjectures—futile, on present evidence—about exact developmental timing
and sequence.

fully is to allow this "pull" to act upon him. From a purely sensory-input standpoint, both S and E_2 are confronted with the same visual data, seen from the same spatial perspective; from this standpoint, the task really has no role-taking character at all. It would rather seem that the task requires, not role-taking skill, but something much more elementary, for example, the ability to make simple interpretations of visual data (from one's *own* point of view). Young children are capable of this kind of behavior. Why, then, should Task ;D pose difficulties for children as old as our Ss?

The answer, obviously, resides in the fact that they have previously encountered the same data in a different setting. There has, in effect, just been a kind of "semantic polarization" of the four cards which now makes it difficult for S to see them in isolation, "as they are," and thereby draw from them their most compelling four-card-sequence meaning. It is solely this previous experience with the same cards which makes the task a role-taking one. That experience has "programmed" S to interpret the data in a particular way, from a particular point of view. Since E_2 is defined as a naïve observer, without such prior experience, he has a different point of view. The task thus creates a gap between two roles or perspectives which S must bridge, and therein lies his problem.

The question then is, what sorts of cognitive abilities might be needed to effect this bridge in perspectives? And correspondingly, what sorts of intellectual dispositions or attitudes might interfere? In reading over the protocols, we were impressed with one factor which seemed to play a particularly crucial role. This was the S's ability (or inability) to regard the cards in rather the same way as a sophisticated adult regards projective test stimuli: as ambiguous, multipotential data, subject to a number of possible constructions or interpretations. For such an observer, the perceptual data are regarded as intrinsically dead things into which he, and he alone, breathes life through his own interpretative act. This attitude implies considerable psychological differentiation between observer and observed, with the observer quite aware of the distinction between the inferences which he makes and the observables from which they are drawn. Piaget, among others, has described this sort of cognitive attitude in many publications and in many different ways: it calls to mind his notions of *operations, reversibility, decentration, relativity,* etc., as contrasted with *pre-operations, irreversibility, centration, intellectual realism,* and the like (Flavell, 1963).

In the present study, this attitude towards data is in force when an S has a clear understanding that the cards and the story he has attributed to them are not irrevocably wedded together; that a given card can be interpreted this way in this setting and that way in that setting; that a card in a given setting could have several different meanings, some with better perceptual support than others. For one who possesses this attitude, it would be wholly natural to suppose that the same four cards could be interpreted differently in the two parts of our experiment. One interpretation is more tenable when they form part of the seven-picture sequence; another is more reasonable when they are seen alone; neither is any more "true," any more "inscribed" in the cards than the other. For such an S, there is no question as to whether E_2 may interpret the cards differently than he—with his prior experience—is prone to do; the only problem is to find out what that different interpretation would most probably be.

An S without this kind of psychological distance from the visual data, on the other hand, may be in for difficulties on Task ID. For instance, he may be inclined to view the seven-picture story as the story, the real one, and thus assume automatically that E_2 will tell that story, or, at most, may wonder only if he will "discover" it. Or if his intellectual realism is not quite that extreme, his inability to maintain proper distance from the observables may hinder him from finding alternative stories, may cause him to "regress" to the original story when pressed about motives (perhaps momentarily losing whatever role-taking set he had had before), and the like. Our conception of the processes underlying performance on this task is a dynamic one (to use a much-abused term). That is, we envision a constant and unremitting pressure of S's previous story on his present cognitions and their verbal expression. Depending upon his ability to remain apart from the givens, to look at them without prejudice, etc. (the ability just discussed), we variously imagine him: succumbing immediately to this pressure without any awareness of its existence; alternately succeeding and failing to rid himself of its influence, with any manner of partial or "compromise" solutions manifest in the resulting story; or successfully combating all tendencies toward a seven-picture story, even to the point of overstressing (a kind of reaction formation?) the irrelevance of the dog as a story element.

To recapitulate, it has been argued that the problem character of Task ID effectively resides in the fact that, when S looks at the four pictures in order to predict E_2's story, these pictures function as insistent cues for cognitive responses which are at variance with that story. It was further suggested that the possession of a certain attitude towards perceptual data, described by Piaget and others as one of the hallmarks of developmentally mature cognition, is of material assistance in suppressing or disregarding these cues. Since children would be expected to possess this attitude in varying degrees, depending upon developmental level and other sources of individual differences, such variability ought to be detectable in our *Ss'* protocols. That is, we ought to be able to see evidence of such things as intellectual realism and its opposite; of struggle and lack of struggle; of failure, partial failure, and success in disregarding seven-picture-story cues; in short, we ought to be able to see traces of the various cognitive phenomena described in the preceding paragraphs. It turned out that about one-fourth of the 160 protocols contained at least something that could be interpreted as evidence of the processes in question (the rest showed little direct evidence of process, for example, a straightforward, unelaborated seven- or four-picture story). The following examples taken from this subset of protocols should provide concrete reference for the previous discussion. We have italicized some of the more illuminating passages in each.

"I can't do it." (Well, you try and see if you can't.) "Well, this little boy is walking down the street and, let's see, *I don't know what to do without seeing the other pictures.*" (After further encouragement, *S* produced a story which, with inquiry, was scored as Category 3.)

"*You mean he'd tell a different one?*" (Well now, I don't know whether he'd tell a different one or not. You'll have to decide.) "A little." (Maybe. You go ahead.) "Well, he's walking down the sidewalk and he sees these—this apple tree. Well, *he lost his dog* and he saw these apple trees and he climbed up this tree *to get some apples* and he sits eating—sitting in the tree eating them." (That's fine. What does Mr. Wright think about that dog there? What does he think that dog is there for?) "Well, *he might—uh—have been somewhere else looking for the boy, and then he's walking back home.* That could be his house in that yellow picture."

(*S* tells a more or less straightforward four-picture story, indicating that the boy climbed the tree because he wanted an apple.) (That's very good. What does Mr. Wright think about that dog, Bonnie? What does he think that dog is there for?) "*He's chasing the boy.*" [Does he (points to E_2) know that?] "*He doesn't know it but he (the boy) does.*"

"Well, this boy was walking and he's started to running up in an apple tree and then this dog started walking away and then he picked an apple and started eating it." (That's a fine story, Mark. Mark, why does Mr. Wright think the boy wanted to climb the tree?) "*Should I tell?*" (Well, you tell me what you think *he* thinks, understand? If I were to ask Mr. Wright, "Mr. Wright, why do you think that the boy's climbing the tree?" now what do you think Mr. Wright will tell me?) "*Wants to get an apple, I guess.*"

(*S* gives a seven-picture story, clearly indicating that the dog is chasing the boy. On impulse, E_1 made further inquiry.) (Does Mr. Wright *see* the dog chasing him?) "*No.*" (So he just—how does he know?) "*By me telling him?*"

"Pulling (the stick) and he's going on the sidewalk. Now, uh, *he's scared* and he's running toward this tree. He's gone up it and he has this stick. Now he's safe up there and *this scary ghost*—and he's eating an apple." (So, what was—why does Mr. Wright think the boy wants to climb the tree?) "Uh, *because he sees a scary ghost.*" (And, now, what does Mr. Wright think about this dog here? What does Mr. Wright think that . . . ?) "*Oh, he's just crossing the sidewalk.*"

"*Not—like the last one or just the way it is now?*" (Just the way it is now. Just the way that he would tell it.) "Well, the boy was walking down. He's whistling. Next he's—uh—he's running and then he gets up the tree. And then this dog starts to walk away and the boy's up the tree eating an apple." (That's good. Why does Mr. Wright think the boy wants to climb the tree?) "*Mean, tell that?*" (Well, why—no—why does Mr. Wright think the boy wants to climb the tree? What do you suppose he thinks?) "*Cause he sees the apple tree and he wants to go and eat it.*"

"Well, *he probably could tell* that he was just walking down the sidewalk whistling one afternoon and then, uh, looks like (incomprehensible on tape) just going up the tree for—he's running up a tree. And then he sees the, uh, that the dog—that there's a dog going back *so then he probably gets the idea that the dog is*" (pause). (That the dog chased him up, you mean?) "*Yeah, I don't know for sure yet, though.* Now—and then he just, uh, then the—after the dog goes back *he feels safe* and gets an apple. And he eats it on the way down." (Okay. That's very good. Now, um, why does Mr. Wright think that the boy wants to climb the tree?) "*To get an apple.*" (And, um, what did you say about this dog here?) "*Uh, well, I've seen the whole thing but to him it would look like he's just climbed the tree and there's a dog in the picture. They took a picture and the dog was right in the picture.*"

"There's the boy walking along. He runs up into an apple tree. Then, while he's standing up there—he's just standing up there—a dog goes across the street and he starts sitting down to eat the apple." (Fine. Now, why does Mr. Wright think the boy wants to climb the tree?) "*Well, he hadn't seen the previous pictures of the dog after him.*" (But why would he think that the boy would want to climb?) "*To eat the apples.*"

"Uh, I think, ah, the boy'd be walking down the street and he sees, uh, apple and he'd go for the apple. And he, uh, gets up in the tree and he sees a dog walking across the street *but he doesn't think much of it.* Then he starts eating the apple."

"Well, the boy's walking down the street and he sees the apple tree and he runs toward it and climbs it. He's still eating—and he climbs up and eats the apple." (Fine. Okay. Now why does Mr. Wright think that the boy wants to climb the tree?) "*Oh, because he doesn't know that the dog was chasing the boy.*" (But why does he think the boy might want to, though?) "*Because he want—he might want the apple.*" (Okay, and what does Mr. Wright think about this dog here. What does he think that dog is there for?) "*Well, he's just walking across the street.*"

"Well, this—this boy was walking down the street whistling and he noticed this apple tree and *obviously wanted to get an apple* so he climbs up it and he noticed a dog *and, uh, well, I presume he'd stay there until the dog would go away* and then finish up eating the apple."

"Well, uh, first of all, this boy was, uh, walking along the sidewalk whistling and, uh, he, uh, was hitting the fence with a piece of wood. And, um, he saw an apple tree so he started running for it and he went up there and uh, he looked around a little while and, uh, he saw a dog across the street *which has nothing to do with it* but—uh, then he decided to eat some apples, so he did. He ate the apples." (Fine. Now why does Mr. Wright think that the boy wants to climb the tree?) "To eat the apples."

"Well, to start off the little boy was walking down the street whistling— appears that he's very happy. And, uh, he came to an apple tree and, uh, *then it looks like, he, well, sh—, should I assume that I've seen these before? Myself?*" (Well, you want to tell the story, only tell the story that Mr. Wright can see.) "And he climbed up the tree, *apparently to get an apple*. And then he found an apple and he ate it." (Uh, uh, what does Mr. Wright think about that dog there? What does he think that dog is there for? (pause) *"Well, he might* (pause) *he sees that the little boy's looking at the dog or looks like he's looking at the dog, so he might assume that—ah—since he's running toward the apple tree that the dog was after him, but it doesn't necessarily mean it because the dog could just be walking across the street."*

Task ID appears to illustrate particularly well two important points about role-taking problems and processes. First, it highlights the assertion made in Chapter 1 and implied in the preceding pages here: that role-taking processes are part of the whole cognitive fabric, that is, they cannot realistically be taken as something apart from and unrelated to other cognitive processes. Take, for example, a child in our study whose perception of the four cards remains indelibly distorted by his previous cognition of their meaning. We can of course describe this state of affairs in purely role-taking terms: he *is* manifestly unable to discriminate a naïve other's role attributes with respect to these pictures. But we can also characterize him as *concrete, stimulus bound, rigid,* or *intellectually realistic* (in Piaget's sense). And we can surely speak of Piagetian *irreversibility* or *inability to decenter* here: having embarked on a certain inferential course this child cannot return to the starting point, "wipe the slate clean," and look at the same pictures from a new and fresh perspective. These characterizations—and we could add to the list—also fit the child's behavior in this situation, even though they do not *sound* like descriptions of a role-taking inadequacy. Can we then relate these various expressions in some cause-and-effect way, for example, irreversibility regarded as the *cause* of role-taking failure or conversely? We think, rather, that the relation is more one of partial synonymity or overlap in meaning, with the choice of terminology depending upon theoretical predilection and the nature of the task in question. In a sense, and within certain limits, a cognitive task becomes a *role-taking* task because its author finds it reasonable to construe the variation in behavior which it elicits in role-taking terms, that is, in terms of some preexisting conceptions about role taking and its development. This state of affairs is, we need hardly add, not unique to this particular domain of psychological inquiry.

Task ID also illustrates, as much or more than any task we have worked with, a psychological obstacle which is more or less indigenous to all role-taking problems. This obstacle consists in the fact that the very act of trying to predict the other's perspective may serve to enliven your own. In the present task, for instance, the child must survey the four cards in sequence in order to find a story appropriate to E_2's point of view. But the very act of surveying them stimulates his own point of view, since the cards have become cues for the seven-picture story. The point is a simple but important one. Role taking usually demands more than just the ability to search and find the other's perspective. It is also likely to demand the ability to counteract the insistent intrusions of one's own during the search. This also holds true where the role-taking activity serves communicative efforts, as was suggested in the last chapter (see Figure 2) and as will be shown in the next.

CHAPTER THREE

Communication in Middle Childhood and Adolescence

This chapter takes up the remaining two tasks of the series administered in Study I. Like the preceding three, these tasks also deal with role taking development, but as it mediates effective verbal communication rather than other behaviors. Task IA treats the problem of adapting a communicative message to the specific input needs of a single listener. Task IE, in contrast, deals with the problem of communicating to several listeners at once, each of whom has different listener role attributes.

TASK IA

The basic elements of this experiment were as follows. Ss are instructed to communicate information about a given set of visual materials to two listeners who differ markedly in listener role attributes: a blindfolded one, whose informational input must consist solely of whatever S tells him; a sighted one, who can supplement this informational source considerably by looking at the materials the child is discussing. The major hypothesis was that the *difference* between these two messages would augment with age, presumably as a function of role-taking development. That is, older children would be expected to be more sensitive to the differing input needs of the two listeners and fashion their messages accordingly, namely, a much more information-laden one to the blindfolded receiver.

Procedure

We shall begin by summarizing the general procedure and experimental design, leaving exact procedural details until later. S was first taught to play a simple competitive game with E_1. Although this game was our own invention, it was intentionally designed to be a familiar prototype which children in this age group would have little difficulty in learning. There is a cube with different colored faces on it which is shaken in a cup and then thrown on the table. If a red face turns up, say, the player moves his "man" (actually, a toy pig) along a board which has colored bands on it and stops at the first red band he comes to. Then the other player takes his turn with the cube and moves his own pig to the appropriate band. The two players continue to alternate in this way and the first player to get up to the end of the board and back to the beginning wins the game. Finally, there is one, more or less self-evident rule which normally comes into force sometimes during the course of play: if the cube turns up a black face, the player cannot move his pig, since it happens that there are no bands of that color on the board. The game was taught to each child *nonverbally*. That is, E_1 and the child simply played through the game together, E_1 using gestures where needed. It turned out that, as we had hoped, even the youngest Ss quickly learned to play it correctly.

After the game had been played twice through, E_2 entered the room. The child was told that he did not know anything about the game and that it would be the child's task to tell him how to play. There would be two "rules," however. First, the child was forbidden to touch any of the game materials as he communicated; that is, he could not teach the game by actually playing it, as he himself had learned it. And second, the listener would not be allowed to say anything during the communication; he would just sit and listen.

For half the boys and girls at each grade level, E_2 was blindfolded throughout the proceedings, a fact that was very carefully brought to the child's attention. For the other half of the sample, E_2 listened without a blindfold.[1] In the case of the second- and eighth-grade groups only, there was a second communication trial, always to a blindfolded listener in the person of E_3. These 40 Ss were told that this man, too, knew nothing of the game and needed to be told how to play it. Thus, for half the boys and girls in these two grades, the listener sequence was sighted E_2-blindfolded E_3, and for the other half it was blindfolded E_2-blindfolded E_3. To recapitulate the design: 80 of the 160 children communicated to a sighted listener while the other 80, matched for grade, sex, and IQ, talked to a blindfolded one; 20 Ss (second and eighth graders)

[1]Each grade group was thus made up of four subgroups of five Ss each: boys who communicated to blindfolded E_2, girls who communicated to sighted E_2, etc. Ss were assigned to the two listener conditions in such a way as to insure that these four subgroups would be closely matched on IQ.

from each of these two subgroups then described the game a second time, invariably to a blindfolded listener.

The following is a more detailed statement of the testing procedure:

At the beginning of the session, the game materials are spread on the table and covered with a cloth. They include: (a) a wooden board, 20 in. $\times$ 15 in. $\times$ $\frac{3}{4}$ in., with eight colored bands or strips running transversely across it in the sequence red-blue-white-red-blue-white-red-blue; the bands are divided by a black line which runs down the middle of the board, simply to give each player a "side" to move his pig on; (b) a cube (1 in. sq.) with two red, two blue, and two black faces, like colors on opposing sides; (c) a plastic cup; and (d) two rubber toy pigs, one white and one brown. Since Task IA is the first of the sequence of five, E_1 has just ushered S into the experimental room, tried to make him comfortable and relaxed, etc., and now begins to instruct him as follows. "We are going to do several things here today and I think you'll find them fun to do. Now the first thing we'll do is play this game (removes cloth). Now this is an easy game to play and I'm going to show you how to play it without using any words at all. We'll just play along together for a while and you'll learn to play it as we go along." Then E_1 performs the following actions:

1. He holds the two pigs out, one in each fist, and indicates by gestures that S should choose one.

2. He places the two pigs in starting position at one end of the board.

3. He points in turn to the two red, two blue, and two black faces of the cube, and indicates that there are also red and blue bands on the board.

4. He shakes the cube in the cup, dumps it on the table, and moves his pig to the first band which corresponds to the color of the cube's upturned face, carefully indicating this correspondence to the child.

5. He hands the cube and cup to the child, indicating that he should do the same thing.

6. The two continue to take turns in this fashion until one of the players has moved his pig up to the other end of the board and then back to the starting point, at which point E_1 *says* that that player "won" the game (the only time he speaks rather than gestures). The game is then played through a second time.

7. The first time someone turns up a black cube face, E_1 indicates that the pig cannot be moved on that turn, since there are no black bands on the board. If such an event appeared to be in danger of not occurring during the two trials (it almost always did), E_1 in best sleight-of-hand tradition saw to it that it did occur on one of his throws.

E_1 covers the game materials again after play is completed. E_2 now enters the room, is introduced, and—with young and/or shy children especially—chats a bit with S. What happens thereafter depends upon the listener role which E_2 assumes for that S.

E_2 **Sighted.** "My friend here doesn't know anything at *all* about this game. I'd like to have you *tell* him how to play the game so he'd be able to play it himself later. Tell him just as *well* as you can—try to tell him *so* well that he would know *exactly* how to play it when he gets a chance to, tomorrow or sometime. There are a couple of rules, though. One rule is that you can't actually *touch* or *move* anything while you are telling him—you can't actually *pick up* any of the pieces. The other rule is that he is not allowed to *say* anything to you while you are explaining the game—he'll just sit and listen. Go ahead now, tell him how to play the game" (removes cloth from game materials). If the child seems hesitant about communicating, E_1 encourages him (without, of course, attempting to direct the discourse). If S asks if he may point, he is told that he may. If he asks a question of E_2, he is reminded that the latter is not permitted to reply. E_2 himself sits there looking friendly and acceptant throughout the communication, but attempts not to selectively reinforce any part of S's message.

E_2 **Blindfolded.** The first three sentences are identical to those of the preceding instructions. E_1 then says: "Now I'm going to put a blindfold on him (ties a black cloth around E_2's head, covering his eyes) so he won't be able to *see* anything while you tell him how to play the game. He'll be able to *hear*, of course, but he won't be able to *see* anything. You know what it's like to have a blindfold on, don't you?" If S appears at all uncertain, E_1 playfully puts a second cloth over S's eyes for a moment to show him. "Fine. Now there are a couple of rules. . . ." The rest of the procedure is identical to that of the sighted condition.

The second and eighth graders gave a second communication to blindfolded E_3 immediately after their message to E_2. The instructions were the standard "E_2 blindfolded" ones, with slight modifications appropriate to Ss' previous experience, for example, "Now *this* man doesn't know anything about the game *either*," ". . . but he won't be able to *see* anything like the other man could," etc.

At the conclusion of each message, E_1 made rough notes of the amount of gesturing and pointing which had occurred (if any), and also noted the extent to which S looked at his listener while he talked.

Results

The data of this experiment could be examined from two different perspectives. First, a search could be made for developmental changes, quantitative and qualitative, in what S says when called upon to communicate to any given listener. One might suppose, for example, that older Ss would tend to give longer, clearer, better organized, etc., messages to *both* blindfolded and sighted audiences. In analysis of variance terminology, this amounts to the approach which we followed in Tasks IB, IC, and ID: an interest in age as a "main effect" with respect to a variety of task performance measures. But one could also approach the data in a different way, a way which the structure of the previous tasks did not permit. That is, one could *compare* the communications given to the two types of listeners and see if there are age changes, not only *within* a given communication situation, but in the *relation between* the two messages. The interest here is no longer centered on age as a *main* effect, but rather as it *interacts* with the variable of listener role, that is, sighted versus blindfolded. Although we analyzed the data from both these points of view, the second type of analysis was of preponderant interest. As mentioned earlier, the major hypothesis in this study took the interactional rather than main-effect form: that there would be a progressively greater *differentiation* between the two messages with age, due to a growing sensitivity to the difference in input requirements involved.

In order to test this hypothesis, it was necessary to find suitable measures of communicative performance. Such measures ought to possess at least two characteristics: they should have some face validity as estimates of communicative adequacy, and they should be amenable to analysis of variance treatment, that is, should appear sufficiently continuous, should promise adequate ranges, etc. The following three measures seemed to meet these requirements.

A. *Different Words.* S's score here consisted simply of the number of *different* words contained in his message; for example, "is" can contribute only 1 point to S's score, even though it may occur many times in the message. The judge scored as "different" words which were in *any* way different, for example; "my," "mine," "pig," "pigs," "take," and "taking" were all regarded as "different" for scoring purposes.

B. *Game Information.* This measure was composed of a series of rating scales, S's final score consisting of the sum of the scores obtained on all scales. Each scale referred to some component of the game and S's score on that scale was intended to reflect how fully and adequately he had informed the listener about that component.[2] The name of each

---

2The phrase "he had informed" is not strictly accurate. The judge was instructed to look at this measure from the listener's rather than the speaker's standpoint. That is, her question was always: how well informed about the game can I assume *this* listener to be at the conclusion of S's message? For the blindfolded listener, this is roughly

component is given below, together with its rating scale. Also presented is a statement of the essential information concerning each component, used by the judge to help define the high end of the scale.

1. *Game Materials*[3]

> (a) *Cup* (0, 1). There is a cup.

> (b) *Cube* (0, 1, 2, 3). There is a little wooden cube with two black faces, two red faces, and two blue faces (which serves as a kind of die in the play).

> (c) *Pigs* (0, 1, 2). There are two little pigs (animals, "men," etc.). Each player has one as his "man" in the game.

> (d) *Board* (0, 1, 2, 3, 4). There is a long, narrow rectangular board with colored bands (squares, stripes, etc.) running transversely across it. These bands—eight in all—are alternatively red, blue, white, red, blue, white, red, and blue.

2. *Method of Play*

> (a) *Method of advancing pig* (0, 1, 2, 3, 4). One player shakes the cube in the cup and dumps it onto the table. If the face which turns up is red or blue, the player advances his pig to the band on the board nearest to him which has the corresponding color (red or blue). If black turns up, the player cannot advance his pig, since there is no black band on the board.

> (b) *Alternative play until conclusion* (0, 1, 2, 3, 4). The other player then takes his turn with the cube, moving his pig as specified by the face of the cube which turns up. The two players continue

---

tantamount to asking how much game information S has conveyed to him in the message. But the sighted listener can be adequately informed about some aspects of the game (not all) by simply looking, that is, independently of the spoken message. Since the listener's input, rather than the speaker's output, was the ultimate criterion here, the judge routinely gave high scores for those components of sighted-listener messages where the listener was not dependent on the message content. For example, if S does not tell a sighted E_2 that the game materials include a cup, he is still given a score of 1 for component 1a (see text). If he fails to describe the cup's *function* in the play of the game (2a), that is of course another matter. This disparity in scoring procedure for the two types of messages explains a fact which might puzzle the reader in subsequent pages, namely, that mean Game Information scores are at all grade levels higher for sighted-listener messages than for blindfolded-listener ones (see Figure 6). It simply reflects the fact that a sighted listener is more easily "informed" than a blindfolded one.

[3]Components 1a and 1c were subsequently deleted from the Game Information measure, since their scores showed very little intersubject variance. E_2, even blindfolded, usually ended up informed of the fact that there was a cup and that each contender played the game with a toy pig.

to take turns in this fashion up to the far end of the board and, turning the pig around when the last band is reached, back to the first band again. The first pig back to this first band is the winner of the game.

3. *Additional Information*

Add one point to S's total score for each item of information, not listed above, which would reasonably be thought to help the listener better understand the game. The following are examples. "This is a game two people play." "There are five items in this game (before describing them separately)." "The white bands on the board are not used."

C. *Inadequate Information.* The judge counted the number of separate communication "units" (word or phrase) in which the listener, on the basis of information available to him at that point or immediately afterwards, could not be expected to get at least a *fairly* definite idea of the unit's referent. Inadequate units were scored repeatedly if they occurred repeatedly during the message. Information scored here had to be more than just mildly inadequate, more than just a little vague and imprecise. As in B above, the judge took account of supplemental visual input in the case of the sighted-listener messages. That is, the frame of references was again the listener's inferred level of comprehension, derived from whatever informational sources were available to him. Inadequate Information was thus conceived as a kind of "negative" of Game Information, that is, a measure of what the listener would *fail* to grasp rather than what he would *succeed* in grasping. Here are some examples of communication units so scored. "*This side* is red (first sentence to blindfolded listener)." "You have to go to the *closest color on your side* (no prior mention of board to blindfolded E_2)." "Shake the block in the glass and *whatever color it is* (no previous mention of throwing block on table and noting the face which turns up)." However, less serious inadequacies were not scored, for example, "Roll the block and *if it comes out black* you can't move (colors of the block previously described)." Note that for this measure, in contrast to A and B, a high score indicates a *poor* communication.

The correlations between the two judges' scorings were .76 for Inadequate Information and .84 for Game Information. The Different Words measure required so little decision making on the judge's part that we did not bother to assess its interjudge reliability. As for intercorrelations among the measures themselves (with age in months partialled out), Different Words and Inadequate Information did not correlate at all, whereas the partial r's for the Different Words—Game Information and Game Information—Inadequate Information pairings were .42 and .37, respectively.

Let us now try to specify the interactional hypothesis more concretely in terms of these three measures. Since sighted and blindfolded listeners manifestly need different amounts of verbally presented information to be adequately informed, the hypothesis asserts that older Ss, more attuned to these disparate needs, will make a greater differentiation between the two messages than younger Ss will. In the case of the Different Words measure, this would simply imply a greater gap in mean scores for the older groups. The same basic reasoning applies to Game Information and Inadequate Information, but yields a different prediction. These measures, unlike Different Words, are defined in terms of the listener's "net" informational state, rather than in terms of message content directly. A communication barely adequate for the sighted listener will necessarily be quite inadequate for the blindfolded listener. And conversely, two messages, each well adapted to its respective listener, must be quite different in content. It follows then that the Game Information and Inadequate Information scores for the two messages, unlike the Different Words scores, should be more *similar* in the older versus younger Ss—this similarity reflecting the fact that the messages *themselves* are actually quite *different*. In statistical terms, of course, the same prediction is made for all three measures, namely, a significant interaction between age and listener role. The above discussion concerns only the *form* which the interaction plot should assume for each measure.

The design of the study permits two tests of the hypothesis for each measure: an intersubject and an intrasubject one. The former takes as its data all the *initial* communications, that is, all those addressed to E_2 but not those made to E_3, the second listener (recall that only the second and eighth graders also communicated to E_3). For each measure, a pair of curves can be plotted from these data: one consisting of the mean scores per grade group for the sighted-listener messages and the other the analogous plot for the blindfolded-listener ones. The six curves actually obtained are presented in Figure 6. It appears that the predictions just given are supported here, most clearly so in the case of the Game Information curves. Support is less unequivocal, however, as one passes from visual to statistical evidence. A $4 \times 2 \times 2 \times 2$ factorial analysis of variance was performed upon each separate measure. The four independent variables were: grade (adjacent grades combined, that is, 2–3, 4–5, 6–7, and 8–11); listener role (sighted versus blindfolded); IQ (above versus below the median within any given cell); and sex. Table 10 shows those main effects and interactions on each measure which proved

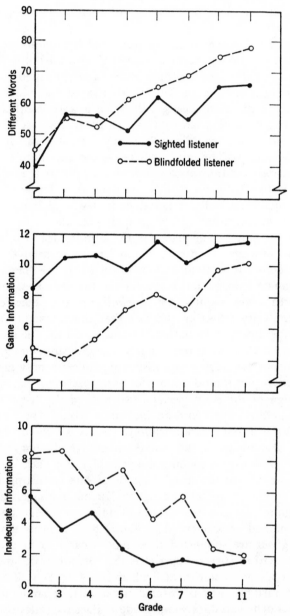

Figure 6. *Mean scores for each grade and listener on three Task IA measures.*

significant at $p < .05$ or better. On all three measures, grade and listener role were highly significant main effects, as would be expected from looking at Figure 6. However, appearances to the contrary, the predicted interaction between grade and listener role reaches statistical significance only in the case of Game Information. Moreover, this interaction is qualified by a significant triple interaction involving these two variables and sex. An analysis of variance performed on the two sexes separately showed that the grade-by-listener-role interaction is significant for boys only ($p < .01$), although the curve for girls also shows a (nonsignificant)

Table 10
Statistically Reliable Sources of Variance in Three Task IA Measures

Measure	Source of Variance[a]	Significance Level
Different Words	G	.001
	L	.01
Game Information	G	.001
	L	.01
	G X L	.01
	L X I	.05
	G X L X S	.05
Inadequate Information	G	.001
	L	.001

[a]The independent variables are: G = grade; L = listener role; I = IQ; and S = sex.

trend to close up in the upper grades. IQ and sex were not significant main effects on any of the three measures, although IQ, like sex, entered one significant interaction in the case of Game Information, that is, L × I. A plot of this interaction showed that the lower IQ Ss tended to have higher scores in the sighted-listener condition and lower scores in the blindfolded-listener condition, as compared with the higher IQ Ss. Although we find this interaction a little more comprehensible than the G × L × S one, we are not really inclined to try to interpret either.

The intrasubject version of the interactional hypothesis can be tested on those second and eighth graders who first communicated to sighted E_2, and then to blindfolded E_3. Figure 7 presents the mean scores for each message of the 10 Ss in each grade group. These data also appear to support the interactional hypothesis. The older Ss compose messages containing more different words when they shift from the sighted to the blindfolded listener; the younger ones do not (interestingly, their mean Different Words scores were virtually *identical* under the two conditions).

Also in accord with the hypothesis, the gaps between mean scores on the other two measures in the second-grade group tend to close up in the eighth-grade group (more clearly so in the case of Game Information). Statistical evidence and visual appearance are somewhat more congruent

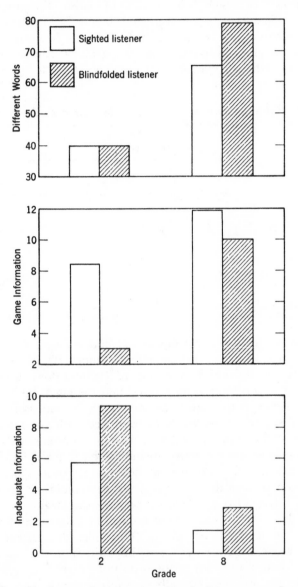

Figure 7.   *Communication to two successive listeners on Task IA:
sighted first and blindfolded second.*

here than was true for the intersubject data. The dependent variable used was no longer S's absolute score but his difference score, that is, the difference between his first and second communication (corrected for sign) on each of the three measures. A two-way analysis of variance was performed on these difference scores, the independent variables being grade and sex (the addition of IQ would have necessitated cells of 2.5 $Ss!$). Grade was a significant main effect for Different Words and Game Information ($p < .05$ and $p < .01$, respectively), but not for Inadequate Information; neither sex nor the sex-grade interaction were significant for any of the measures. The hypothesis was thus supported for the first two measures but, once again, not for the third.

It will be recalled that the other half of these two age groups also made two communications, in the sequence blindfolded E_2 then blindfolded E_3. This particular experimental design was the outcome of a series of tentative hypotheses, both developmental and nondevelopmental, about sequence effects in communication situations. As one example, it was conjectured that a previous sighted-listener experience would make for a more inadequate blindfolded-listener message than would either another, previous blindfolded-listener experience or no prior experience —especially in the younger group (due to perserverative tendencies, etc.). It scarcely makes sense to add other examples, however, because none of these hypotheses received any experimental support. That is, the blindfolded-listener communications within each age-group cell had rather similar scores, whether given first, given after a sighted-listener message, or given after another blindfolded-listener message.

A secondary hypothesis in this study asserts age trends in message content generally, apart from listener-role interaction effects. This hypothesis has been strongly confirmed in the data already presented. Older Ss tend to produce messages containing a greater variety of verbal content (Different Words) than younger Ss do, and in this sense can be said to send more total information.[4] Furthermore, much of this total information is useful to the listener: their messages clearly do a more adequate job of telling the listener what he needs to know about the game (Game Information). And conversely, the older Ss utter fewer statements which

---

[4]We chose to work with the number of different words (that is, the Different Words measure) rather than with the total number of words because we expected it to be a more sensitive barometer of communicative adequacy. The latter would probably have worked out equally well as a communication measure, however. Although we did not calculate the correlation between them, it must have been very high: the developmental curves for total words were plotted and are highly similar to those shown at the top of Figure 6. Thus, "greater variety of verbal content" and "greater quantity of verbalization" mean about the same thing in this study, and both show a strong age dependence.

would serve only to puzzle rather than inform the listener (Inadequate Information).

Additional analyses of the data were carried out in hopes both of discovering other types of developmental change and of clarifying further the nature of the changes already described. The overall yield, however, turned out to be disappointly low. Most of the measures tried showed no developmental changes or/and low interjudge reliability. A few did show weak trends which might serve as points of departure for further research. Examples of the former were measures of the smoothness (versus "jumpiness") of the communicative flow, the inclusion of statements about the game's objective, and the inclusion of erroneous, misleading information (as opposed to inadequate, incomplete information). We did find that younger Ss (especially grades 2 and 3) were more likely to make statements which the typist could not decipher from the tape record ($p < .10$), a phonetic rather than semantic form of communicative inadequacy. Younger Ss were also judged more likely ($p < .05$, but with an interjudge agreement level of only 72 percent) to narrate the game as though they were reliving their previous play of it rather than simply giving an impersonal, abstract account, for example, statements like "then I get blue and move here," and "then he got red and moved here." Finally, there was a weak ($p < .10$) but regular increase with age on a measure entitled Introduction to Game Materials, applied only to the blindfolded-listener messages. S received a score for this measure whenever he introduced the listener to the *existence* of some game object prior to describing its *function* in the game, for example, "There is a block here" (followed by an account of its appearance and function) versus "First you take your block. . . ." A number of Ss actually introduced several or even all of the game materials to the blindfolded listener before going into details about any of them, for example, "We have here a cup, a block, two toy pigs, and a long board"; this behavior also showed a nonsignificant but regular age trend. This style of message construction is highly interesting because it so clearly implies a sensitivity to the blindfolded listener's special predicament. The speaker who engages in it seems to be reasoning somewhat as follows: first I'll tell him what he would see if the blindfold were removed, thus bringing him up to the initial position of a sighted listener; then, I'll describe how the players and the materials behave, as would be necessary in communicating to any audience unacquainted with the game.

Discussion

The findings just presented are generally in agreement with our theoretical ideas about the nature and development of verbal communication skills. There is evidence that the ability to tailor message content to listener needs does, as predicted, increase with age across middle childhood and adolescence. When faced with a listener who has special informational requirements, the older children did appear more capable of fashioning messages adapted to these requirements. Needless to say, this ability was by no means a function of chronological age *alone*. Interindividual variation was high at every grade level. Some of the youngest Ss were quite sensitive to the listener's needs; some of the oldest ones were relatively insensitive. Likewise, the evidence was obviously not equally compelling for all measures of listener role adaptation tried; Inadequate Information, for instance, did not turn up as a statistically significant variable in either the intersubject or the intrasubject test of the interactional hypothesis. It would be unduly severe, however, to say that this state of affairs puts the basic hypothesis in serious jeopardy. What was predicted, after all, was that the two messages would be more *different* in the older groups, and that this difference should make sense, that is, it should go in the direction of more verbal information conveyed to the listener who most needs it. The results for the Game Information measure alone could "carry" this prediction. They plainly show that the two messages *were* "more different" in the older groups, and more different in a way which is eminently sensible.

We have so far offered an hypothesis about the development of communicative behavior, described an experiment designed to test it, and presented summary data (developmental curves and statistical findings) which, according to the argument just given, provide good support for the hypothesis. It now remains to cite and discuss some live examples of the processes in play. As in Task ID, the Ss' individual communication protocols here form a rich and instructive supplement to the group data; many of them vividly exemplify—with minimal inference required—how powerfully the presence or absence of role-taking activity can affect the communicative product. We shall preface these examples with a brief review of the basic conceptualizations from which the experiment derived (see Chapter 1, Figures 1 and 2, plus accompanying text).

The theory states that where role-taking activity plays no part in the communicative act, the message is little more than an audible self-coding. The speaker says to his audience roughly the same thing he might say to himself, for example, in silently reviewing the message data for some purpose. The listener is a relatively unimportant cognitive object for such a speaker (not much more than a stimulus for speaking), and the resulting message will be adapted to the listener's informational needs only by happenstance—particularly by dint of a congruence between their two perspectives regarding the message data. Where role taking does play an effective part, however, several important things are assumed to occur. First, the speaker attends very carefully to the listener, attempting to discern his powers and limitations as an audience for the data in question. Second, the resulting image of listener role attributes functions continuously to shape the organization and content of the message. The image acts as a monitor, a sort of communicative servomechanism, which dictates a recoding wherever the speaker's spontaneous self-coding would be likely to fail to communicate. And finally, this monitoring activity is assumed to require real vigilance and effort on the speaker's part, because a recoded message is never the path of least resistance. Quite the contrary, the easiest and most natural message to send is, by definition, the speaker's self-coding, presumed to remain in the forefront of consciousness throughout the communicative act. To express it in a psychoanalytic metaphor: the monitoring activity is the superego which inhibits what corresponds to id expression in communication situations, namely, the direct, unrecoded externalization of the speaker's own private coding.

The following three protocols illustrate the relative absence of such monitoring activity, that is, they appear to be little more than audible self-codings. The speaker in each case is a second grader who talks first to sighted (S) E_2 and then to blindfolded (B) E_3.

(S) "You put that in here and you take—then you pour it out and then you move yours up—the pig up and put it back in there and then shake—put it out and then you move your pig up. Okay? Yes. Sometimes you can't move it up." (The child looked at E_2 as he talked, and pointed occasionally.)

(B) "You put that thing in the cup and then you pour it out and you move your pig up and then you put it back in and then you move your pig up again. And when you put it in there sometimes you can't move it up." (S neither looked at E_3 nor pointed during this communication.)

(S) "Well, if you get a red one you should go here, if you get a blue one you should go here, if you get a black one you shouldn't go. If you get another blue one you go up to here, if you get a red one you go up to here, if you get a black one you don't go again. If you get a blue one you go here, and then you turn around and then if you get a red one you go here, if you get a blue one you go here, if you get another red one you go here." (S looked carefully at E_2 throughout and pointed to each thing referred to.)

(B) "Well, if you get a red one you should go here, if you get a blue one you should go here, if you get a blue one again you should go here, if you get a red one you should go here, if you get a blue one you—go here and you have to turn around, if you get a blue one you have to go here, if you get a red one you have to go—go here, and you win." (As before, S pointed at each referent, but did not look at E_3.)

(S) "First you put, um, these on here and then, um, you put that in the glass and you, um, you just, um, hop it a little and you turn it over and whatever color it is, um, you take one of the pigs and you move him to the color. So then, um, you have to go up and you—then when you get up you have to go down again and the one that gets down first wins." (The child looked at E_2 and gestured and pointed carefully, tracing the pig's movements, etc.)

(B) "Well, first you put, um, the pigs over here on the starting line, then you put the blocks in the glass and you juggle it up a little and whatever color it is you put, um, the one that, um, has the color, then you move the pig to the color it has. And you have to go up and then turn around and come back and the one that comes back first is the winner." (S made roughly the same gesture as before, but looked at E_3 less.)

Perhaps the most striking thing about these protocols is the extreme *similarity* between the two messages in each pair (see again the bar graphs presented in Figure 7). One gets the impression that the listener was indeed a minor figure in the whole proceedings so far as these children were concerned. The psychological situation appears to have been more dyadic than triadic, the only really important relationship being that between S and the game materials. It seems likely that the presence of the game materials coupled with a request to communicate simply unleashed a private verbal codification, different for each child, this codification having more the character of a set of free associations than of an intentional and focussed communicative act to which one listens with the ears of one's audience. Had each of these children been put alone in a room and told to describe the game to and for himself, we doubt if a hidden tape recorder would have given a very different record.[5]

These protocols also illustrate the fact that the communicative adequacy of self-codings depends upon the gap between the role attributes of speaker and listener. These messages are fairly low in informational value for the sighted audience, but not completely worthless. By listening to what S says, watching what he points to, and making some guesses, the listener might achieve at least a partial grasp of the rules of play. But it is hard to see how a blindfolded listener could make much sense

[5]That is to say, the record would not be very different provided the child *could* freely describe the game aloud without the support of a listener's presence. We would not of course argue that a live audience is unimportant in *eliciting* verbal behavior from an egocentric communicator. What we are suggesting is that the *content* of what is elicited is largely independent of the nature of the audience for such speakers.

out of what he hears. One has only to read the B messages to see why. The most interesting source of difficulty, from our point of view, resides in the "verbal gestures" which these Ss employed, namely, the indefinite references which, supported by physical gestures, might be useful to a sighted listener but could only lead to puzzlement in a nonsighted one. The first S, for example, speaks of putting "that thing" in the cup and of moving the pig "up." The second talks of getting "a red one," of moving "there," of going "here," etc. And the third S's message (the least inadequate of the three, perhaps) makes reference to "over here on the starting line" (of what ?), to moving the pig "to the color it (what ?) has," etc. It is hard to see how such expressions could have been uttered if their authors had really paid much attention to who was receiving them. It is doubtful that they actually lacked the necessary verbal equipment to have been more communicative at these points; more likely, they simply were not at that moment aware of any *need* to do so. We cannot resist quoting another, more extreme case of the same communicative malady. The S is a second grader, giving the first of two messages to blindfolded Es:

"This side is red and you're supposed to put it, um, go on these. This side is blue and you're supposed to go on these. You put these in your hand, um, you choose, um, which pig you want. Told ya!"

Needless to add, his second message was no more informative.

Contrast the following records with those just discussed; the two Ss are from the eighth-grade subgroup which had the S-B listener sequence:

(S) "What you do is pick up the two pigs in your hands and you mix them under the table and you hold them up and you let the other person, uh, pick which pig he wants. You have them in your hand so he can't see them. And so you put them right there, one on each, uh, red square. Then you put the block in there and you shake it up and you—when you put it out and if it's, uh, blue you put it on the blue square and if it's, uh, black you don't get a turn and if it's, uh, red you put it on your red square up there. And, uh, when you get down to the end you turn around and come back." (S pointed and gestured slightly, but did not look at E_2.)

(B) "The items in this game are a cup, a block with four—three different colors on it—black, blue and red—two pigs, one's white, one's brown, and there's a long board with seven—fourteen squares on it. Uh, the colors are red, blue, and white. Uh, first thing that you do on beginning the game is one person—he picks up the two pigs one in each hand and, uh, shuffles them under the table. Then he lets the other person pick which pig he has with, uh, the pigs inside his fist so the person can't see it. Then, uh, they put them on the first squares which are both red and, uh, they put the blocks with colors in it in the glass and they shake it up and if it happens to turn up blue they go to the blue square and if it goes black they, uh, you get the turn. He doesn't move any place. When they get down to the end they turn their pigs around and, uh, start back, keep on following the same thing, putting the block into the glass and shooting it out on the table." (No gesturing or pointing, and did not look at E_3.)

(S) "Mr. Fry, now there's two pigs there you could see and we put each of 'em on the—each one of these lines here and that little thing like a dice—that cube has different colors on them as you can see and you roll it—you put it in that cup there and you shake it up and you drop it on this board here.[6] Now, see the—you're over here and the color comes up red. You move to the red. If it comes up black you don't move at all. The black's, uh, dead (garble).[7] Okay, so you're on the red here so you shake again and you get a red you could come over here and you shake again and it's blue then you move ahead and then you get to the end you turn around and you come back the same way like that and the thing you do mostly is just put it in the cup and shake it and

[6]The child refers here to a small, felt-covered board which rested on the table. The cube was dropped onto it, rather than onto the table itself, simply to reduce the noise. This child was almost the only S to mention its existence.

[7]The typist inserted "(garble)" whenever a small portion of a message was incomprehensible on the tape.

[8]An intercorrelational analysis of the five Study I tasks was also attempted, age variance held constant insofar as possible. Since the Tasks IA and IC scores could be regarded as continuous measures, it was possible to use partial correlation to estimate intertask relationships. The data from Tasks IB, ID, and IE had to be treated dichotomously, however. Since partial correlation could not be used in any comparisons involving these data, it was necessary to test for covariation at each "age level" separately, defined as grades 2–3, 4–5, and 6–7 (grades 8 and 11 are of course too disparate to be treated as one "level"). The statistical techniques used here were biserial correlation, for continuous-dichotomous comparisons, and chi square, for dichotomous-dichotomous ones. There were therefore three types of analyses in all: partial r's for continuous-continuous comparisons (IA-IC); biserial r's for continuous-dichotomous comparisons, computed for each age level separately (IA-IB, IA-ID, IA-IE, IC-IB, IC-ID, IC-IE); and chi squares for dichotomous-dichotomous comparisons, also computed for each age level separately (IB-ID, IB-IE, ID-IE). These analyses are reported here, in a footnote, rather than in the text because they yielded results which were wholly inconclusive. Of 108 intertask relationships tested in these various ways, only 13 were statistically significant. Moreover, most of even these 13 were hard to interpret, for example, two tasks significantly correlated at one age level only, significant negative correlations where one would have expected positive ones (sic), and the like. We think it would be wholly unjustifiable to conclude from these negative findings that the five tasks tap no common abilities or skills. Study I was never designed with this question in mind, and the present analysis was done simply out of curiosity, to see what might turn up. A proper study of the question would surely require a very different experimental design, for example, a large group of Ss of the same age, general intelligence well controlled for, and continuous measures on every task. The problem of the structure of abilities in this area is certainly an interesting and important one, but we do not believe that our study sheds any light on it.

drop it on this board right here with the black tape. Well, that's about it." (S pointed and gestured throughout, looking carefully at E_2.)

(B) "You (garble) over here. Toward you is a board, it's, uh, oh I don't know, kind of wood like. Then it's got shellac or varnish on it to give it that stain, I believe. Forget about that. It's not the board but it's what's on the board. There's four different—five different colors—four different colors on the board. There's red, blue, and white with black lines dividing the cubes. Like there's two, four, six, eight, ten, twelve, fourteen, sixteen cubes altogether. Which means there's eight on each side now. There's two pigs here. Now I take one side where there would be eight of those little cubes and you take the other side. There's just like clean lines on the board with (garble) in there so you have four cubes you know. And you have like property—I forget the name of the game—but. So now, suppose you got the brown pig and I got the white pig. Now we got a cup here. It's a white cup with designs on it. Looks like stars. And they got a cube like a dice and it has six sides, I believe, yes. There's red, there's blue and there's black on it. I think that's all, yeah, red, blue and black. Now you put that cube into the cup and you shake the cup and you drop it on the mat, there's another mat here—just a little piece of— I don't know what it is but it's there. Now your pig is on the board so, say— the first color on the board, by the way, is red, then there's blue, there's white which is the neutral color which don't mean nothing. You can't move, there ain't no white. There's the black. Okay, so I say 'go' so you shake it up and you drop the cube. The cube comes out blue. Okay, you move your animal up to the blue—the blue color on the—the blue blotch on the board. Then I shake it and say mine comes up red. I move it to the first red spot. We go like that all the way down the eight numbers. No, when we get to the, uh, far one, we turn our animals around and come back and the first one to make it back is the winner, of course. So that's the, uh, major idea of the game." (As before, S gestured and pointed frequently, looking at E, as he talked.)

These protocols are clearly not beyond criticism as communications. As one example, the first S twice fails to mention that the object of the game is to beat one's opponent back to the starting point; the second mentions it only at the end of the B message. Nonetheless, they are indisputably much more adequate and effective than those quoted previously. And more important, they give clear evidence that these Ss were very much aware of the difference between the two listeners, and made valiant efforts at role-appropriate recoding. Both Ss adopted the Introduction-to-Game-Materials strategy when they shifted to the blindfolded listener. For instance, notice the difference between the first S's two opening sentences: "What you do is pick up the two pigs. . . ." versus "The items in the game are. . . ." Throughout both of his messages the second child continually reminds us both that he is talking *to* someone and that he knows full well the *kind* of someone who is listening. Thus, the S message contains expressions like "there's two pigs there *you could see*" and "that cube has different colors on them *as you can see*," in addition to the usual role-appropriate verbal gestures ("there," "here," "this board," etc.). Correspondingly, the B message is full of painstaking descriptions of what the game objects look like, beginning with the revealing phrase "*Toward you* is a board." Indeed, so obsessed does he seem to be with the listener's state of sensory deprivation that he "overcommunicates" in places, that is, encumbers the listener's already-overladen memory storage with irrelevant information, such as the appearance of the cup.

We have quoted, for purposes of illustration, three communicative protocols which show little evidence of monitoring activity and two which show a great deal. The three are taken as concrete examples of the type of communication schematized in Figure 1, while the two correspond to that given in Figure 2 (Chapter 1). Where does the subject sample as a whole lie in terms of these two paradigms? Studies IB, IC, and ID suggested that most Ss in this age range can demonstrate at least some role-taking activity under laboratory conditions, and the same thing appears to hold true here. Whereas the two protocols given above are better than average for this group, few Ss did as poorly as the three second graders did. So far as we could judge, most of the children constructed messages in which one could infer at least *some* attempt at adaptation to the listener's role. In the case of many of the younger ones, the monitoring activity impressed us as minimal and intermittent, with role-appropriate message units only appearing here and there within a stream of role-inappropriate ones. But the very grossest and most obvious forms of maladaptation (the "pick this up and put it here" sort of utterances, made to the blindfolded listener) were nowhere highly frequent, and virtually disappeared beyond the early grades. There might be practical problems in administering Task IA to, say, 4- to 6-year-old children. But if it could be done, we strongly suspect that communicative performance of the "pure" Figure 1 variety would be found in much greater abundance.

It must be admitted, however, that the task of diagnosing role-taking capacities from communicative performance is not really as simple as the preceding discussion may have implied. Suppose S makes an assertion, at point X in his message, which is judged to be poorly adapted to the listener's needs. Of what psychological process is this assertion the outcome? One can conceive of at least three possibilities. First, S might at that moment be wholly incognizant of his audience; the fact that the latter is, for example, blindfolded, is simply not a psychological fact for him at point X. The assertion is therefore an unrecoded, "top-of-the-head" utterance of the classical Figure 1 variety. On the other hand, *S* might indeed keep his audience in mind, but nonetheless be unable to grasp the precise implications of the listener's role for this portion of the message data. While knowing that the listener needs special information at point X, *S* does not know exactly *what* information he needs. And finally, *S* might grasp these implications quite clearly, that is, he does know just what information this particular listener must have at point X. However, for one reason or another he is unable to compose a communicatively effective verbal formulation of this information. That is, he knows what he wants to tell his audience, but he lacks the verbal machinery, the *mots justes,* to express it clearly.

Needless to say, it is difficult to be sure which of these three possible sources of communicative inadequacy is operative in the case of any given component of any given message. The present data suggest that the first source is likely to be especially prominent in the communications of young children. In older ones, the second and third types of difficulty probably become increasingly important, that is, difficulties due more to an insufficiently penetrating analysis of the listener's role and to insufficient skill in verbal expression than to a gross and outright insensitivity to the audience. But even here, however, the first source undoubtedly intrudes from time to time. We suspect that the average communication is a medley of all three processes, especially where the audience has, as in this study, unusual listener role attributes. That is, the average speaker will occasionally and momentarily forget to whom he is talking; and when he remembers, he will occasionally not know exactly what needs communicating; and where he does know, he will occasionally be unable to verbalize it effectively. The efficacy of the resultant message ought then to be largely dependent upon the frequency and distribution of these "countercommunicative" events. Task IA was obviously not amenable to analyses of this fine a grain. What is needed, perhaps, is a procedure in which *E* questions *S,* gets his reactions to suggested alternatives, etc., at various points in the message. Such a procedure has its hazards, of course, especially with young children. But it does at least offer the possibility of finding out which of the above three processes underlay *S's* overt communication behavior.

TASK IE

This study was designed to investigate developmental changes in the ability to communicate effectively to several individuals at once, that is, to a multi-listener versus single-listener audience. There appear to be three major paradigms here, three prototypical situations in which a single communicator addresses a plural audience. For purposes of illustration, we shall suppose that a speaker S has the task of sending a single message to three listeners, L_1, L_2 and L_3. The first and simplest paradigm obtains where the three Ls all have the same listener role attributes, so far as this particular message is concerned. That is, any given message which S constructs affects them all equally, brings them all to an identical level of comprehension. This multi-listener situation is obviously indistinguishable from the single-listener one, from S's standpoint. While he may well have problems in constructing an effective message, none of these problems derive from the fact that his audience consists of more than one listener.

Special difficulties arise, however, where the several Ls are assumed to differ in listener role attributes. There are two prototypes here. In the first, the informational content given in the message is such as to be susceptible to quite different interpretations by different listeners. One kind of listener may construe or assimilate it quite differently than another listener would. The content is in one or another sense "interpretatively plastic," rather like a projective test stimulus, and can therefore affect different listeners in different ways. As such, it is quite literally a *multiple* communication, in that—psychologically speaking—it "fractionates" into a series of different messages as the audience decodes it. Certain literary productions, for example, fables, parables, and allegories, are extreme examples of this paradigm. *Gulliver's Travels*, for instance, is a message which communicates one thing to a child, something quite different to a sophisticated adult, and still an additional set of meanings to the student of English literature. One can also find ready examples in spoken messages. A psychology professor describes an important experiment to his class. The brighter students, those with more psychological background, etc., may see immediately how it relates to other, existing research, may see implications for further research, and so on; the other students may do little more than remember its bare, factual details, if they succeed in understanding it at all. The speaker's problem in this genre of multiple-listener situation is, as in any communicative task, to attain a measure of prediction and control over what his audience assimilates. But here the problem is complicated by the fact that several different messages depart under the guise of a single one, and S wants to blend his communication so that it fractionates in the manner desired, that is, so that L_1 will really assimilate X and L_2 will really assimilate Y, as S intended. It would be highly interesting to study the ontogenesis of the relevant abilities here, for example, the ability to imagine how several different listeners will differentially interpret one's multi-level message. The present investigation, however, dealt with developmental changes with respect to a third multi-listener paradigm.

We said that the message content in the second paradigm is highly plastic: subject to diverse interpretations, full of implications which one L grasps and another does not, and so forth. That of the third paradigm is the opposite. The prototype here is a set of utterly banal and prosaic items of information, such as a shopping list, an enumeration of the contents of a room, a set of directions as to how to get from here to there, or—the communicative content of Task IE—the combination to a safe. Although the "interpretative plasticity" of message content is a graduated rather than all-or-none quality in real-life communication situations, we are discussing the extreme case where it is virtually absent. Thus, S's message does not resolve into several different ones when it reaches his listeners, as it did in the previous paradigm. It remains, phenomenologically, one and the same message for each and every listener. Having an obvious, per se character, with a simple, common meaning for all, the informational items are simply received as such, to be summated with whatever information on the same topic each listener may already possess. However, as in the preceding case, the listeners really do have different role attributes, in the sense that they differ in the amount of relevant information which they possess prior to S's communication. And despite the simplifying property just mentioned (that S need not be concerned here about his message having different meanings for different listeners), this heterogeneity of listener role attributes poses genuine problems for S—problems which are uniquely group communicative in nature.

We shall illustrate this paradigm with some communication situations of the type actually employed in Task IE. Suppose S possesses the five items of information (a, b, c, d, e). Suppose also that his listeners already have diverse portions of this information set: L_1 has (a), L_2 has (a, b), and L_3 has (a, b, c). S's task is to communicate items from the set, via a single message delivered to all three Ls at once. It is stipulated that two restraints are to govern his message. First, it should contain *enough* information so that, after receiving it, all three Ls would be in possession of the entire set (a, b, c, d, e). Second, it should not contain any *more* than is needed to accomplish that communicative end, that is, it should not be redundant in terms of that end. There exists a unique solution to this problem, and it consists of sending the message (b, c, d, e). There is, moreover, a logical procedure which guarantees a correct solution in this and all similar multiple-listener tasks. One must carry out a *set* or *logical multiplication* of the three sets and then communicate the com-

plement of the set *intersect* or *product* resulting from this multiplication. In the present instance, multiplication of the three sets (a), (a, b), and (a, b, c) yields the product (a), whose complement is (b, c, d, e). In simple terms, the solution resides in first listing the items which all three *L*s already possess *in common*, and then communicating all *remaining* items. In the example just given, the three *L* sets can be called *transitive*: that is, (a, b, c) subsumes (a, b) which in turn subsumes (a). The same logical procedure works equally well with what we shall term *nontransitive* sets. If, for instance, the three *L* sets are (a, c), (a, b, c), and (a, c, e), set multiplication yields the product (a, c) and its complement (b, d, e) is thus the correct message content.

In the foregoing situations there is the implicit assumption that each *L* obtains the information he needs from *S*, and from *S* alone. But one can imagine situations where the *L*s *themselves* assist in the communicative process. Let us assume once more that *S*'s task is to see to it that all the *L*s end up maximally informed with the briefest possible message. This time, however, suppose we let the *L*s intercommunicate freely among themselves before or after receiving *S*'s message, that is, they can *pool* all the information they have. By what method can *S* insure an adequate but nonredundant message under these circumstances? There is again a general procedure which works in all such cases, but it entails *logical* or *set addition* rather than *multiplication*. The procedure consists of *adding* the three sets and then communicating the complement of their *union* or *logical sum*. Given the sets (a), (a, b), and (a, b, c), for instance, logical addition yields the union or sum (a, b, c) and the message should therefore contain only (d, e). This method amounts to first making a list of all the different items found in the three sets and then using the complement of that as the message content. Since the three *L*s can share their information freely, all three can be considered as already possessing the set (a, b, c) in the above example; they lack only (d, e), which is precisely what *S* provides in his message. The nontransitive case here is handled in exactly the same way, for example the communicative solution for sets (a, c), (a, b, c), and (a, c, e) is (a, b, c, d, e) minus (a, b, c, e), or (d). We shall refer to these tasks where the *L*s may intercommunicate, as *communicating* situations, and refer to the preceding ones as *noncommunicating* situations.

The above examples illustrate the essential properties of the third group-communicative paradigm. First, there is the requisite heterogeneity of listener role attributes in the audience: the *L*s are differentially informed about what *S* knows at the outset and thus have differing informational needs with respect to it. Second, *S*'s message does not fractionate into basically different communications to different *L*s; it consists of a series of items, presumed to be of a humdrum, factual sort, which all Ls would interpret in essentially the same way. And finally, it places certain cognitive demands upon S which derive specifically from its multiple-listener character, that is, which could not arise in single-listener problems such as Task IA. Imagine that our S were confronted with only one L, who possesses, say, the set (a, b, c). S's communicative problem here is an easy one. Taking note of what L already possesses relative to what he wants L to have (a simple form of role-taking activity, appropriate to this simple problem), he communicates the complement (d, e). But in the multiple-listener situations we have been describing, there need not be *any* single L in the group, the complement of whose informational set would be the correct message for the group as a whole. And yet S must send a single message with a single, fixed meaning, just as he would if there were only one listener. How to do this? As we analyze it, S solves the problem by, in effect, resolving the several Ls into a single one, in terms of whose listener role attributes he tailors his message. The L in question is entirely a product of S's cognitive activity and will only by accident have listener role attributes identical to any real L in the audience. This conceptual resolution of group into individual is done in the manner described above, that is, by logical multiplication in the case of noncommunicating Ls and by logical addition in the case of communicating ones. Where the listeners are described as $L_1 = $ (a, d), $L_2 = $ (a, d, e), and $L_3 = $ (a, b, d) and may not intercommunicate, for example, the "imaginary listener" in question is $L = $ (a, d) and thus coincides with the real listener L_1. Given the same conditions, however, save that the Ls may intercommunicate, the listener has no real counterpart, since he is defined as $L = $ (a, b, d, e).

To recapitulate, it has been suggested that multiple-listener problems of this general type are apt to require the utilization of certain logical operations for their solution. In order to find a message which meets the adequacy and nonredundancy criteria which may be set for such problems, S must first resolve his several listeners into a single one to which he can direct his communication. This conversion is a cognitive-logical process, carried out either by adding or by multiplying Ls' information sets, depending upon whether or not the Ls are assumed to share their information. The present investigation was designed to find out how well children of various ages cope with this genre of group-communication task. It was predicted, of course, that coping ability here would be strongly age dependent. In particular, it was expected that the younger Ss, hardly skilled at adapting messages to a single listener, would be very hard put to deal effectively with several at a time.

Procedure

The highlights of Task IE are as follows. The child assumes the role of a police chief who communicates by radio to his subordinates in police cars. Various ploys were used to make the task interesting and realistic, especially for the younger Ss: we pinned badges on them, showed them toy police cars to illustrate the instructions, and had them talk into a real microphone (the microphone to the tape recorder). The subordinates were to drive to the city bank vault and open the safe. Each already had a specified portion of the safe combination and the chief's job was to send the necessary remainder by radio in a single message. This message was to be adequate to the subordinates' informational needs but minimally redundant (since nefarious others might be listening in, and the chief would not want them to hear the *whole* combination).

There were six such messages altogether. The first two were essentially practice trials and involved only one listener. The remaining four each entailed a group of three listeners. Two of the four were sent under *noncommunicating* (NC) conditions. The chief was to say just enough of the combination so that any one of the three policemen could go to the bank *alone* and open the safe by adding the information received from the chief to that portion he already possessed. The other two were delivered under *communicating* (C) conditions. The chief was to say just enough of the combination so that the three policemen could open the safe *together*, by pooling the information they already had and adding to it that contained in the chief's message. One member of each pair of tasks involved a *transitive* (T) ordering of information possessed by the three subordinates; the other involved a *nontransitive* (NT) ordering. We shall thus refer to the four multiple-listener tasks as: CT, CNT, NCT and NCNT, that is, communicating—transitive, communicating—nontransitive, etc. Although all Ss began with the two preliminary, single-listener subtasks (called 1 and 2), the four multiple-listener ones were taken in one of the following four sequences: (a) CT-CNT-NCT-NCNT, (b) CNT-CT-NCNT-NCT, (c) NCT-NCNT-CT-CNT, or (d) NCNT-NCT-CNT-CT. One-fourth of the Ss at each grade level were assigned to each sequence, in such a way that the resulting subgroups were roughly matched for IQ scores and sex distribution.

The "equipment" used in this study included a policeman's badge, three toy police cars, and a combination padlock used for demonstration purposes. The most important items, however, consisted of a set of cards listing the turns of the safe combination. The content of these cards is indicated in Table 11. Proceeding from left to right in the table, S's own card was 8 in. long and 3 in. wide. The entire safe combination of 8 turns was listed on it, from top to bottom, in large ($\frac{1}{4}$ in.) black print: thus at the top was printed "1. R-10" (that is, first turn right to setting 10), then just below that "2. L-20," and so on. There were eight other cards, each 8 in. $\times$ 2 in., containing the combination turns which the various L's already possessed. These turns were printed in the same relative positions as their equivalents on S's card, with spaces left for the missing ones, for example, L_2's card contained first a space, then

Table 11
Speaker's (S) and Listeners' (L) Information in Task IE

S's Information	L_1	L_2	CT and NCT			CNT and NCNT		
			L_a	L_b	L_c	L_d	L_e	L_f
1 (R-10)	1		1	1	1			1
2 (L-20)	2	2	2	2	2	2	2	2
3 (R-90)	3		3	3				
4 (R-50)	4	4	4	4			4	
5 (L-40)		5	5			5	5	5
6 (R-00)			6					6
7 (L-30)						7		
8 (L-80)		8						

"2. L-20," then a space, etc. Columns L_1 and L_2 in Table 11 show the information available to the first and second L, respectively, in the initial, single-listener subtasks. The next three columns give the informational sets for the two transitive subtasks (the same three cards were used for both CT and NCT). The last three columns give the corresponding data for the two intransitive subtasks. In each multiple-listener subtask, S saw the three cards side by side in the left-to-right order shown in the table. The solution to each of the six problems can also be inferred from the table. S's message should consist of turns (5, 6, 7, 8) for subtask 1, (1, 3, 6, 7) for 2, (7, 8) for CT, (3, 4, 5, 6, 7, 8) for NCT, (3, 8) for CNT, and (1, 3, 4, 6, 7, 8) for NCNT. The exact details of instructions and procedure are given below.

"Now this is the last game we are going to play today. Do you know what this is (holds up the padlock)? It's a combination lock. This is how it works. You see you can't pull it open now—it's locked tight. This is how we open it. First (demonstrating) we turn this middle part to the *right* like this until we come to 40. Then we turn it to the *left* all the way around until we come to 20. Then we turn it to the *right* again to 30 and it opens. You see how it works? Let's do it again; you hold the

wheel and I'll guide your hand (older Ss were permitted to do it themselves, E_1 simply calling out the direction). Now the turns we make to
open a lock are called the *combination*. The combination to this lock is
this (E_1 lists 'R-40,' 'L-20,' and 'R-30' in a column on a piece of paper).
You see—right-40, left-20, right-30. That's the combination.

"Now *different* locks have *different* combinations. Let's imagine there
is a lock with this combination here (shows the S card). To open *this*
lock we'd have to first turn *right* to 10, then *left* to 20 (E_1 continues
through the rest of the combination). Now the lock wouldn't open if you
did just a *few* of these turns—you have to do them *all*. Also, you have
to do them in just the right order, just like on the card—*first* turn right
10, *then* turn left 20, etc.—or the lock won't open. Now let's imagine you
are the police chief and that this (microphone) is a radio (E_1 also pins
the badge on the second and third graders). On this radio you can talk
to all the policemen in these police cars (points to toy cars) and to anyone else who has the right kind of radio. Now there is a lock down in
the city bank which has this combination and you want a policeman
named Bill to go down and open it. Now Bill, who is riding around in
his police car, has part of the combination but not *all* of it. He has just
this part here (show card L_1). Now you want to talk over the radio to
Bill and tell him *only* what he needs to know to be able to open the
lock. You certainly do not want to give him the *whole* combination—all
this (points to S card)—because then *anyone* listening could open the
lock, and you wouldn't want *that* to happen! So tell Bill *only* those parts
of the combination that he *has* to know to be able to open the lock by
himself—but don't tell him any *more* than he *needs* to know." If the
child communicates incorrectly to L_1, E_1 corrects him by saying that Bill
would have to be told "this" (points) in order to have the whole combination. "Fine. Now let's imagine there is another person named Sally
listening in—you could imagine she is a woman policeman! Now *she*
has *this* much of the combination (shows card L_2). Tell her over the
radio here *just* what *she* needs to know so that *she* could open the lock
too—but don't tell her any *more* than she needs to know." E_1 corrects
any errors here, just as in subtask 1.

The instructions for the four multiple-listener subtasks were as follows,
apart from slight modifications due to the particular sequence in which
they were presented.

NCT and NCNT. "Now I want you to imagine there are *three* people
in *three different* police cars. These cards (L_a, L_b, and L_c for NCT, and
L_d, L_e, and L_f for NCNT) show how much of the combination each one
has already. Now you want to speak into the radio and tell *just enough*
so that *each one* of them could open the lock, all by himself—say *just*

enough so that *each one* of them could hear what you say and go to the bank all by himself and open the lock. Don't say any *more* than you *have* to, though."

CT and CNT. "Now I want you to imagine that there are *three* people in *three different* police cars. These cards (L_a, L_b, and L_c for CT and L_d, L_e, and L_f for CNT) show how much of the combination each one has already. Now they want to drive down to the bank and meet there. When they all get there they want to open the lock *together*—and of course when they get there they'll be able to *talk* to each other about the parts of the combination they know already. However, they *still* won't be able to open the lock—even helping each other—unless you *tell* them certain parts of the combination. Speak into the radio now and tell them *just enough* so that, when they get to the bank and talk to each other, they'll be able to open the lock. Don't say any *more* than you *have* to, though."

E_1 carefully noted the contents of each message (it did not prove necessary to tape record them). If the child simply pointed to the turns (on the S card) he wanted to communicate, rather than actually reciting them aloud, this was perfectly acceptable.

Results

A category system was devised for classifying Ss' message responses to each of the six subtasks. Some of the categories applied to all subtasks; others applied to certain ones only. The categories and the subtasks to which they referred are described below.

Category 1 (all subtasks). No response.

Category 2 (all subtasks). S gives the entire combination (all 8 turns) once through.

Category 3 (all multiple-listener subtasks). S gives the entire combination three times through.

Category 4 (all subtasks). S gives all the turns which the listener or listeners already possess, each turn given only once.

Category 5 (all multiple-listener subtasks). S reads off the contents of each of the three L cards, that is, identical to Category 4 except that certain turns are given more than once.

Category 6 (all multiple-listener subtasks). S recites the turns which are not present on each of the three L cards (thus some turns are necessarily given more than once). S may do this in either of two ways:

(a) *Horizontal.* S recites the turns by "rows." for example, for CT or NCT, he reads "3, 4, 5, 5, 6, 6, 5, 7, 7, 7, 8, 8, 8" (see Table 11).

(b) *Vertical.* S recites all the absent turns for one card before turning to the next, that is, he recites by "columns" rather than by "rows."

Category 7 (subtasks NCT and NCNT). S gives a single communication for all listeners but it contains too little information.

Category 8 (subtasks NCT and NCNT). Same as Category 7, except that the "too little information" consists precisely of that which would be correct for the corresponding C subtasks: turns 7 and 8 in the case of NCT (the correct message for CT) and turns 3 and 8 in the case of NCNT (the correct message for CNT).

Category 9 (subtasks CT and CNT). S gives a single communication for all listeners but it contains too much information.

Category 10 (subtasks CT and CNT). Same as Category 9, except that the "too much information" consists precisely of that which would be correct for the corresponding NC subtasks: turns 3, 4, 5, 6, 7, and 8 in the case of CT (the correct message for NCT) and turns 1, 3, 4, 6, 7, and 8 in the case of CNT (the correct message for NCNT).

Category 11 (subtasks CT and CNT). S communicates to some *one* listener (that is, gives the information which that listener does not possess), as though assuming that he can then inform the others. If the listener so selected on subtask CT is the one possessing turns 1 and 2, however, S's message is scored for Category 10 instead, since this particular message happens to be the correct one for subtask NCT.

Category 12 (all subtasks). Any incorrect message not scorable for the preceding categories.

Category 13 (all subtasks). The correct message.

Each S's performance on Task IE was recorded on a special scoring sheet. This sheet took the form of a double-entry table or matrix, the six subtasks forming the columns and the 13 categories forming the rows. Some of the cells were inked out, of course, since not all categories applied to all subtasks. The judge's task was simply to put a checkmark in the appropriate row of each column, representing S's performance on that subtask. The two judges made identical scorings in 93 percent of the 240 columns rated in common (that is, 40 Ss, 6 columns per S).

The first analyses to be discussed are those which dealt with Category 13, that is, correct messages versus all others. Five chi square analyses were computed for each of the three independent variables: grade (adjacent grades combined); sex (boys versus girls), and IQ (above versus below the median). One of these analyses concerned overall performance across the six subtasks, the cut being made between those Ss who correctly solved at least five of the six and those who solved four or fewer.

The remaining four chi squares dealt with correct versus incorrect performance on each of the multiple-listener subtasks separately. Where grade was the dependent variable, all five chi squares were highly significant ($p < .001$), confirming the hypothesis of strong age dependency for Task IE, IQ was significant ($p < .05$) for overall performance across subtasks (and in the expected direction), but not for the multiple-listener subtasks taken separately. Sex was not a significant variable in any analysis.

Table 12

Number of Subjects per Grade Giving Correct Communications on Each Subtask of Task IE

Subtask	Grade								Σ
	2	3	4	5	6	7	8	11	
2	18	17	20	20	18	19	17	19	148
1	12	14	16	18	18	18	20	17	133
NCT	7	7	15	16	15	17	17	18	112
NCNT	8	7	12	17	15	16	16	17	108
CT	4	6	8	13	12	9	13	16	81
CNT	2	5	6	11	10	9	9	16	68

Table 13

Number of Multiple-Listener Subtasks of Task IE Correctly Solved at Each Grade Level

Number of Subtasks Correct	Grade								Σ
	2	3	4	5	6	7	8	11	
0	10	10	3	2	2	2	1	0	30
1	0	0	3	1	0	1	1	2	8
2	9	7	7	5	8	7	8	3	54
3	1	1	4	2	4	4	2	1	19
4	0	2	3	10	6	6	8	14	49

Tables 12 and 13 give a more detailed picture of the developmental changes here. The most abrupt improvement in overall performance appears to take place between grades 3 and 4 (with perhaps another "spurt" between grades 8 and 11). From Table 13, for instance, it can be seen that fully half of the second and third graders failed to solve even a single one of the four multiple-listener problems, and only a tiny minority solved three or more. Beginning with the fourth grade, on the other hand, only a few Ss proved unable to solve any, and almost two-fifths of them gave correct messages on all four subtasks.

Examining the six subtasks separately, the "warm-up," single-listener problems were of course the easiest to solve, as they were intended to be (Table 12). Even the youngest Ss negotiated subtask 2 with ease, perhaps as a result of corrective feedback from E_1 regarding any mistake or misunderstandings on subtask 1. Of more interest are possible differences in difficulty level among the four multiple-listener problems. The rightmost column of Table 12 suggests that such differences might exist, and the data given in Table 14 confirms this impression. The order of diffi-

Table 14
Relative Difficulty of the Multiple-Listener Subtasks of Task IE

Subtasks Compared	Response Pattern		Significance Level
	L+, R−	L−, R+	
CNT-NCT	12	56	.001
CNT-NCNT	14	54	.001
CNT-CT	3	16	.01
CT-NCT	15	47	.001
CT-NCNT	18	45	.001
NCNT-NCT	6	10	NS

Note. Pattern L+, R− consists of a correct message on the left-hand subtask in the first column together with an incorrect message on the right-hand subtask; L−, R+ refers to the converse pattern. Thus, for example, the figures in the first row assert that 12 Ss communicated correctly on subtask CNT but incorrectly on NCT, while 56 Ss did the opposite.

culty appears to be, from hardest to easiest (CNT) > (CT) > (NCNT ~ NCT). This indicates that the communicating subtask is decidedly more difficult than its noncommunicating counterpart in both the transitive and the nontransitive pairs, whereas a nontransitive ordering of listeners' information appears to be harder to manage than a transitive one only in the more difficult, communicating condition.

We also examined the difficulty level of these four subtasks as a function of the sequence in which S encountered them. It might be hypothesized, for example, that the C subtasks would be more difficult when they follow rather than precede the NC ones, because the latter might induce a solution set inappropriate to the former. Similarly, one might expect differences stemming from the sequence in which the T and NT subtasks were taken, and so on. It will be remembered that these subtasks were administered in only 4 of the 24 distinct orders possible, thus limiting any search for sequence effects. For those effects available to investigate, however, nothing significant emerged. We could find no positive evidence whatever that the difficulty level of any subtask depended upon its ordinal position in the series and/or the particular subtasks which preceded it.

The scoring system employed in this study made possible a developmental analysis of Ss' unsuccessful as well as successful communicative efforts. The incorrect messages described in Categories 2–11 do not appear homogeneous from the standpoint of performance level; that is, some attest to more group-communication skill, more understanding of multiple-listener task requirements, than others do. Categories 2–5 certainly constitute the most immature errors from this standpoint. The child who composes such messages even fails to grasp an elementary principle common to single- and multiple-listener problems alike, namely, if the message aims to be nonredundant, it must consist of the complement of some corpus of information already in the listener's (or listeners') possession. The exact definition of this corpus may well constitute a problem for S, but *some* corpus *must* be defined if S is to achieve a communicative solution even remotely like the correct one. A message which either includes the whole combination (Categories 2 and 3) or the turns which the Ls already have (Categories 4 and 5) suggests that no such attempt at definition has taken place, and that S has failed to understand even the most fundamental requirements of the task.

Category 6 (a or b) is clearly an error of a higher order, since the message is now composed of information which each L lacks. But it nonetheless indicates a failure to grasp the problems unique to a multiple-listener as opposed to a single-listener situation. What the child does here, in effect, is to reduce the multiple-listener problem to a *succession* of single-listener ones; that is, he treats the last four subtasks of Task IE as though they were identical in structure to the first two. It is difficult to know exactly how the Category 2–5 child has defined these problems for himself, and how well he has solved the problems so defined. But in the case of the Category 6 S, it is easy to see that he has restructured the multiple-listener task into a trio of single-listener ones, each of which he solves correctly.

An interpretation of Categories 7–11 is undoubtedly more hazardous than of Categories 2–6, but we believe that these errors reflect a third and still higher level of performance. They suggest that the multiple-listener problems are now being construed in something like the terms in which they are posed, that is, as communicative situations which have a structure and attendant problems different from those of the single-listener type. Category 8 (and perhaps 7) errors may indicate that S has falsely interpreted NC tasks as having C structure, and the converse for Category 10 (and perhaps 9). And Category 11 errors may reflect an attempted solution to C problems which, although insufficiently nonredundant, is scarcely illogical. In summary, Categories 2–5 and Category 6 are both interpreted as indicating a basic failure to grasp the nature and demands of multiple-listener communication problems, with the Category 2–5 errors regarded as the more primitive of the two. In contrast, Categories 7–11 are thought to reflect at least a minimal understanding of the requirements of such problems, at least the understanding that these requirements are different from those encountered in single-listener problems.

Table 15 gives the relevant developmental data on these three classes of errors. Categories 2–5 and 6 are relatively frequent in grades 2 and 3

Table 15
Multiple-Listener Subtasks of Task IE: Distribution
of Subjects by Grade across Scoring Categories 2–11

Category	Grade							
	2	3	4	5	6	7	8	11
2–5	5	4	1	1	1	3	0	2
6	8	8	4	3	2	1	3	0
7–11	11	8	14	9	10	12	11	4

Note. Each cell contains the number of Ss who show one or more instances of one or more of the categories in question.

but rare thereafter. The decline with age is statistically significant in the case of Category 6 ($\chi^2 = 18.99$, $df = 3$, $p < .001$). Categories 7–11, on the other hand, continue to occur in force right up to grade 11 (where there are few errors of any kind, as Tables 12 and 13 show). We have already seen that the frequency of correct responses increases with age. It can now be concluded that the proportion of mature to immature errors does too—another index of the older child's greater ability to grasp what is involved in multiple-listener situations.

The 12 error categories varied widely in frequency of occurrence. Half of them were quite rare. Thus, the number of Ss showing one or more instances of Categories 1, 3, 4, 5, 8, and 11 was only 1, 2, 2, 4, 5, and 6, respectively. And within Category 6, only 3 Ss recited the turns by rows (6a) rather than by columns (6b). Frequency data for the other categories is presented in Table 16. It can be seen that Category 2 is the predominant error in the 2–5 group, as might be expected. Five of the 10 Ss who commit it are first or second graders. The data on Category 6 have already been considered, and those on Category 12 tell us little beyond the fact that our scoring system did not succeed in classifying all of Ss' messages. As for Categories 7–11, it will be recalled that we interpreted Category 8 (and perhaps 7) as indicating that S may have construed NC problems as C ones, and Category 10 (and perhaps 9) as indicating the reverse assimilation. It is interesting to note that Cate-

Table 16
Multiple-Listener Subtasks of Task IE: Distribution of Subjects by
Grade across the More Frequently Occurring Scoring Categories

Category	Grade								Σ
	2	3	4	5	6	7	8	11	
2	3	2	1	1	1	2	0	0	10
6	8	8	4	3	2	1	3	0	29
7	0	1	2	1	1	1	1	2	9
9	4	2	5	2	3	0	3	1	20
10	8	6	6	5	6	11	8	3	53
12	3	1	2	1	2	1	2	2	14

Note. Each cell contains the number of Ss who show one or more instances of the category in question.

gories 9 and 10 occurred much more frequently than 7 and 8; indeed, more Ss made Category 10 errors than any other single type, despite the fact that there were only 2 subtasks (CT and CNT) on which such errors could occur. We shall discuss the possible significance of this finding presently.

Discussion

The evidence just presented supports the view that the ability to cope successfully with multiple-listener communication problems develops with age during the middle-childhood and adolescent period. This view is supported both by the data on correct responses and by the data on preponderant types of incorrect responses. The older child is more likely than the younger, both to compose a correct message and also, when he errs, to construct an incorrect one which reflects at least some understanding of what the task demands. Moreover, for these specific problems, at least, there is a suggestion that much of this developmental progress occurs across grades 3–4, that is, during the age period 8–10 years, approximately.

It will be recalled that we felt justified in describing the results of Task IB in qualitative, stage-developmental terms, but did not feel that the Task IC data merited this kind of interpretation (Chapter 2). What about the data from the present task? Does the evidence here warrant any attempt to go beyond the simple statement, made above, that performance on Task IE *is* age dependent, and particularly so during a certain portion of middle childhood? We think there is such evidence, and that one can make a case for a certain amount of developmental discontinuity. Specifically, we believe that the ability to solve these problems develops in three rough stages:

Stage 1. The child is unable to solve multiple-listener problems of either the NC or the C type. He may or may not be able to solve single-listener problems of the same format. And if he can solve them, he is likely to generalize the same solution strategy to the multiple-listener tasks, thus composing messages of the sort described in Category 6.

Stage 2. The child is able to solve NC problems, but not C ones. When he attempts the latter, he is likely to apply the NC solution to them, in analogy with the overgeneralization just described for the Stage 1 child.

Stage 3. The child is able to solve NC and C problems alike, utilizing the solution procedure appropriate to each.

The inclusion of Stages 1 and 3 in this schema probably needs little defense. There of course must be a period where all such problems are beyond the child's capabilities (Stage 1), and the data of Tables 15 and 16 strongly suggest that, probably during the latter part of this period, single-listener strategies are liable to be misapplied to these tasks. Likewise, it is hard to believe that any of these problems would be too difficult for most adults (or near-adults—witness the fact that 14 out of 20 eleventh graders correctly solved all 4). But the assertion of an intervening Stage 2 does need justification, and we shall try to provide it by a reexamination of the data presented in the results section. First, there is the fact that both C tasks were significantly more difficult than both NC tasks (Tables 12 and 14). More than that, however, there is an important peculiarity in the last column of Table 13: a mere 8 Ss solve only 1 multiple-listener problem, whereas 54 Ss solve only 2. Which 2 do they tend to solve? There are 6 possible pairings here, equiprobable under a null hypothesis. But in fact no less than 42 of the 54 Ss in question solved the 2 NC tasks. Table 14 also hints at the notion that NCT and NCNT have a certain psychological unity for our Ss: in contrast to all NC-C pairings, there are only a few cases where NCT is correct and NCNT incorrect, or conversely. And finally, there is the evidence presented in Table 16: by all odds the most frequent error (Category 10) is one in which S seemingly generalizes the NC solution procedure to C problems. Taken together, these facts support the belief that children do not go immediately from an inability to solve multiple-listener problems to a generalized ability to solve any and all. On the contrary, there appears to be an intermediary acquisition of a definite sort: the discovery of a method for solving NC problems, whether T or NT in format, accompanied by a proclivity for generalizing this method to tasks where it does not apply.

We can only speculate about the problems involved in passing from one of these stages to the next, that is, about the difficulties posed by each new, higher-level task and about the skills needed to surmount them. There is first of all the problem of transition from Stage 1 to Stage 2. The child can solve subtasks 1 and 2 but not NCT or NCNT. Why not? The most likely reason, we think, is that the operation of logical multiplication has not yet become a serviceable instrument within his cognitive repertoire, readily brought into play when the problem demands it. It is difficult to find any other feature of subtasks NCT and NCNT which would constitute an equally important obstacle for a child who can solve subtasks 1 and 2. These subtasks absolutely require a train of reasoning of the following type: "I obviously do not have to communicate turn X, because all three listeners already have it, and the same is true for Y and Z; so I only have to describe the remaining turns, those which one or more listeners lack." The concept of joint attributes, lowest common denominator, "what they all have"—however expressed —is the indispensable key to such communication problems, and the child simply must be able to think in these terms to solve them.

There is, moreover, some evidence that the ability to "think in these terms" is in fact a relatively tardy acquisition, one which is only gradually elaborated during the primary school years. The operation of set multiplication has an important place in Piaget's theoretical analysis of the cognitive structures characteristic of these years (that is, the concrete operational "groupings"), and he and his co-workers have made a number of studies of its ontogenesis (Piaget and Inhelder, 1959, ch. 6; Flavell, 1963, pp. 177-179; 192-193; 300; 309). In one study (Piaget and Inhelder, 1959, pp. 178-187), for example, the child was shown a horizontal row of pictures of different colored *leaves* which almost joined, at right angles, a vertical row of pictures of *green* objects of different kinds. The two rows thus formed an L, but with a blank space at their juncture. The child's task was to decide what picture should be placed in this blank space, that is, the picture which would "go well" with *both* the rows. Not until about 9-10 years of age does there tend to be a systematic preference for a *green leaf*, that is, an object which possesses the defining attributes of both sets.

In another study *(ibid.,* pp. 190-195), S was shown two large, overlapping circles. One circle contained 10 *round* chips (5 red and 5 blue) and the other contained 10 *blue* chips (5 round and 5 square). The nonoverlapping portion of the first circle contained only red (round) chips, and the nonoverlapping portion of the second circle contained only square (blue) chips. Hence, the overlapping, common portion contained only round, red ones, 5 in number. The display as a whole therefore gave a visual representation of 2 classes or sets (round objects versus blue objects) which possess a subset in common (round, blue objects). *E* asked the child to describe the contents of the 2 circles, to explain why the round, blue chips were placed in the overlapping area, and the like. Children in the early school years found this task difficult also, again suggesting that the concept of set intersect is a relatively late achievement. It would hardly be surprising, in view of these results, to find among our *S*s a number who lacked this concept—or who, having just recently acquired it, could not readily apply it to a logical multiplication problem "embedded," so to speak, in what purported to be a multiple-communication task.

There are several obstacles which the C problems might pose for *S*s who can already solve NC ones. One possibility is that the relative *brevity* of correct C messages might of itself lead *S* to believe them to be insufficiently communicative. Both C subtasks demanded a message containing only two combination turns, a mere one-quarter of the total available, and many *S*s may simply have doubted that a message this brief could be adequate. The same problem would of course not arise in the NC tasks, both of which demanded a message composed of six turns. There is perhaps some evidence for this possibility in Table 16: 20 *S*s *overcommunicated* in the C tasks (Category 9), whereas only 9 *S*s *undercommunicated* on the NC tasks. It is probable that a strategy of overcommunicating when in doubt would be a popular one in any group of *S*s, and also that problems demanding very brief messages would tend to be doubt producing.

There is second difference between the C and NC problems which might also make the former harder to solve. The NC tasks are in one sense more similar to single-listener ones than the C tasks are. Just as in the single-listener case, *S*'s object in the NC task is to make sure that *each L* ends up fully informed, in possession of the entire set of combination turns. If *S* turns his attention to any given *L* after giving the correct message, he can satisfy himself that this *L* does have the entire set, exactly as he would in subtasks 1 and 2. But this is obviously not the case in the C problems, since one or more *L*s are bound to remain only partially informed after *S* sends the correct message. Here, it is only the *group as a whole* which needs to be fully informed, and this peculiar property of the C problem may be hard for the child to grasp. He sees that one or more *L*s still have an incomplete set of turns and the temptation to communicate additional information, that is, to deal with him as an individual listener, may be strong. Group communication situations where the aim is to inform each individual listener are frequently met with in the child's daily life, for example, in the classroom.

But situations where the aim is to inform the audience *qua* collectivity, with subsequent intragroup exchanges explicitly "budgeted for" in S's message, are not often encountered.

There remain another obvious possibility: that set addition is a more difficult, later-developing skill than set multiplication. Piaget has repeatedly argued that these two operations are psychologically related and developmentally synchronous (for example, Piaget and Inhelder, 1959, pp. 197-198). In his theoretical system, class addition is a central operation in certain intellectual structures which develop during middle childhood, while class multiplication plays the same role in others; neither can be said to be a more "mature" operation than the other. We wonder, however, if this equivalence would hold true over all task settings where these operations are required. Piaget worked with class addition problems where the subordinate classes did not overlap and where the superordinate classes had ready labels, for example, collections of blue squares (A) and red squares (A') which together form a set of "squares" B, under the additive operation $A + A' = B$. Neither of these simplifying properties held true in our C problems. On the one hand, the sets to be added had common elements, for example, turns 2 and 5 in the CNT problem (Table 11). On the other hand, the "name" of the set union turns out to be a rather complicated, multiword affair— something like "all the turns which at least one L already possesses." We cannot of course be sure that the special characteristics of our tasks rendered one operation more difficult to carry out than the other. On the other hand, we see nothing in Piaget's data on the question which rules out the possibility.

Bruner, Goodnow, and Austin (1956) report some evidence which may be relevant to this question. They conducted a number of concept formation studies with college student Ss. The concepts investigated were of three types: *conjunctive, disjunctive,* and *relational,* of which only the first two are of concern to us. A conjunctive concept is made up of concept instances which fall within the *intersect* of two or more overlapping classes, for example, objects which are *both* red *and* square. A disjunctive concept, on the other hand, is defined by the *sum* of two or more classes. Positive instances of a disjunctive concept might include, for instance, nonred squares, nonsquare red objects, and red squares. The authors report two interesting findings regarding the acquisition of these concepts. First, disjunctive categories turn out to be *much* harder to attain than conjunctive ones. And second, Ss frequently err by assimilating disjunctive situations to conjunctive ones, that is, prematurely and erroneously structuring the concept as conjunctive on the basis of commonalities found in the instances initially encountered.

(Both of these findings hold true, by the way, in task situations where *S knows beforehand* that the concept he is looking for is disjunctive rather than conjunctive!) The second finding recalls to mind the high frequency of Category 10 errors in our data (Table 16), also taken to indicate an assimilation of set-union (disjunctive) problems to a set-intersect (conjunctive) strategy.

Task IE illustrates a point about communication and role-taking problems which we have mentioned before, but which is worth reiterating. Although role-taking skills are believed to be essential to the solution of such problems, they are seldom if ever the *only* skills demanded. In the present case, for instance, we have argued that certain logical operations play an important, perhaps paramount role in the solution of one category of group communication tasks. To solve these problems S must pay attention to listener-role attributes, but this is only a first step (and a less important one here than in the other Study I tasks). The core of the problem lies in the second step: to reduce the group of Ls to a (conceptualized) single L for communicative purposes. It is difficult to see how S could manage this resolution by role-taking activity alone, that is, without carrying out certain intellectual operations which are essentially unrelated to role-taking activity.

There is finally the question of the similarity between these tasks and multiple-listener problems encountered in everyday life. The tasks were of course artificial, laboratory affairs, designed only to represent in a clear way certain problems an individual may face in communicating to a group audience. And it is doubtful, as we said, whether the C tasks have many real-life analogues, although a few might be imagined. In contrast, situations resembling our NC problems are often encountered. This kind of task structure obtains whenever someone wishes to make sure, with minimal redundancy, that *all* members of his audience achieve (at least) a specified level of information. If there is the minimal-redundancy restraint (and there usually is), he must engage in something akin to a logical multiplication operation. That is, he must make some guesses about the informational corpus which his diverse listeners already possess in common. This then becomes the information he can assume instead of communicate, and it forms the point of departure for his message. In educational parlance, we would say that he intends to "teach to the bottom of the class," although of course the same strategy often occurs in communicative settings other than the schoolroom. It is difficult to see how we could consciously pursue this strategy without being able to "think in terms of" set intersects, in some sense.

Of course, one does not always aim to "teach to the bottom." Where it is not absolutely essential that each and every listener be adequately informed and where the heterogeneity of listener-role attributes is great, the speaker may want to strike for some compromise which avoids boring (or insulting) an undue proportion of the audience. But even here it seems that there must be some implicit logical multiplication involved, that he must first have an idea of what the "bottom" is in this situation before he can move his communicative sights upward. In other words, although the set intersect itself need not always constitute the communicative point of departure, the speaker's cognition of it must assist him in finding any other point of departure.[8]

CHAPTER FOUR

Further Investigations of Role Taking and Communication in Middle Childhood and Adolescence

This chapter reports another study (Study II) of role-taking and communication development. It is best introduced by comparing it with its predecessor, described in Chapters 2 and 3. Like Study I, its orientation was developmental-descriptive rather than antecedent-consequent (see Chapter 1); the principal aim was simply to extend our previous exploration of this problem area by investigating a new and different set of tasks. The tasks were again five in number, administered in a constant sequence (IIA-IIB-IIC-IID-IIE) to a single group of school children of approximately the same age range as in Study I. And finally, the research was carried out in the same school system, under the same general experimental conditions, and with about the same pre-experimental instructions and procedures as before (see Chapter 2).

Study II differed from Study I in several respects, however. Limitations of time and personnel together with competing research commitments led us to search for economies of design, procedure, and analyses in this particular investigation, economies which would not, however, seriously jeopardize our developmental-descriptive objectives. Accordingly, the subject sample was smaller than it was in Study I, with wider gaps between adjacent age groups. The Ss were 60 in number, 20 at each of grades 3, 7, and 11. Likewise, sex and IQ were not used as independent variables. All Ss were female and were drawn randomly from class lists.[1] Also, pilot studies had suggested that children in this age group do not necessarily require a "live" other to perform appropriately

[1]The three grade groups turned out to be quite closely matched on group IQ scores nonetheless, with mean scores of 107–109.

on communication and role-taking problems. In consequence, the "listener" in most of the tasks to be described was a life-sized photograph of a human face which the child was told to *pretend* was a real person, sitting there listening to her. This permitted the experiments to be conducted by only one *E* (Patricia T. Botkin). As in Study I, *Ss*' responses were tape recorded and subsequently typewritten. Scoring was done either from typescript or from the tape itself, depending upon the scoring category (typescript except where otherwise indicated). Unlike Study I, however, the interjudge reliability of the scoring categories was not assessed. Only one individual scored the protocols (Ellin Kofsky). She was not a member of the research group and of course performed all scoring operations without knowledge of the *Ss*' identities. Although every effort was made to write clear and unambiguous scoring instructions, to define scoring concepts which a judge could readily grasp and apply, etc., it is naturally possible that at least some of the scoring categories in this study were of low reliability, the likeliest contenders probably being the few that failed to show clear developmental trends.

TASK IIA

This task was very similar, in both form and rationale, to Task IA (Chapter 3). In the latter, the child was required to construct a message which would be communicatively effective for an individual whose listener needs were usually high, that is, a blindfolded listener whose information about the game had to come entirely from the child's verbalization. Analogously, the *Ss* in Task IIA had to adapt a message to the—also high—input requirements of a very *young* listener, one to whom, as with the blindfolded person, it was necessary to explain the obvious, give abundant detail, and so forth. In both cases the communicator is faced with what is, in effect, a "listener disability" for which he must make special allowances in his message. And here, as in Task IA, it was predicted that the younger *Ss* would be less prone to make these allowances than the older ones would.

Procedure

S is shown a sheet of paper on which a familiar fable appears in extra large typescript:

The Fox and the Grapes
One hot summer's day a fox was strolling through an orchard till he came to a bunch of grapes just ripening on a vine which grew along a lofty branch. "Just the thing to quench my thirst," quoth he. Drawing back a few paces, he took a run and jump, but just missed the branch. Again and again he tried

to get the tempting morsel, but at last had to give it up, and walked away with his nose in the air, saying "I'm sure they are sour."

In the case of the third graders, *E* begins by slowly reading the passage aloud, with *S* looking on. Then *S* herself reads it aloud once through (or more than once if she has particular difficulty). While she reads, *E* corrects any errors, briefly defines any words which *S* appears not to understand, and generally tries to insure that she has mastered the story content. In the case of the seventh and eleventh graders, *S* is simply told to read the fable once through to herself.

E then shows *S* a large photograph of a man's face. "I'd like you to pretend this is a real man sitting here. Now I'd like you to read the story to him so he'll know it too. Go ahead."

When *S* has finished reading, *E* presents a similar photograph of a four-year-old boy. "Okay, that's fine. Now here is a picture of a little boy. He's probably three or four years old. I want you to pretend he is a real four-year-old boy sitting here. Now tell *him* the story so he'll understand it just as well as you do. You can use the paper or not, whichever you want. The important thing is for you to tell him the story so he understands everything—be sure he *understands* what everything in the story *means*. Go ahead."

Results

The judge scored each child's (second) message for the number of *Simplifying Recodings* which it contained. A Simplifying Recoding was defined as any deviation from the original fable text which could reasonably be interpreted as a deliberate attempt to make the story easier for a juvenile listener to grasp. Not all deviations were to be scored here—*only* those which appeared to stem from a motivated attempt to communicate more effectively. We defined three varieties of Simplifying Recodings.

Substitutions. An expression in the text is replaced by a simpler one, more easily comprehended by a young child. Examples: "said" substituted for "quoth," "steps" for "paces," and "grapes" for "tempting morsel."

Additions. Something is added, presumably to clarify or supplement the text. Example: "This is a story about a fox and some grapes."

Deletions. Something is deleted, presumably because it is judged unessential to the story line but potentially confusing to the audience. Example: the omission of the expression "just ripening."

Table 17 shows the number of *S*s at each grade level who showed one or more instances of any type of Simplifying Recoding, and of each type separately. Chi squares were calculated for the data given in each row,

Table 17
*Number of Subjects per Grade Showing One or
More Instances of Each Category in Task IIA*

Scoring	Grade			Significant Level
	3	7	11	
Simplifying Recodings	6	18	18	.001
Substitutions	5	18	18	.001
Additions	5	10	10	NS
Deletions	1	8	5	.05

with the results shown in the rightmost column. There is a striking increase in recoding activity generally between third and seventh grade, with no apparent change thereafter. Most of this increase is accounted for by the Substitutions subcategory, although the other two also show developmental trends. As the table indicates, Substitution was by far the preferred method of recoding in this communication task: 173 instances of it were scored altogether, as against 64 Additions and 40 Deletions.

Discussion

The evidence for some sort of developmental change in this investigation is very strong. Only about one-fourth of the youngest Ss altered the fable for the listener's benefit, even minimally, whereas almost all of the older ones did. How can we account for such a poor performance by the third graders? It may have been partly due to insufficient reading or vocabulary skills, at least in the case of some Ss. That is, some children may still have been so preoccupied with trying to read the fable correctly or trying to comprehend its archaic terminology—despite all E's attempts to reduce these difficulties in previous readings—that no surplus energy remained to cope with the communicative problem. However, a number of Ss did seem to be able to read and understand the fable easily enough and yet made no effort at all to reword it for their young listener. And conversely, other Ss had considerable difficulties of this sort but nonetheless tried valiantly to recode (even, in some cases, to the extent of actually asking E for help in redefining troublesome words). Thus, although reading and vocabulary problems may partly explain the third graders' low level of performance, we cannot credit them with being the whole explanation.

A more important factor, we believe, was a relative inability to take the listener's role, to hear the message with the ears of a preschool auditor. Their behavior suggests that the majority of the younger Ss, but very few of the older Ss, either failed to grasp the recoding implications of the task situation from the outset or else could not keep these implications in mind once immersed in actually reading the fable. Reminiscent of the younger Ss in Task IA, they appeared to function as if the situation were dyadic rather than triadic for them, that is, as if fable alone, rather than fable and audience, preempted their field of awareness. Accordingly, they simply read the text aloud, word for word—"lofty," "quoth," "tempting morsel," and all.

The recoded messages stand in sharp contrast to the above. A few Ss made extremely free translations, essentially retelling the fable in their own words. Most, however, adhered quite closely to the text, only departing from it at points of potential difficulty for the listener. It was these latter messages which we found most interesting from the standpoint of role-taking and communication development. More than in any of the Study I protocols—even those of Task IA—one gets the feeling here of actually seeing role-taking activity *in vivo*, as it occurs in S's thought. S comes to a difficult word in the text, and one can almost sense the warning light go on. Typically, S would either read the difficult word aloud, pause, and then recode it for the audience, or alternatively, pause and redefine without ever uttering it at all. The following is a sample of such messages. The first four were composed by seventh graders and the last one by an eleventh grader.

"The Fox and the Grapes. One hot—one hot summer's day a fox was strolling, that means walking, through the orchard, that's where there are lots of trees, till he came to a bunch of grapes just ripening on a vine which grew along a lofty branch, that means high. 'Just the thing to quench his thirst,' that means satisfy his thirst, quoth . . . that means . . . quote a little or something like that. Drawing back his— drawing back a few paces, he took a running—a run and jump, but just missed the br-branch. Again and again he tried to get the tempting morsels, that means get the tempting . . . food. But at last—last he had to give it up, and walked away with his nose in the air, saying 'I'm sure those—they are sour.' "

"The Fox and the Grapes. One hot summer's day a fox was walking through the orchard till he came to a bunch of grapes just . . . ripening on a vine which grew . . . along a high branch. 'Just the thing . . . to satisfy my thirst,' said he. Drawing back a few paces, he took a run and jump, but just missed the branch. Again and again he tried to get the tempting . . . fruit, but at last he had to give it up, and walked away with his nose in the air, saying 'I'm su-sure they were sour.' "

The story is about a fox and the—bunch of grapes. A fox was walking through an orchard, which is a . . . group of trees, when he came to a bunch of grapes ripening on a vine which grew high in the air. 'Just the thing . . . ah . . . to satisfy his thirst,' said he. Backing up a few . . . steps he took a run and a jump, but just missed the high branch. Again and again he tried to get the bunch of grapes, but at last he had to give it up, and he walked away with—with his broken dignity, saying 'I'm sure they are sour.' "

"Well, today we're going to have a little story about the Fox and the Grapes, and it goes like this. One hot summer's day a fox was strolling through an orchard till he came to a bunch of grapes just ripening on a vine which grew along a lofty branch. Now ripe . . . wait a minute . . . strolling is when you're walking just leisurely—well, you don't know what that is, probably—nicely, rather, just slowly, and orchard is a, could be an apple orchard or a place where they grow apples, or grapes, as we were talking about. And he was walking along until he came to a bunch of grapes and a . . . bush. So he said, 'Just the thing to quench my thirst.' And that means just the thing to—take care of my thirst, so I won't be thirsty any more. And drawing back a few paces he took a run and a jump, but just missed the branch. That means he went back a little bit, and he ran and he tried to jump up and catch the grapes in his mouth. Again and again he tried to get the tempting morsel. That means he tried over and over again to get this—these grapes on the vine—they taste very good. But at last he had to give it up, and walking away with his nose in the air, saying 'I'm sure they are sour.' That means that at last he knew he couldn't get it, so he had to give it up. Then he walked away and tried to make himself think that he could have done it. He said 'I'm sure they are sour.' "

"The Fox and the Grapes. One hot summer's day a fox was strolling through an orchard, strolling means walking or—just moving along slowly, strolling—ah—strolling through an orchard until he came to a bunch of grapes just ripening on a vine, which grew along . . . a lofty branch. Lofty means very high or—he can't reach it very easily. 'Just the thing to quench my thirst,' quoth he, meaning just the thing to give him—so he wouldn't be too thirsty, and he was saying it to himself. Drawing back a few paces, drawing—which means moving back a few paces, just getting a little ways back from where he was so that he could take a running jump, and he took a jump, took a run and a jump, but just missed the branch. Again and again he tried to get the tempting morsel, tempting means something very good to eat, but at last had to give it up and walked away with his nose in the air, saying 'I'm sure they are sour.' That means they were very, very bitter."

These protocols need little commentary, and an extended discussion of the study as a whole would simply repeat points already made in previous chapters. Like Tasks IA and IE, the results here argue for an intimate working relation between role-taking and mature communicative activity, and for the view that this relation is progressively constituted during middle childhood and early adolescence. One special feature of Task IIA deserves brief comment, however. Good performance here depended in part on having some idea about the verbal equipment of a four-year-old, that is, on being able to guess which words would need to be defined in order to be understood and which would not. It appeared that most of the Ss who recoded did have fairly good intuitions about a young child's verbal capabilities; see, for example, the protocols quoted above. As was stated in Chapter 1, Milgram and Goodglass (1961) also found that Ss of 11–12 years and upward were able to make accurate inferences about the verbal capabilities of younger children, in this case their word association habits rather than vocabulary knowledge.

TASK IIB

An effective communication has been defined as one which is nicely adapted to the listener's informational requirements. The nature of these requirements will of course vary from situation to situation. In communicative problems like Task IA (and, to an extent, Task IIA) they are certainly very high, but at the same time one would be hard put to specify just *how* high. Consequently, S need not worry unduly about communicating too much, that is, about being redundant from O's point of view. On the contrary, it is sound strategy here to send as complete and detailed a message as possible, in hopes that one will at least come close to meeting L's exorbitant needs. In Task IE, on the other hand, it was overcommunication which presented the major danger. Because of the peculiar structure and demands of this task, each trio of Ls had a precisely definable set of informational requirements which S was supposed not to exceed in his message. An able communicator, then, should respond to the first type of problem with a compulsive, all-stops-open effort to verbalize fully, but to the second with a deliberate and selective laconicism.

Task IIB was designed to confront S with both species of problem, given in quick succession and involving a common body of communicative raw materials. S had first to describe a visual display as completely as possible, so well that her listener could draw it accurately on the basis of what she said. Immediately thereafter, she was told to describe it again to a second listener, in barely enough detail to permit him not to draw it sight unseen, but merely to identify it among a set of four displays in front of him. It was hypothesized that there would be an age-dependent increase in the difference between S's communicative behavior in response to these two problems, somewhat in analogy with the predictions made in Study IA (Chapter 3). That is, we expected that the first message would become more, and the second less information laden as a function of age—both trends reflecting an increasingly more precise communicative adaptation to the listener requirements in each case.

Procedure

The visual displays used in the study are reproduced in Figure 8. Display X was the one which S was to communicate in both the first

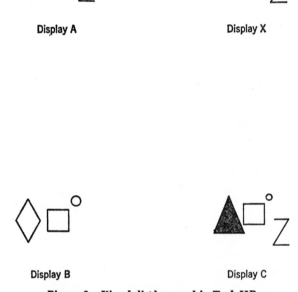

Display A   Display X

Display B   Display C

Figure 8. Visual displays used in Task IIB.

(Description) and the second (Discrimination) subtask; Displays A, B, and C were the ones from among which the listener was to distinguish X in the Discrimination subtask. The display designs were drawn in blue ink. The two subtasks were administered as follows, Discrimination immediately following Description:

Description. E shows S a photograph of a man's face, and then turns it around so the face is no longer visible to E and S. "I want you to describe this design (Display X, mounted on a card) to this man as well and completely as you can—so well that he could draw it later himself just from listening to what you say, so that he could draw it *exactly* as it is. Remember, he can't *see* the design you are describing, he'll only have your description to go on when he tries to draw it later. Go ahead."

Discrimination. "Now, here is a set of *four* designs (a single sheet of paper containing all four displays, arranged as shown in Figure 8). This is the one you described to the other man. Look carefully at each design—see how they are alike and how they are different." After S has had a chance to inspect them closely, E presents another photograph of a man's face. "Now, here is another man. He has a set of designs that are just like yours." (The set consists of the four displays, each mounted on a separate card. E carefully points out that S has the same displays on his sheet that the man has on his four cards). "This time I want you to describe this same design to this man, so he'll know just which one of the *four* you are talking about. Describe it so he can pick out the right one from the pictures he has. This time, I want you to see how *short* a description you can give, and still make sure he'll choose the right one. Tell him *enough* so he can be sure to find it—but no *more*. For instance, if you were this man, what information would you need in order to choose the right picture? How many things would you have to be told? *Remember*, he doesn't have to *draw* it or anything. He just has to find out *which* one of the four pictures you are talking about. So of course you don't have to tell this man as *much* as you did the other man. Go ahead."

Results

S's two messages were scored for the quantity of information about Display X they contained, in analogy with the Game Information measure of Task IA. The display consisted of four elements, as Figure 8 shows: a circle, a square, a triangle, and a "Z." For each element, S received a score of one point for each of the following attributes mentioned.

Presence. The child gives an at least approximately correct designation of the element in question.

Size. The child gives some indication of the absolute or relative size of the element.

Position. The child gives some directional indication of where the element is, relative to at least one other element. Simple contiguity statements without direction (for example, "next to") are not scored.

Color. The child indicates that the element is or is not colored in, is "blue," etc.

Other. The child says something which is communicatively useful, but is not covered by any other category, for example, the particular shape of the triangle.

All statistical calculations were based upon S's summed score for each message. Table 18 presents the means of these scores, by grade and subtask.

Table 18
Mean Information Scores per Grade on Each Subtask of Task IIB

	Subtask	
Grade	Description	Discrimination
3	6.20	5.60
7	8.65	8.25
11	10.20	4.90

Simple analyses of variance were performed on the scores of each subtask, that is, on the data represented in each table column. Both F ratios were highly significant ($p < .001$, $df = 2,57$). Accordingly, t test comparisons were carried out for each pair of grades within each subtask. All three comparisons were significant ($p < .01$) in the case of the Description messages; two of the three, that is, grades 3–7 and 7–11, were significant ($p < .01$) in the Discrimination subtask.

A difference score was next computed for each S, consisting of the Description score minus the Discrimination score (plus a constant). The simple analysis of variance performed on these scores also yielded a significant F ($p < .001$, $df = 2,57$). Subsequent t tests showed that the eleventh graders had significantly higher ($p < .01$) difference scores than either the third or seventh graders, the latter two showing no reliable intergroup differences.

Finally, it was possible as in Task IE to define a "perfect" communicative solution to the Discrimination subtask, that is, the least informative message which would permit the listener to distinguish Display X from the other three. S needed only to say that the critical display was the one which contained the colored square, or the noncolored triangle, or the second largest (or third-from-smallest) circle. Only 5 of the 60 Ss discovered the solution (in all cases the "colored square" version), and all 5 were eleventh graders.

Discussion

Table 18 shows that the Ss behaved completely in accord with prediction in the case of the Description subtask. That is, there was a regular, grade-by-grade increase in amount of information sent in response to this high-listener-need problem. Developing intellectual and verbal skills must certainly have played a substantial part in this increase. As the child matures, he would be expected to become more and more skillful at accurately discriminating and encoding the forms and form attributes (size, position, etc.) encountered in Display X. However, our previous studies would lead us to believe that a burgeoning sensitivity to the listening other must also have exerted an influence here. The interpretation of these data which we find most reasonable, therefore, is that the older children gave more informative communications both because they were more attuned to the listener's needs and because, so attuned, they had better cognitive-verbal equipment with which to fulfil them.

The Discrimination data pose more of an interpretative problem. There is strong evidence that the eleventh-grade group considerably reduced its informational output in accord with the second listener's reduced informational requirements and with E's exhortations against redundancy; the other two groups, on the other hand, showed no evidence of doing this. The performance of the youngest and oldest groups came as no surprise. We had guessed that the third graders would give relatively meagre communications in the Description subtask and, unable to grasp or keep in mind the special requirements of the Discrimination problem, would give approximately the same—again meagre—message there. The results of Tasks IA and IIA had already convinced us that children in this age group are likely not to alter their communicative behavior very much as a function of changes in listener role, and we would therefore have been rather surprised to see them do it on this task. Likewise, we had predicted that the eleventh graders would sharply curtail their messages in the second subtask, as would be expected of a mature, near-adult communicator in this situation.

The performance of the seventh graders was in no sense predicted, however, and is difficult to explain after the fact. Children of this age level generally acquit themselves quite well on role-taking and communication tasks, according to our previous research experience, and had been expected to show at least a trend toward message reduction in the Discrimination problem. The instructions, after all, strongly and repeatedly implied that such a reduction was in order here; furthermore, there was ample "room" for reduction in the case of these Ss, given the relatively detailed messages they had composed just previously in the Description subtask. One might think, perhaps, that it was the logical demands of the problem which prevented them from shortening their messages, that is, an inability to grasp the notion that the minimal-length, adequate communication here must consist of some property or properties which Display X *alone possesses*. We have no doubt that this was in fact beyond their capabilities, but it scarcely accounts for their complete failure to reduce information. There were 5 eleventh graders who found this "perfect" solution, to be sure, but the other 15 also showed a substantial mean reduction. If these 5 Ss are omitted from the group, the eleventh-grade average information score only rises from 4.90 to 5.80, still well below the seventh graders' mean of 8.25—and still far below the eleventh grade Description mean of 10.20. What happened was that a number of these 15 Ss described only 1 or 2 Display X forms, simply named all 4 forms, or constructed other "nonperfect" but relatively low-information messages. Thus it was that 10 of the 15 eleventh graders achieved scores in the 3–6 point range, whereas only 4 out of the entire group of 20 seventh graders achieved scores as low as 6. A reduction in message content was therefore not wholly contingent upon the discovery of the systematic, logical, solution procedure in this task. A number of the older Ss managed quite well without discovering it; whereas only a few of the younger ones did.

How, then, to account for the seventh graders' difficulty? Our present hypothesis is that the ability to *inhibit* ready-to-emit communicative behavior when operating under a communicative set may be a difficult, tardily acquired one, and the reasons for its tardiness may be sought in the child's previous reinforcement history. It is reasonable to suppose that children are fairly frequently rewarded for giving "all out" communications, that is, for saying all they can think of to say, the better to approximate, at least, what the listener requires. In contrast, frequent and consistent sanctions against overcommunication are much harder to imagine. In the first place, the child's undeveloped explanatory and role-taking powers make it unlikely that overcommunication will even occur very often. And second, when it does occur, it seems less likely to be negatively reinforced than undercommunication would be. If mild, overcommunication will doubtless pass unnoticed; if severe, it will probably elicit nothing more serious than a certain amount of impatience or boredom. Even in the latter case, in contrast to that of undercommunication, the listener will learn what he needs to learn for the purpose at hand, and may not tarry to supply the speaker with the needed feedback about his overcommunicative tendencies.

It seems probable, therefore, that this subtask was harder than most because it went so strongly against the grain of the child's previous communicative experience.[2] Consider what the problem required of S. She was first told to communicate as "well and completely" as she could on the Description subtask. Immediately after, still operating under a communicative set and with her previous codification fresh in mind, she had deliberately to *withhold* elements of it from the listening other, elements

2Recall that Task IE also showed behavioral change up through the eleventh grade, and overcommunication errors were common in that minimal-redundancy problem as well.

which would definitely be helpful to him under ordinary circumstances and which it would certainly do him no harm to know under any circumstances. Viewed in this way, it becomes a little easier to postdict the seventh graders' difficulty. The ability not to say more than is necessary begins to look like a high-level communicative refinement rather than a low-level fundamental, something which is probably acquired—to the extent that S does acquire it—only after more basic things are firmly installed. We find it an interesting and important refinement, however, and deserving of further investigation.

TASK IIC

We have so far reported four studies (IA, IE, IIA, and IIB) of the developing relation between role-taking and communication processes. In all of these, S's task was simply to *inform*, that is, to impart information to another individual in a more or less neutral and disinterested way. It occurred to us, however, that the growing ability to discriminate listener attributes might also perform an important instrumental function in communicative situations where the primary intent is not so much to inform as to *persuade* the audience to some course of action.[3] The ability to persuade another person effectively ought to presuppose the ability to identify those of his role attributes which are persuasion-relevant, that is, the particular needs in the listener to which appeal might profitably be directed, the sorts of arguments to which he might be susceptible—in general, the "chinks" in his sales resistance which the persuasive message ought to seek out and enter. There has been some previous research (Abelson and Lesser, 1959a, 1959b) on *persuasibility* in children, that is, their reactions to persuasive messages directed towards them by others. We know of none, however, which deal with what might be called their *persuasability*, that is, their ability to persuade others.

Procedure

There were two subtasks, administered in quick succession in the order given below.

Tie. "Suppose you were on one of those TV programs where they give away prizes for doing funny things. Suppose the thing you had to try to do is to sell this necktie (*E* presents a woolen, handwoven necktie with red, blue and grey stripes) to this man (photograph of a man's face). If you sell him this particular tie you'll get a prize of $500 on the pro-

[3]See Hovland, Janis, and Kelley (1953, chs. 1 and 9) for an analysis of the similarities and differences between informative and persuasive communication, as well for their discussion of theory and research concerning the latter.

gram. But of course this man doesn't know that and you can't tell him. But since you want the money you'd try just as hard as you could to talk him into buying the tie, you'd say *everything* you can *think* of to talk him into buying it. So here's the man just coming into the store. Go ahead and sell it to him the very best you can." When the child appears to have finished, *E* says: "Is there anything else you can think of to say which *might* help to make him buy it?"

TV. "Now suppose you wanted a TV set for your own room real *bad,* and you are trying to get your father to buy one for you. Once again, you'll try to use *every* argument you can *think* of which might talk him into buying it for you. We'll let this man (another photograph) be your father. Go ahead and try to talk him into it." When the child appears to have finished, *E* says: "Is there anything else you can think of to say which *might* help to make him buy it?"

Results

Ss' communications were scored in the manner described below. Two items of information are presented in parenthesis at the beginning of each scoring category. First, there is the subtask(s) to which the category applies: Tie, TV, or Tie and TV. Second, the kind of measure involved is indicated: continuous; seven-point rating scale (1–7); or dichotomous (0, 1). The judge worked from the actual tape recordings as well as from the typewritten transcript in the case of two categories: *Persuasive Effectiveness* and *Hard versus Soft Sell.* For the other measures the transcript alone was used.

Number of Different Arguments (Tie and TV; continuous). One point was given for each different argument contained in the message. Exactly what constitutes an "argument" was left to the judge. She was simply to derive her own working definition in surveying the protocols and attempt to apply it consistently throughout. Not to be scored, however, were unelaborated appeals to buy, for example, "Please buy me a TV set." That is, there had to be some minimal selling point, some content which might induce the listener to buy.

Type of Argument (Tie or TV; 0,1). A perusal of *Ss'* protocols suggested a further differentiation within the ensemble of arguments scored in the previous category. In each subtask there were certain classes of arguments which occurred frequently enough to be analyzed individually. These were:

Personalization (Tie). S personalizes the appeal, that is, addresses this buyer specifically, refers to his particular attributes, etc. For example: "It will look good on you"; "It will go with the suit you have on."

Prestige (Tie). S asserts or implies that the tie is a high-prestige product by alluding to its stylishness, exclusiveness, etc., by suggesting that others will esteem it or its wearer, and the like. For example: "It's the kind of tie well-dressed men are wearing these days"; "People will think you look nice in it."

Advantage to Others (TV). S mentions an advantage or benefit which someone other than herself might derive from the purchase of the TV set. For example: "If I have my own TV set, I won't be bothering you and Mom when you're watching programs I don't like."

Economic Objections (TV). S anticipates and attempts to deal with sales resistance relating to the cost of the TV set. For example: "I know they are expensive but . . ."; "I can pay for part of it myself."

Bandwagon (TV). S asserts or implies that the family will not be conforming to some social norm if she does not have her own TV set. For example: "All the other kids have their own, why can't I?"

Persuasive Effectiveness (Tie and TV; 1–7). The judge was to listen to each tape as though she were the buyer and simply make a global estimate regarding persuasive effectiveness, that is, how much the message would incline her to buy the product. She was, however, to try to disregard any sort of influence stemming solely from the apparent age of the speaker, for example, giving a high rating to a young speaker simply *because* she sounded so young, and so appealingly inept.

Hard versus Soft Sell (Tie and TV; 1–7). This was also a global, impressionistic rating. We attempted to define the meaning of these terms in rough correspondence with their usage in contemporary advertising parlance. Thus, a "hard sell" message (low rating on the seven-point scale) was defined as one which involved: (a) "high pressure" tactics, with the seller pushing, imploring, dogging the buyer to buy; (b) repetitive, unsubtle appeals, with the speaker clearly and undisguisedly in a seller role; and (c) loud and insistent voice quality on the tape (a less crucial criterion). In contrast, a "soft sell" communication (high rating) entailed: (a) "low pressure" tactics, with an attempt at gentle and subtle manipulation of the listener; (b) the use of indirection, understatement, and carefully phrased appeals to reason, the seller to some extent disguising or soft-pedaling the fact that he is a seller; and (c) soft and lulling voice quality on the tape (a less crucial criterion). The judge was told that she need not use all of the scale unless the protocols warranted it. That is, we were interested not only in measuring intersubject differences but also in obtaining a crude *absolute* estimate of the "hardness-softness" of these messages.

Table 19 presents the mean scores for Number of Different Arguments. Since the two subtasks show very similar age trends, statistical analyses were performed only on the summed scores (bottom row in the table).

Table 19
*Mean Number of Different Arguments per Grade
on Each Subtask of Task IIC*

	Grade		
Subtask	3	7	11
Tie	2.15	4.40	4.80
TV	1.20	3.25	3.25
Total	3.35	7.65	8.05

A simple analysis of variance showed highly significant differences among the three groups ($p < .001$, $df = 2,57$). Subsequent t test comparisons yielded reliable ($p < .01$) differences between the third graders and each of the older groups, but not between the latter two. The data on specific Types of Arguments are given in Table 20. It can be seen that all categories show at least some *prima facie* increase with age. Only one (Advantage to Others) does so reliably ($p < .02$), however, with two more (Prestige and Bandwagon) yielding chi squares which approach significance ($p < .10$). Parallel with what is shown in Table 19, there was a significant ($p < .01$) age increase in the number of Ss who produced three or more of these five types of arguments in their two messages.

Tables 21 and 22 present the group mean ratings for the two more global and impressionistic measures. These data were submitted to chi square analyses, using suitable cutoff points (number of Ss rated x or higher versus those rated x — 1 or lower, with the value of x dependent upon the particular measure and subtask). The chi square values were highly significant ($p < .001$) on both subtasks in the case of Persuasive Effectiveness, as the distribution of mean scores in Table 21 would suggest. The trend shown in Table 22 is obviously much weaker, and the

Table 20
*Number of Subjects per Grade Showing Various Types
of Arguments in Task IIC*

Subtask	Type of Argument	Grade			Significance Level
		3	7	11	
Tie	Personalization	11	15	17	NS
	Prestige	5	12	11	.10
TV	Advantage to Others	6	9	15	.02
	Economic Objections	6	9	12	NS
	Bandwagon	2	8	4	.10
Both	3 or More of Above	3	12	12	.01

Table 21
Mean Persuasive Effectiveness Ratings per
Grade on Each Subtask of Task IIC

Subtask	Grade		
	3	7	11
Tie	1.70	3.70	4.85
TV	1.75	3.80	4.40

Table 22
Mean Ratings of Hard versus Soft Sell
per Grade on Each Subtask of Task IIC

Subtask	Grade		
	3	7	11
Tie	3.00	3.10	4.30
TV	2.75	3.00	3.80

chi square for Hard versus Soft Sell reaches significance ($p < .05$) only in the case of the Tie subtask. The mean values here (Table 22) suggest that, in the rater's judgment, the messages as a whole tended to be of the high-pressure, hard-sell variety. Of the 120 messages sent by the 60 Ss, for instance, 37 received scale ratings of 1 or 2 whereas only 9 were rated 6 or 7. Even if we were sure that these absolute ratings were valid, we would hesitate to interpret them. It might be, for example, that they indicate a general tendency for children (and perhaps many adults as well) to employ hard-sell techniques in persuasive-communication situations. On the other hand, they may mean no more than that these particular tasks did not favor the utilization of more subtle and indirect methods, whereas others might have. Of more interest to us than these absolute scores is the trend, weak and uncertain though it is, for the messages to become relatively less "hard-sell" with age.

Discussion

The instructions in Task IIC had an explicit quantitative emphasis. S was told to "say everything you can think of," "use every argument you can think of" to persuade the imaginary listener. The study was thus structured to provide a rough estimate of S's persuasive repertoire, that is, of the number and variety of appeals she could muster when confronted with specific persuasive-communication problems. The results just presented indicate that the size of this repertoire is strongly age dependent. This age dependency, moreover, seems to be particularly marked across the grade 3–7 interval, as has tended to be the case for most of the tasks reported in this volume. The key measure here is doubtless that of Number of Different Arguments. Table 19 shows a marked increase from third to seventh grade in the number of "real arguments," that is, those which go beyond mere pleas or simple "mands" (Skinner, 1958). Part of what is involved in this increase can be seen in Table 20, which shows developmental trends in the major classes of arguments given in response to each communication problem.

It is likely that age changes on the remaining two measures are partly, and maybe primarily, the result of this increase in genuine argumentation. The persuasive impact of the messages (Persuasive Effectiveness) must have been at least partly a function of the sheer variety of appeals contained therein, although there probably were more subtle determinants also—phrasing, tone of voice, message organization, etc.—which contributed in many cases. Likewise, a shift from pleading to reasoned argumentation would by itself make for some movement toward the soft-sell end of the scale, although again there probably were other contributing factors.

We interpret this growth in persuasive repertoire as one more expression of the growth of role-taking skills. The creation of an argument intended to persuade O implies some recognition of those of O's attitudes, needs, or other attributes which are relevant to his present role of "persuasee." A persuasive argument, just like an informative communication, has a specific set of functions to perform, a specific job description, and this job description is defined in terms of the listener's putative characteristics: what he may and may not want or need, his counterpersuasive resistance, etc. To pose a persuasive argument is implicitly to imagine in advance O's response to it—and also, perhaps, to have just imagined his (negative) response to some alternative argument for which the present one was judged a more effective substitute.

This interpretation does not of course demand that S has actually to engage in a complex role-taking cognition each and every time he presents an argument. Persuasive appeals, like other responses, must attain a certain degree of efficient automaticity with continued exercise in persuasive-communication situations, and may thus be "run off" more or less mindlessly when certain cues are present. Calling attention to the superior qualities of the tie was probably an immediate and effortless response for many of our Ss, for example. What the interpretation does state, however, is that a rich repertoire here implies that a considerable amount of role-taking *skill* has previously been achieved, regardless of whether that skill needs to be *exercised* in the here and now verbalization of any given argument. This distinction between having, and having to use, role-taking abilities probably figures to some extent in our other role-taking and communication tasks. But it may be especially prominent here, since there exist categories of appeals which could be applied with little change in a wide variety of persuasion situations. With continued application, therefore, they might eventually come to be emitted without the role-taking activity which—according to our interpretation—functioned importantly when they first occurred.

We shall now examine the two subtasks separately, quoting examples of various levels of performance. The Tie subtask is interesting in that it may call forth in S two different sets of role-taking responses. There is first of all the usual prediction of O's attributes, in the role of potential buyer. In this particular case, these attributes consist of his needs, wishes, and tastes as regards haberdashery. With these attributes as his target, S tries to weave a message which will overcome whatever sales resistance O brings with him to the situation. We have already presented evidence and arguments to the effect that the older Ss showed more skill at this sort of role taking than the younger ones did.

S may also discriminate and actually *enact* the role attributes of a professional seller. We would hesitate to speak of role *enactment* in describing S's behavior on the previous tasks, although the distinction is not a hard and fast one. Explaining a game (Task IA) or a fable (IIA), describing a visual display (IIB), telling a story (ID), trying to persuade one's father to buy one a television set (second subtask of IIC), and the rest could all be viewed as role-appropriate behavior for children.[4] Acting out the part of a tie salesman is hardly role-appropriate behavior for girls, however, and could thus be termed role enactment if it occurred. Task IID (the next to be described) was expressly designed to study the development of role-enactment skills, but the present one was not. It would nonetheless be interesting to see whether any of our Ss took advantage of the role-enactment opportunities which it presented and, if so, whether there was any age trend in this respect.

The answer to both questions appears to be affirmative. A perusal of the messages shows that a number of Ss seemed to get actively involved in the task, using salesmanlike expressions such as, "May I help you?" "How do you do," "Yes, sir," and the like. A simple count of the protocols containing the word "sir" may serve as a rough and ready index of role-enactment behavior here, although it surely underestimates its frequency. Seventeen children used the word: 2, 6, and 9 Ss in grades 3, 7, and 11, respectively. There is tentative evidence, then, that there was an age

---

[4]Task IE could have been a role-enactment situation but was not in fact. That is, none of the children actually *behaved* like an adult law enforcement officer in broadcasting the safe combination.

trend, not just towards a cognitive assessment of the buyer's attributes, but also towards a behavioral assumption of the seller's. It is reasonable to suppose that the second process may have had a facilitative effect on S's performance. That is, actively entering the seller's role—actively getting "into the spirit of the thing"—may have lent an assist to the (other) role-taking process and/or increased the "habit strength" of the responses in S's persuasive repertoire. The following protocols illustrate developmental changes in both processes: the Ss were from the third, third, seventh, eleventh, and eleventh grades, in the order presented:

"Here's a tie. . . . Do you want to buy it? . . . Give it to him, he don't say no more." (Inquiry).[5] "Here, buy it."

"Would you like to buy this tie? It's a pretty tie. I think you—you would look very nice. . . . Would you like to buy it?" (Inquiry). "It's a very pretty tie. I like it very much, and maybe you would like it just as much."

"Ah . . . oh, ah . . . hello, sir. I'd like to introduce a new kind of tie that we have brought out. I'm sure that you would like it. It's a—it would be a wonderful Christmas present, or a birthday present, and of course you could wear it anywhere you want yourself. It doesn't cost very much. It's a very handsome tie, and you could match it with all your shirts, I'm sure." (Inquiry). "No."

"Well, you're the perfect type. Oh, you notice in this tie this blue is the exact color of your eyes. Oh, I bet you could never find a match like that again. Oh, that grey shirt you've got on, the grey is the exact same color. Oh, it would just go so nice with that shirt. All the people have been trying to get this tie but I've been saving it because I liked it so much I thought I might buy it myself, but seeing it looks so good on you, I guess I'll sell it to you." (Inquiry). "I wouldn't want to say it was—ah—low priced—ah. . . . I'm sure this is a tie that all women would like, and—ah—you could wear it with a lot of different suits, I think. It's got many different colors in it."

"Well, the look of—the best dressed man is a tie. Right, sir? . . . I have here a very, very beautiful tie. It has very nicely designed stripes on it, which will contribute much to any—any suit that you might have at home. And I'm sure that your wife and everyone around you would like it very much. They'd probably all pay you very nice compliments on it. It doesn't cost much—it's not—not very expensive tie, but—by looking at it you might think it was. I'm sure that you must have millions of ties at home but—ah—one very outstanding tie is always better than a—millions of just common ties. And by looking at this one I'm sure you—might agree with me." (Inquiry). "No."

The writer, for one, would just as soon keep out of the persuasive toils of the last two females quoted!

There are obvious differences between the Tie and TV persuasion

[5]As described earlier, the inquiry for all Ss consisted of the question: "Is there anything else you can think of to say which *might* help to make him buy it?"

problems. In both cases, of course, O is to be persuaded to buy something. But in the Tie situation he gets to keep what he buys, whereas in the TV problem the purchased object will revert to the persuader. To balance this disadvantage, the buyer is S's father instead of a stranger, and she may count on some extra persuasive leverage on that account. These differences importantly influence what S is likely to say in each case. Since O does receive something tangible for his money in the first sub-task, it is altogether likely that S would dwell on the object's merits, that is, the advantages to O in owning it. Virtually all of the children did this in one fashion or another, even the younger ones. Analogous arguments are possible in the TV case. O will not receive the object he paid for, to be sure, but its purchase may nonetheless benefit him in indirect, less obvious ways. With his daughter securely ensconced in her own room with her own television set, Father will have more freedom to watch his favorite programs on the family set, more peace and quiet, etc. Since these advantages are more subtle and indirect, one would not ex-pect arguments based on them to occur as frequently, in the younger group especially, as did their counterparts in the Tie problem. This appears to have been the case: the Advantage to Others category showed a significant increase with age, only six instances occurring in the third-grade group (Table 20).

One would also expect S to trade on the special relation between herself and the buyer, a relation not available for exploitation in the Tie sub-task. At the level of genuine arguments, S can point to the advantages which she, rather than he, would gain from the transaction. Such argu-ments are potentially effective because of the listener's paternal, altruistic, acquiescent, etc., attitudes regarding the persuader and her requests. Reasoned appeals of this nature were of course very common on this subtask: S should have her own TV because the other girls do, because it would make her happy, because it would help her scholastically (edu-cational programs), etc. But the special relation might also increase the probability of nonargumentative appeals of the sort all parents are familiar with: simple nagging and begging, cajoling and threatening, and whatever other contentless forms of pleading behavior children are capable of. One would expect this to be true with the younger Ss particu-larly, whose argumentative repertoire has been shown to be more limited. A casual perusal of the protocols suggested a simple but face-valid measure of pleading behavior: the occurrence of the word "Please" two or more times in the message. One such instance might be ordinary politeness; two or more begin to look very much like begging. The frequencies here were 8, 2, and 0, for the third-, seventh-, and eleventh-grade groups, respectively.

The verbatim messages in this subtask make interesting reading. There are two things particularly worth noting in those of the older Ss which we are about to quote. First, they illustrate varieties of persuasive subtlety, finesse, and ingenuity not caught in our scoring procedures— so frequently the case when your data consist of free and extended verbalizations. Second, they give rather direct evidence of ongoing role-taking activity, evidence of a sort we had not expected to obtain when we planned the study. Analogous to the overt role-enactment behavior on the Tie subtask, several of these Ss actually appear to be responding to O's imagined verbalizations, as though they were engaging in an ongoing discussion with him, for example, "What do you mean we can't afford it?" near the end of the fifth protocol. This is impressive when one considers that the instructions did not mandate such behavior and that the "interlocutor" was a photograph of a stranger. The authors of the following messages were three third graders, three seventh graders, and three eleventh graders, in that order. We have in each case left out anything the child may have added following the Inquiry.

"Oh Daddy, oh Daddy, please let me buy a television. I always wanted a television. Oh please, Daddy, please."

"Come on, I want a television for my own room. Come on. Please. Daddy, come on. Buy me a television. I want one for my room. Come on. Come on, Daddy. I want you to. There!"

"Daddy, would you buy me a TV set? . . . If you don't I'm gonna make the money, and go around selling things. And I . . . I know it looks nice in my room, and I think I should have it. . . . And if you don't get it for me, I won't bring you any birthday or Christmas present. . . And if you don't I won't— I won't like you and . . . if you don't get me a TV set . . . I'll get. . . . If you don't get me a TV set I'll get. . . . I'll make my money . . . or if you won't get me a TV set I'll just say you just better."

"Say, Dad, a lot of kids at school I know are getting televisions for Christmas. Can I have one? Gee, I know a lot of kids that want one, gee. I could really use it, you—for some of the educational programs, you know, that are on TV, and they're real good, and for homework at night some of our teachers want to watch 'em, and—you know, Johnnie always wants to watch cowboys, and . . . and everything, and I—I'll never get a chance to watch it down there, so why can't I have it in my room? C'mon Dad, please."

"Oh Father—er, wait a minute—oh, Dad. I just was down shopping and I saw this most lovely, most beautiful TV I ever saw and it's a portable too. And I was wondering—it didn't cost very much, and you could put it on your charge account down there, and I was just wondering if you could kinda buy it for me, for my birthday or Christmas present to have in my own room. Ah—I'm sure that you'd like it, and well, if you want it, you could buy one for your room too. They're kinda cheap, I mean, well, what you can get out of a TV, they're pretty nice, and oh, it'd just match all my furniture in my room. And I promise I wouldn't let any of my friends come in and watch it, or any of my sisters and brothers to wreck it."

"Oh, hello Dad. How are you today? Do you want your slippers changed or something? Here, have a cigarette? Oh, you don't want one? Oh, okay. Do you want me to do anything for you? Ah—let's see—hey, Christmas is coming. I'll review my list for you. Now there's only one thing I want and that is a television set. Ah—if you get me that you don't have to get me anything else, unless you want to, of course. But you know I need one real much, and ah— and if I don't feel good I don't have to come into the living room and watch the TV. I can stay right in my room and be very rested. And ah—you know—I can use it a lot. And ah—and when my friends come over they don't have to pack in front of the television. They could stay right in my room and be very quiet. Um, yeah, yeah. And they're real pretty and they make a room look real nice, and they're real small ones too, that you can use if you want—wanted. They wouldn't take up any room and—well, you could get a pretty cheap one. Maybe a used one, a second-hand one. They're only be used a few times. Anything you want to get me, as long as it's a television set. Okay?"

"Hi Dad, guess what? Janie next door just got a television in her room. Don't you think I could have one? What do you mean, I wouldn't sleep at night? Sure I would, I'd go to bed real early and I could sit there and watch it. And I could rest while I'm watching it. Oh, I'd turn it off before I went to sleep . . . I'm sure I'd get my homework done. I could do it in the den instead of in my room, and that way I wouldn't get to watch television. Then, don't you think I could have one? All the other girls have got them in their rooms."

"Dad, ah . . . it gets pretty lonely up there in my room at times, and—it'd be very nice if I could have a companion. I know I have my radio but—I can only listen to my radio, I can't see. And I'd like to have—well, maybe a small little TV set . . . But it doesn't cost that much, I mean. After all, I could use some of my allowance to pay for it . . . You could only finance me a little bit of it. I could—I could get a job even—'cause I really want that TV set. I'll give up my radio. I'll even clean up my room every day. I'll make my own bed in the morning . . . Well, I know, I should make my bed, but—I want that TV set and I'll—I'll make everybody's bed in the morning if I can have that TV set . . . Oh, I don't like the one downstairs. Everybody's down there, and there's lots of things I have to watch on TV for school, and—really, the kids want to watch kiddie programs all the time, and I don't get a chance to see much educational ones. So I—no, I won't listen to Dick Clark all the time, I'll listen to educational ones, too. What do you mean we can't afford it? I think we can afford it, if I pay with my allowance. I'll even get a job, anything."

"Well, Dad, I have a problem. Since we here in Rochester have only two stations, uh—for a choice of television watching, and—uh—we have a very large family, and—so we probably have many different interests. You like to watch the baseball game, I like to watch Alfred Hitchcock, and if they come at—at the same time . . . somebody's going to be left out. Since I have the largest room in the house, all the conveniences of the room and everything—to put another television, wouldn't it be a very good idea if I had one up there? I don't know what he'd say. Well, the expense wouldn't be bad, because you could buy it on installments, or you could even get a second-hand one. Probably pick one up very cheap at a second-hand store, maybe you'd have to sink a little money into it, but—it probably wouldn't be bad at all. And the kids could come up there and watch their programs, while we—while you're watching yours, and—and there's only two stations anyway, so—two TV sets would be just fine."

The ontogenesis of persuasive skill impresses us as an exceedingly interesting and important subject for research. It appears first of all to be a salient, frequently exercised skill in its own right, one which may make up a substantial minority of the average child's (and adult's) daily verbalizations. More than that, however, the child's ability to persuade others appears to lie at the crossroads of numerous other developing behaviors. It ought therefore to constitute a valuable index of such things as his social perception, his understanding of human motivation and cognition, his role-taking prowess, his social-interactional skills—perhaps his social development as a whole. It is obvious that the present study constitutes only a small first step in our understanding of this behavior. There remains, for example, the intriguing question of the causal antecedents of persuasion, that is, the various factors and forces which make for (or interfere with) the genesis of the skill (Chapter 7).

Even at the developmental-descriptive level, however, there is much more to be learned. Our task instructions encouraged S simply to produce all the persuasive arguments she could think of, given a particular listener and persuasion goal. Stressing sheer quantity as it did, the task could provide little direct information about the child's evaluation of the relative efficacy of different types of appeals, of different temporal or structural organizations of a given set of appeals, etc. One could perhaps better obtain this kind of information by presenting already-constructed persuasive material and having the child make choices: for example, present two arguments and ask him which he would judge to be more effective in a given situation, and why. Methods of this sort might demonstrate interesting age changes in the preference hierarchy: younger children prefer argument-type X above all others; older ones opt for Y, judging that X would either be ineffective or would increase sales resistance; still older Ss detect subtle flaws in Y and find reasons for preferring unlikely looking Z, given the particular persuasee, and the like. There is the merest hint that age-dependent preference shifts of this type may lie hidden in our data. Compare, for example, the apparent developmental trends for Bandwagon versus the other two TV-subtask categories. It is hard to believe that more seventh graders than eleventh graders were able to *think* of the possibility of adding Bandwagon arguments to their battery. More likely, in our opinion, a number of the older Ss may have decided that this kind of appeal simply would not accomplish anything—except, perhaps, to irritate the father and cause a persuasive backfire. In contrast, they may have judged Advantage to Others and Economic Objections to be innocuous at worst and very useful at best. The father is after all bound to ponder the cost involved, and the child might as well try to neutralize, or at least minimize, his economic objections in advance. Similarly, the child may gain some persuasive mileage by calling attention to certain benefits to other family members which might not occur to the father.

Whatever the best research tactics may be, it is clear that research problems abound in this area. Social psychologists have only just begun to obtain precise data about the persuasive efficacy of various types of messages, as a function of listener, speaker, and other relevant variables (for example, Hovland et al., 1957, 1959). Developmental psychologists could provide an important complement to these data, namely, information about the nature and sequence of the steps which the growing child takes in moving toward these adult "norms" of persuasive behavior.

TASK IID

The previous task was designed to measure persuasive behavior, conceived as an expression or reflection of the child's role-taking development. An incidental finding in that study was that a number of Ss responded, not only by covertly *assessing* the *persuasee*'s role attributes, but also by overtly *enacting* those of a *persuader*, for example, using phrases that an actual sales clerk might use in talking to a customer. While overt role enactment was only of passing interest in that investigation, it was the major subject of study in the present one. Our own previous research and that of others have shown that the ability to discriminate O's role attributes is strongly age dependent. It therefore seemed reasonable to predict that the ability to go beyond discrimination into accurate enactment or portrayal would also increase with age.

Procedure

As in Task IIC, there were two subtasks which were administered one right after the other, in the order shown below.

Shy. "Now, I want you to do a little acting, as though you were in a play. I'm going to play the part of a teacher and you are to play the part of a little girl, say in the first grade. You have just returned from a trip to the zoo and I, the teacher, am going to ask you about it. Now I want you to take the part of a particular *kind* of little girl. This girl is *very shy*. She doesn't like to talk up in class, and she is not very good at putting things into words—she isn't a very good talker. I want you to *be* just like this little girl, even to *sound* just like her as you talk. Here goes. I'm the teacher and I say to you: 'Mary, tell me about your trip to the zoo— what you saw and did there.' "

Bold. "Now, we have the same situation again—you are a first-grade girl who has just come back from the zoo. But you are a very *different* kind of girl from the first time. You are very *bold,* not at all *shy;* you like to talk in class and you can express your ideas very well in words; you are a *good* talker. Again, I want you to be just like this kind of girl, *sound* just like she would talk. I'll repeat the teacher's question (*E* repeats). Go ahead."

The predictive strategy here was similar to that of Study IA. *S*'s task is to behave as two quite different children would behave in a common situation, that is, describing a recent visit to the zoo. The extent to which *S*'s behavior corresponds to that of each of the two "models" designated by *E* may be difficult to measure in any absolute sense. One can, however, confidently assert that she should behave *differently* in the two enactments, and one can at least guess at some of the dimensions on which these differences should lie. As in Task IA, therefore, the hypothesis that role-enactment skill increases with age translates into the prediction that these two enactments would in various ways become more different with age.

Results

The following is a list of the dimensions on which differences were measured, together with their rationales. A more detailed description of the dimensions will be given subsequently. First, a child (Bold) who enjoys and is skilled at talking should give a fuller, more detailed account (*Words and Different Words*) of her adventure than one who lacks these traits (Shy). For the same reason, one would expect her verbal delivery to be more rapid (*Rate of Speech*). Since she is supposed to be a bold, expressive, relatively uninhibited individual, one would also anticipate that her speech would be louder (*Loudness of Speech*) and more variable in pitch and volume (*Intonation-Stress*); likewise, the behavior which she reports having engaged in at the zoo might be braver (or less fearful) than that of her shyer counterpart (*Behavioral Audacity*). And finally, one would expect the latter to have more word-finding difficulty (*Verbal*

Facility), since she is characterized as "not very good at putting things into words."

The Words and Different Words measures were continuous variables. All the others were dichotomous. Rate of Speech, Loudness of Speech, and Intonation-Stress were judged directly from the tape, while the rest were rated from its verbatim transcript.

Words. S is scored for the total number of words contained (in each narration).

Different Words. S is scored for the total number of different words, that is, with each word counted only once, regardless of how often it may have been repeated.

Rate of Speech. S is scored only if her Bold narration is judged to have been delivered at a higher average rate of speech than her Shy narration, that is, more words emitted per unit time, on the average.

Loudness of Speech. Same as above (Rate of Speech), except that the dimension rated is the average loudness or intensity of speech.

Intonation-Stress. Same as above, except that the dimensions rated are intonation (variation in pitch) and/or stress (variation in loudness)—in general, the extent to which the narration seems to depart from an unstressed monotone.

Behavioral Audacity. Same as above, except that the dimension rated concerns expressions of audacity or boldness and fearfulness or timidity in the child's reported behavior at the zoo. As in the other dimensions, it is the relation between the two enactments which counts. That is, S is scored here if timid, fearful behavior were reported in the Shy narration and not (or less so) in the Bold, *or* if bold, audacious behavior were reported in the Bold narration and not (or less so) in the Shy.

Verbal Facility. Same as above, except that the dimension rated concerns the actor's apparent ability to find suitable verbal expression for her thoughts. More specifically, S is scored here only if word- or phrase-finding difficulties occurred in the Shy narration and did not occur in the Bold. For example, the child said "I don't know what they call it," "I don't know how to tell it," etc., in the Shy role but not in the Bold.

Table 23 presents the mean number of Words and of Different Words per grade and subtask. It is clear that the Bold instructions generally elicited much longer and more detailed narrations at all grade levels. Only 3 of the 60 Ss, for example, produced more words in response to the Shy subtask. There is also a suggestion of an interaction effect of the sort predicted: the differences between subtask means are larger in the two older groups than in the youngest group. It cannot be regarded as more than a suggestion, however. A difference score was computed for

Table 23

Mean Scores per Grade and Subtask for Words,
Different Words, and the Different Words–Words
Ratio (DW/W) in Task IID

	Words		Different Words		DW/W	
Grade	Shy	Bold	Shy	Bold	Shy	Bold
3	86.35	147.65	38.25	62.85	.44	.42
7	51.55	171.30	31.25	77.10	.61	.45
11	62.80	169.10	37.25	75.75	.59	.45

each S on each measure, consisting of Bold score minus Shy score plus a constant to correct for sign. Simple analyses of variance were then performed on each set of difference scores ($df = 2,57$). The F ratio for the words measure was 2.84, only significant at $p < .10$; the corresponding figure for Different Words was a nonsignificant 1.99. Table 23 also shows the mean Different Words—Words ratios, calculated as part of a post-

Table 24

Number of Subjects per Grade Scored for
Various Measures in Task IID

	Grade			Significance Level
Measure	3	7	11	
Rate of Speech	12	18	19	.01
Loudness of Speech	8	13	11	NS
Intonation-Stress	10	13	16	NS
Behavioral Audacity	3	4	9	.05
Verbal Facility	6	6	5	NS
3 or more of above	8	13	15	.10

experimental search for group differences.[6] These ratios were analyzed in the same fashion as their two components, that is, the differences between each S's ratios were computed and a simple analysis of variance was performed on them. The resulting F ratio was 2.67 ($p < .10$). Data on the remaining measures is presented in Table 24. All except Verbal Facility show trends in the predicted direction, but only Rate of Speech and Behavioral Audacity yielded chi squares which reached statistical

---

[6]Also calculated were the following ratios: adjectives to total words; nouns to total words; verbs to total words; self-referential pronouns ("I," "me," "we," "us," "mine," and "ours") to total words; and personal-action verbs (those expressing the narrator's actions) to total verbs. None of these measures contributed any evidence for intergroup differences.

significance. There was also a developmental trend, of borderline ($p < .10$) significance, with respect to the number of Ss who availed themselves of 3 or more of these methods of role differentiation.

Discussion

Although the intergroup differences are not as clear cut here as in other tasks investigated, the data nonetheless suggest that some increase in role-enactment skill probably occurs across the age range studied. There is, for example, a near-significant trend for the older Ss to make a better adjustment of narrative length (words) to the implied requirements of each role. Thus, their Shy messages are briefer, on the average, than those of the younger Ss. These messages also appear to be relatively more compact or less redundant (have higher DW/W ratios), perhaps indicating an attempt to include a reasonable minimum of information while still maintaining a role-appropriate brevity. Likewise, their Bold narratives tend to be wordier than those produced by the third graders. The dichotomous measures also offer a certain amount of support for the developmental hypothesis. There is clear evidence, for example, that the older groups are more prone to increase their rate of speech when enacting the Bold role, and most of the remaining indices of role differentiation at least show trends which conform to prediction. Behavioral Audacity strikes us as a particularly subtle method of distinguishing between the two roles; it appears to be a much less obvious technique, for example, than simply changing message length. It seemed reasonable, therefore, to find the use of Behavioral Audacity largely concentrated in the eleventh-grade group.

We believe these developmental trends may be interpreted in the same general way as the others reported in this volume: as children mature, they tend to become more and more adept at inferring and subsequently maintaining in awareness the role attributes of others; this adeptness mediates good performance in a wide variety of situations to which it is relevant, including—as in this task—the special case where the inferential process is followed by overt enactment of the other's role. One should not, however, gloss over possible differences between role enactment and other behaviors which also entail role-attribute discrimination. It is our suspicion that it may, in one sense at least, be a less demanding psychological operation than most of the others. In role enactment, S need only cope with one role during the period of time he is performing, namely, that of the individual or role position he is portraying. He can "forget himself," as it were, and devote all his attention to "being" the other. This is not the case where S discriminates the other's role attributes in order to carry out a role complementary to his, for example, where S

functions as his communicator, game opponent, and the like. Here, S cannot expend all his psychological resources in a single role, but must instead divide them between two. When communicating, for example, he must continually alternate between his own role and that of the audience if the message is to be adapted to the latter's needs.

Role enactment, then, appears to differ from other role-taking-relevant activities in that it is more of a one- versus two-process affair. One might expect, therefore, that *in general* (that is, other contributions to difficulty level held constant) role enactment ought to be a somewhat easier, earlier-appearing skill than the others. It may be worth noting in this regard that almost all of our youngest Ss were able to demonstrate some noticeable competence in the present task. For instance, only three of the twenty third graders failed to produce a longer message in the Bold sub-task, and Table 23 shows that the group mean difference in message length was substantial.[7] Moreover, a fair number of these young Ss found other, perhaps less obvious ways of distinguishing between the two roles (Table 24). And apart from this study, it is well known that primitive manifestations of role-enactment activity enter the child's behavioral repertoire very early in life, for example, dramatic play, and imitations of the mother's speech and gestures (Maccoby, 1959). We would expect that the difficulty level of a role-enactment task would rise markedly if it were given something resembling the two-process structure of the other role-taking tasks. It would be interesting, for example, to see how easily children could enact two or more distinct and different roles in quick alternation, as in carrying out the puppetmaster function in an impromptu puppet show (supplying the dialogue for the various personalities as they interact, etc.).

We have previously alluded to the substantial within-age-level individual differences which are omnipresent in all our research data. This sort of variation was, if anything, even more noticeable than usual in this study and undoubtedly had much to do with the relative paucity of statistically reliable developmental trends. The following two protocols —both produced by third graders—will serve to illustrate the magnitude of these differences as well as to convey the general character of the Task IID raw data.

[7] Of course part of the increased length of the Bold messages at all grade levels may have been due to the fact that they always constituted the *second* communication on the same topic, with S perhaps thinking of additional experiences to report the second time around. Other measures may also have been similarly influenced by sequence, for example, Rate of Speech and Verbal Facility. There is no convincing reason we can find for supposing that this factor would have spuriously affected *intergroup* differences to any significant extent. It may, however, be causing u° to overestimate somewhat the third graders' role-enactment skill in the present discussion.

(Shy). "I, er, I seen a kangaroo. I seen a giraffe, an elephant, some lions, a tiger, some rabbits, monkeys, an alligator, some snakes—and some seals . . . and some—zebras . . . and some chimpanzees . . . and some birds . . . and lots of people I seen . . . and lots of trees and merry-go-rounds . . . a building . . . that's all."

(Bold). "I seen some monkeys, chimpanzees, some rabbits, some giraffes, and some kangaroos . . . ah . . . some giraffes, some elephants, some seals, some—some chimpanzees, an alligator, and . . . and zebras, some birds, some big buildings, a fence, little reindeers—goats . . . um . . . lots of people—lots of cars and that's all."

(Shy). "Well . . . we saw—we saw animals, and—an—well . . . we saw some lions . . . and saw some birds—and saw parrot and some horses, and we saw—well, we saw some ah . . . some elephants eating hay, and we saw lots of other stuff."

(Bold). "We saw some elephants eating hay, and the man got on his trunk and, and the elephant waved him around like a swing. And we saw some lions, and they—they were at their meal, and boy, that was fun to watch 'em. And we saw some birds with all their pretty colors, and we saw a peacock, and it spread its wings out. And we saw lots of other stuff too. We saw lions and tigers, and we saw . . . we saw some . . . the lions and tigers were fighting sorta—well, sorta playing, not fighting, and ah—they—the man let us stay there for a long time and watch 'em. And then—finally—finally fed 'em. Then we—we went over and saw the monkeys, and they were playing very happily on a—on a tree, and they were—the mothers were carrying their babies, and then we ate, and they threw banana skins all over. And we—we saw all different—and we saw—we saw some things that are real skinny and some that are real fat. We saw a gorilla—I mean a chimp—well, a squirrel and we saw a—a chipmunk, and we saw a chimpanzee, and we saw a laughing hy-hyena, and we saw a—we saw lots of other stuff too."

The written record does not catch all of the differences between these two Ss' role-enactment skill, however. Not only was the second S's Bold message much longer than her Shy one, it was also judged from the tape to be louder, more variable in intonation-stress, and more rapid in delivery; the first S, on the other hand, was not scored for any of the five dichotomous measures.

We can of course do no more than make educated guesses about the major sources of such individual variation. A particularly likely contender in the present case might be the cluster of personality characteristics vaguely described by terms such as "social anxiety," "self-consciousness," "shyness," and the like. S was, after all, almost literally "onstage" here, called upon to act out another's part before a "live audience" in the person of a strange adult (*E*). To do so skillfully, she may well have needed something more than the intellectual ability to make shrewd inferences about how this or that type of child would narrate a recent experience to her teacher. She may have needed among other things, the spontaneity, the emotional freedom—the "ham" quality even—to translate these inferences into overt enactment in the presence of an audience.[8] She may have needed, in short, some of the same personal qualities she was to portray in the Bold role. This is not to suggest that these and related noncognitive factors were unimportant sources of individual variation in the other tasks as well, but only to suggest that they may have been exceptionally potent in this one.

TASK IIE

We have described five tasks (IA, IE, IIA, IIB, and IIC) designed to investigate developmental changes in communicative skill. In each instance, *S* was instructed to compose one or more messages, the quality of which were subsequently assessed by the investigators. The converse obtains in the present study: *E* presents *S* with an inadequate communication already prepared by the investigators and *S*'s task is to try to diagnose its inadequacies. In the previous studies, it was hypothesized that the ability to construct an effective, listener-adapted message is age dependent across middle childhood and adolescence; here, the same prediction is made concerning the ability to detect communicative maladaptations in a message constructed by someone else.

Procedure

The task materials consisted of a typewritten message and two copies of the map shown in Figure 9 (minus the designations of *O*'s present location and destination). *E* instructed *S* as follows:

"Now suppose there were a man in his car out in the country some place who got lost—he didn't know where he was or how to get to the house he wanted to go to. Now suppose he had this map (points) and I had *exactly* the *same* map here (points). These are the roads and these are the houses (points). Now he calls me up on the telephone and from what he says I can figure out where he is now. He is here (points to bottom X on the map), and I can also tell him how to get to where he

---

[8]It occurs to us that the older *S*s might have needed *more* of such qualities than the younger ones, inasmuch as the roles to be enacted (a shy and a bold *first grader*) were more dissimilar to their own. This may have served as an artifact which further attenuated group differences.

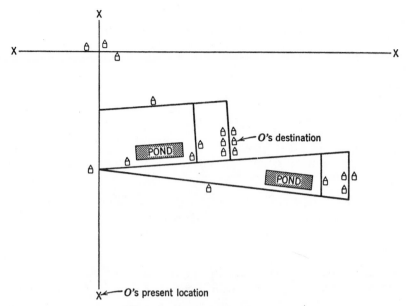

Figure 9. Map used in Task IIE.

wants to go—there (points to second house on the right on the street which contains a cluster of six houses). I'm going to read out loud what I might tell him over the phone, and you may look along with me as I read. When I get through I want you to tell me what's *wrong* with the way I gave him the directions, why he'd have trouble getting there from what I say. Okay, now I'm going to talk to him on the phone."

E then proceeds to read slowly the following message, tracing the correct route with a pointer as she reads.

"If you look on your map you'll find an X. That's where you are right now. You go down the road until you see a house on your left. Turn right there and keep going until you pass a pond on your left. Then you make a left turn and the house you want is the second one on the street."

E then says:

"Here are the directions I just read (*E* places them before the child). Okay, now you tell me all the things wrong with those directions you can think of—all the things which might confuse him."

With the younger children especially, *E* gave encouragement and support freely, for example, urging *S* to find additional errors, and rereading parts of the message or the instructions as needed. If, despite such assistance, *S* still could discover no communication errors, *E* explained Error A (see below) and urged *S* to try to find others. Of the eight *S*s so

Table 25
Number of Task IIE Communication Errors
Detected at Each Grade Level

Number of Errors	Grade			
	3	7	11	Σ
0	8	0	0	8
1	7	3	2	12
2	3	9	9	21
3	1	7	4	12
4	1	1	5	7

treated (all third graders, as Table 25 will show), only two were then able to find any additional errors on their own.

Results

The data analysis centered principally on the communication errors which S was to discover. We identified the following four errors in E's communication.

Error A. "That's (that is, X) where you are now": since there are *four* Xs on the map, this fails to establish O's initial position.

Error B. "Turn right there": there are *two* roads which branch off to the right at this juncture.

Error C. "Then you make a left turn": the correct street is the *second* left after the pond.

Error D. "The house you want is the second one on the street": O's destination is the second house on the *right*.

We indicated at the beginning of the chapter that an individual unconnected with the research project served as judge in Study II. While this was true for the preceding four tasks, it was not the case here. Pilot work indicated that E herself was in the best position to judge whether or not some Ss had identified a particular error, since their gestures gave important supplementary evidence. An error detection was thus counted if S had convinced E, by verbalization, gesture, or both, that she had indeed really identified it. In the great majority of cases, actually, such judgments could have easily been made by anyone, from the typewritten record alone.

Table 25 shows the number of Ss per grade level who discovered 0, 1, 2, 3, and 4 of these errors. There are clear-cut group differences in evidence here, notably between the youngest group and the two older ones. For example, 15 of the 20 third graders found no more than 1 error; the corresponding numbers for the seventh and eleventh graders were 3 and 2, respectively (chi square significant at $p < .001$). Similarly, all of the older Ss found at least 1 error, whereas only three-fifths of the youngest ones did. There is only a slight difference between the achievement levels of the two oldest groups, largely consisting of a shift in the relative number of Ss discovering 4 versus 3 errors.

There appears to have been some variation in ease of discovery among the 4 errors. The number of Ss detecting them were 15, 28, 38, and 37 for Errors A, B, C, and D, respectively. There is a distinction between Error A and the other three which may partly explain its relatively greater difficulty. In perceptually following the route from O's present location to his intended destination, S must at least *see* the visual basis for Errors B, C, and D. That is, his eye will inevitably encounter the two right forks, the two left turns after the pond, and the houses on both sides of the street. He will not, however, necessarily perceive the other three Xs, located some distance away at the top of the map (see Figure 9). A number of Ss, therefore, may have failed to detect Error A for no more profound reason than that they did not register the fact that there *were* four Xs on the map.

How did the children go about trying to detect the errors? A logical and orderly procedure would be to peruse message and map route step by step from origin to destination, picking up errors along the way as noticed. This appears to be exactly what most of the Ss did. Of the 40 children who discovered at least 2 errors, 37 reported them in the sequence in which they occurred in the message, that is, BD, ACD, ABCD, etc. versus DC, BDC, BACD, etc.

Discussion

Task IIE presents certain features in common with Task ID (Chapter 2). In both cases S is initially provided with a certain perspective vis-à-vis the task materials. In Task ID, this perspective consists of a seven-picture-story interpretative context for the subset of four pictures; here, it consists of a knowledge of O's location, destination, and intervening route as depicted on a map. And in both cases S's task consists principally of ignoring or suppressing his initial perspective in order to apprehend, and function in terms of a second, quite different perspective. In ID, this second point of view is that of an O who sees the four pictures naïvely, that is, with no knowledge of their previous seven-picture setting; in IIE, it is that of an O who, unlike S, cannot identify on the map his own location, destination, and route.

It is difficult to see how S could detect inadequacies in E's message without in some degree trying to hear it as O would hear it, without in some degree imagining how O might respond—covertly and at the steering wheel—to each of its instructions. She must see that he might feel puzzled, and might end up making the wrong turn, on being told simply to "turn right" at an intersection which presents two right forks. Such imaginings clearly entail a representation of his behavior, not her own. It is not she who must drive from X to the house; and even if it were, she already knows how to get there and could thus disregard the defective message entirely. But the message, in conjunction with the map, will surely stimulate O, and in ways which are in part predictable. S must therefore disregard her own assimilation of these stimuli in favor of trying to assess their probable impact on O, and this entails role-taking activity on her part. We think that a relative inability to engage in such activity was largely responsible for the third graders' difficulty on this task, although we would not rule out the possible contributions of other perceptual and cognitive factors. In being sufficiently able or prone to extricate themselves from their own perspective, they were insufficiently able—as in Task ID—to simulate O's reactions, that is, to cause the communicative stimuli to elicit in them the conflicts and confusions these stimuli would be likely to elicit in O. The findings of this and our previous studies taken together may support a general developmental conclusion: young children appear to be relatively incapable of predicting other people's responses to stimuli if these responses differ substantially from their own; this holds equally for verbal-communicative versus other stimuli, and for stimuli produced by others versus those produced by the child himself.

The map and its accompanying message were designed in such a way that the inadequacy of a given message unit would not necessarily be apparent to O upon receiving subsequent ones. Suppose, for example, that O had assumed from the initial instructions that he were located at some X other than the bottom one on the map. The next subsequent instructions would not correct his mistake: if he proceeded from *any* of the four Xs he would discover a house on the left side of the road and a possible right turn nearby. This would not have been the case if, say, the road leading from his chosen X had presented no intersecting roads or no houses on its left side. Suppose further that O had located the correct X but then had taken the incorrect (lower) right fork. He would still find the reassuring presence of a pond on his left, could still take one of two left turns thereafter, and could on either of these turns find a "second house."

Situations fitting this paradigm must abound in real life. The world and the people in it are simply not constructed so that an initial erroneous cognition is always corrected, quickly and unambiguously, by subsequent events; all too often, these events have the necessary malleability to be nicely misconstrued in accord with the initial cognition—and may indeed serve to reinforce it. It would be interesting to investigate the child's growing recognition that information sequences often possess this property. In surveying Ss' protocols, we noted—using rough and perhaps unreliable criteria—that some 17 Ss verbalized such recognition more or less explicitly. They might indicate, for example, that if O took the wrong right fork he would *still* find the expected pond on his left, or that if he took the first instead of the second left turn he would *still* find a series of houses from which a second could be selected, and the like. Of the 17, 2 were third graders, 8 seventh graders, and 7 eleventh graders. These figures surely underestimate Ss' sensitivity to this communicative property, if they can be said to measure it at all, and we regard them only as indications that more careful studies of the problem might yield something interesting. We conclude study and chapter with the verbatim record of one of the 7 eleventh graders.

"Well, first of all you state that you'll find an X on the map. Consequently there are four of them. You don't denote which one you want. Then you say, you go down the road till you see a house on your left. Of course, if you don't know which place you're starting out at you don't know which road you're going down, which house is supposed to be on your left. But say you're going down the right road anyway, and you see the house on your left, and you take—you turn right there, as it was stated in the directions, but there's a fork in the road and they both go right. You do not denote which way to go, either take the left or the right fork. You tell him to make—to take this turn, and he doesn't know which one to take, so consequently when he goes down the road and makes another left—no matter which one he took there would be a left-hand turn at both, and of course, there would be a second house on the street, no matter which one he took. So he could end up at the wrong place, by taking that wrong turn at the fork."

CHAPTER FIVE

Role Taking in Early Childhood

Studies I and II were designed to investigate changes in role-taking and communication skills which take place during middle childhood and adolescence. Thus, the youngest Ss tested in these studies were 7–8 years old. About midway through the research project it was decided to attempt a small, pilot-type investigation (Study III) of role-taking development during the preschool years. The results of our efforts are described in this chapter.

The investigatory strategy was essentially the same here as in the two previous studies. That is, we tried to think of a variety of tasks which would be appropriate to very young children, but which would nonetheless be face-valid measures of role-taking skill as we have been defining it. These tasks were then given to small samples of children in the 3–6 year age range. In a few instances, analyses of the resulting data or a reexamination of the task itself led to task revisions and subsequent readministration.

The details of Study III were as follows. All Ss were individually tested by 1 project member (Patricia T. Botkin). Two of the Ss were neighbors of hers; all the rest were drawn from 2 nursery schools (one of them a day care institution which included preschool children above nursery school age).[1] The children came from intact, mostly middle-class homes and all were judged to be of at least average intelligence by their teachers (no formal IQ or other ancillary data were available, however). Six brief tasks (Tasks IIIA–F) were administered in random sequence[2] to each S during a single testing session. The sample consisted of 40

[1]The authors wish to express their thanks to the staffs of the Rochester Children's Nursery and the University of Rochester Medical School Child Study Center for their cooperation in providing Ss and facilities for this study.
[2]Tasks IIIC and IIID were exceptions to this random sequence. Since they had initially been conceived as two parts of a single task, they were always administered one right after the other, in the order named.

children (19 boys and 21 girls), 10 at each of ages 3, 4, 5, and 6. Three of the 6 tasks (IIIA, C, and F) were later revised and readministered to 10 three-year-olds and 10 five-year-olds. All of these 20 children were drawn from the 2 above-mentioned nursery schools, and 16 of the 20 had been tested in the original study. In the data tables to be presented, the reader will note an occasional group N of less than 10; this means that 1 or more Ss in that group were judged to have given invalid data on that particular task for some reason (for example, failed to follow instructions, or failed to respond at all) and were therefore not included in the analyses.

We shall begin by describing the procedure and results for each task in turn. Following this, we shall briefly cite some supporting data from another study, not directly connected with the research project described in this book. And finally, we shall conclude the chapter with a general discussion of our various findings.

TASK IIIA

As will be seen, all but one of the Study III tasks were of the "perceptual role taking" variety, analogous to Task IC (Chapter 2). That is, S was tested on his ability to predict or otherwise take account of E's *perceptual* (as opposed to *cognitive* or other) experiences, under conditions where those experiences differed in some way from S's own. Task IIIA attempted to measure a very simple behavioral expression of this "taking account of" E's perceptual perspective: with E seated facing him, S was to show a picture to E; our question was whether S would spontaneously orient the picture so that E would see it right side up (with S himself, of course, having to view it upside down in so orienting it).

Procedure

The test materials consisted of two sets of three brightly colored pictures, each picture mounted on 9 $\times$ 12 in. tagboard. One set consisted of pictures of animals: a squirrel eating nuts, a rabbit eating a large carrot, and two kittens standing side by side. The other set showed various winter scenes: a girl on a sled, children gathered around a snowman, and a Christmas tree with children opening presents. S and E are seated on opposite sides of a small table.

E says, "I have some pictures to show you," and presents the three animal pictures right side up to the child. S is urged to name them, with E coaching and supplying names where necessary. "Now we are going to play a little game. You blind your eyes, like this (shows S), and I will choose my favorite picture." After the child blinds his eyes, E chooses a

picture at random, tells the child to open his eyes, and shows him the
picture so he sees it right side up. "It's your turn now. I'll blind my eyes,
and you choose your favorite picture and show it to me." E hands S the
three pictures (oriented correctly for him), covers her eyes while the
child makes his choice, and then observes the orientation in which S
presents the chosen picture to her.

If S presents it upside down to her, she says: "Show it to me so I can
see it as you see it." If S presents it in side view (so that both E and S
can see it right side up if they turn their heads), E says: "I like that one
too—will you put it on the table so I can see it?" If S fails to orient the
picture correctly on his second trial (that is, after one of the above hints
has been given), E says: "It doesn't look right side up to me; can you
show it to me so it does?"

S is then presented with the other set of three pictures and the entire
procedure is repeated.

Results

A total of 21 Ss made at least 1 orientation error on the 2 subtasks, 16
Ss made no errors, and 3 Ss were judged to have given invalid data. Of
the above 21 Ss, 11 positioned the picture(s) upside down from E's point
of view (thus, "egocentrically"), 3 Ss positioned it in side view to both S
and E, and 2 Ss did it one way for 1 picture and the other way for the
other. There was no suggestion in the data that the side-view orientation
was a more "mature" kind of error, in the sense of being more frequent
at the higher age levels.

Table 26
*Number of Subjects Showing Various Numbers of
Incorrect Responses on Task IIIA*

Number of	Age			
Incorrect Responses	3	4	5	6
None	3	3	3	7
One	2	1	3	3
Two to five	1	5	4	0
Six	2	0	0	0

Table 26 shows the number of Ss at each age level making various
numbers of placement errors. Since there were 3 trials potentially available to S for each set of pictures, the maximum possible number of incorrect responses is 6. The data shown here suggest that performance on

this task probably improves with age during the preschool years.[3] Two of the 8 "testable" three-year-olds never succeeded in orienting either card correctly, despite multiple hints. All of the six-year-olds did so, either immediately (7 Ss) or with minimal help (3 Ss).

TASK IIIA (REVISED)

Although the data of Task IIIA did show the expected age trend, their interpretation may be clouded by what in retrospect appeared to us to be a possible ambiguity in the demand character of the task. That is, a case might be made that the instructions ("show it to me") do not absolutely *require* a right-side-up presentation to E. E has, after all, already seen what each picture looks like in its proper orientation, and S might justifiably feel that he need only "show it to E" in the sense of indicating *which* of the three he had in mind—"show" here being construed more as "point out" than as "present-for-proper-viewing." The fact that several of the incorrect responses were of the side-view variety may also point to this instructional ambiguity.

It was therefore decided to revise Task IIIA in such a way that its adaptation-to-E's-viewpoint requirement might be more unequivocally communicated to S. The hope was, in effect, that successes and failures on the revised version could be more unambiguously interpreted as role-taking successes and failures, rather than something else.

Procedure

The task materials consisted solely of a black-and-white picture of a standing human figure, drawn in childlike fashion on a 9 × 12 in. piece of tagboard. E and S are again seated on opposite sides of a small table. E takes the picture over to S's side of the table and says, "In this game I have just one card. It is a picture of a child. He is standing up. Now, let's turn the card around (that is, upside down). How does he look now?" If S does not indicate that the child is "upside down," "standing on his head," or something equivalent, E says, "He is standing on his head, isn't he?" E then rights the card. "Now he is standing up again. Can you make him stand on his head?"

After S does so, E returns to the opposite side of the table, takes the card and places it crossways (that is, with the figure in lying-down position) in front of S. "Now, *you* take the picture and show it to me so I can

---

[3]It seems superfluous, and perhaps misleading to the reader, to present formal statistical analyses of the Study III data. It was a pilot study, using a very small sample of children, and nothing in our presentation of it should hint otherwise.

see the man standing on his head. Be sure to show it to me so I see the man standing on his *head*."

Results

Six of the 10 three-year-olds succeeded in orienting the picture correctly (that is, right side up for him, upside down for *E*), 5 of them immediately and 1 after an initial egocentric placement (thus, a self-corrected error). Nine of the 10 five-year-olds made an immediate correct placement. The task thus appears to be a somewhat easier one than IIIA for both age groups, perhaps because its exact requirements were in fact more clearly communicated. Moreover, although firm generalizations based on only 20 Ss are of course impossible, there is at least a suggestion of the expected age trend in performance.

TASK IIIB

In introducing Task IIIA, it was stated that all but one of the tasks used in this study demanded role-taking activity of the perceptual variety. The present task is the one exception. Here, the child is called upon to predict, not the immediate perceptions, but the more enduring preferences or wants of others where these differ from the child's own.

Procedure

The task materials consisted of several exemplars of each of the following objects: silk stockings, necktie, toy truck, doll, and adult book. *E* places one of each kind of object on the table. "We're going to pretend this is a little store." *E* encourages *S* to identify each object. "Let's pretend. If you could choose one of these gifts for your ———'s birthday, which one would you choose?" This question is asked successively for the child's father, mother, teacher, brother or sister (if any), and self for one-half the Ss at each age level, and in the order mother, father, teacher, brother or sister (if any), and self for the other half. After the child makes each choice, the object chosen is replaced by another of the same object category. When all choices have been made, *E* inquires about each by saying: "Why did you choose ——— for your ———?"

Results

We shall first consider the presents which the Ss chose for themselves before considering what they chose to give to others. So far as we could judge, not one of the 40 children made a choice which could definitely be labelled as role-inappropriate, from either the standpoint of sex or of age. Fifteen boys chose a truck; none chose a doll. Nineteen girls chose

a doll; none chose a truck. Two boys chose ties, 2 girls and 1 boy chose
a book, no child chose stockings, and 1 three-year-old boy insisted that
he wanted a pair of boots, which were lying in a corner of the testing
room, and refused to settle for anything else!

As for the gifts selected for others, it was possible to sort Ss' responses
into 4 categories according to the level of role-taking skill they appeared
to reflect:

Level A. S selects a truck for his mother or a doll for his father (or
both).

Level B. S shows no instances of Level A, but selects a truck for his
father or a doll for his mother (or both).

Level C. S shows no instances of Levels A or B, but selects an adult
gift (for example, a book) for his sibling or (much more frequently) a
child gift for his teacher. The former selection was judged to be less
clearly role-inappropriate than those of types A and B, both because of
our uncertainty as to the sibling's age and because several Ss, as we have
indicated, actually chose adult gifts for themselves. The latter selection
was so judged because a number of children rationalized it in the inquiry on the basis that the teacher would want or need things like trucks
and dolls for classroom use. While these two kinds of choices did not
appear to be as unequivocally role-appropriate as other readily available
selections would have been, neither did they appear to be as manifestly
unreasonable as those defined in A and B.

Level D. S shows no instances of Levels A, B, or C, that is, all of his
gifts are clearly appropriate to the age and sex of the recipient.

Table 27
Number of Subjects Responding at Each
Level of Role Taking Skill on Task IIIB

Level	Age			
	3	4	5	6
A	6	0	0	0
B	2	1	4	0
C	1	6	1	0
D	1	3	5	10

Table 27 shows the distribution of Ss across the four levels. These data
suggest both that skill on this task is very much a function of age during
the preschool years, and also that one may be able to speak of developmental differences in the degree or kind of skill involved. For example,
it is only the three-year-olds who ever show what looks like a really ex-

treme disregard for both the age and sex of the gift recipient. Two of these 6 children, by the way, actually selected a doll for the father—just about the most inappropriate matching of gift and receiver possible in this situation! Conversely, not one of the 10 six-year-olds ever made a choice with even a hint of role inappropriateness about it. The B and C responses, mostly found in four- and five-year-old groups, may reflect some sort of transitional level, one which lies between a complete or near-complete absence of any role-attribute discrimination and an intellectual differentiation of the other's wants and needs which is wholly adequate to this simple task. Further speculation as to the exact nature of this intermediate-skill level seems unwarranted on present evidence, however; a careful scrutiny of the response patterns and associated inquiry data on these Ss has simply not yielded any clear picture of what may have mediated their overt choices.

TASK IIIC

Tasks IIIC, IIID, and IIIE were essentially variants of IIIA, designed to test the child's ability to predict a visual perspective which differed from his own.

Procedure

The task materials consisted of two 9 × 12 in. pieces of tagboard. Each board had a colored picture of a cat on one side and a colored picture of a boy on a rocking horse on the other. E and S were seated on opposite sides of a small table. "I have two cards here. I want to show them to you. On this side is a cat, and on the other side is a boy on a rocking horse. This other card is just like it. See, here is a cat, just like this one (the two cards are shown side by side), and on the other side is a boy on a rocking horse, just like this one (the two cards are turned over). Now let's play a game. One card will be mine, and one will be yours. I'll take my card and look at it (E holds the card up so that she sees the cat and S sees the boy). You take your card (E hands S the duplicate card so that he sees the boy side) and see if you can look at the same picture I am looking at."

If the child fails to turn his card to the correct side, E says: "That is the picture I have on *one* side of my card, now can you hold your picture so *you* can see, on your *own* picture, the same thing I am looking at on *my* picture?"

Results

Table 28 shows the number of Ss at each age level who: immediately turned the card around to the correct side; held it incorrectly initially,

Table 28
*Number of Subjects Showing Various Response
Patterns on Task IIIC*

Response Pattern	Age			
	3	4	5	6
Correct immediately	5	7	8	8
Correct after false start	2	2	0	0
Correct after E's prompt	1	1	0	1
Incorrect after E's prompt	1ª	0	2	1

ªAnother three-year-old performed this way, but may not have been attending to the task.

but then spontaneously turned it around; made a correct positioning only after *E*'s standard prompt ("That is the picture I have on *one* side. . . ."); never turned the card, even after *E*'s prompt. The table gives little evidence of age changes on this role-taking task. The majority of even the youngest *S*s appear to be able to solve it correctly, and a minority of even the oldest ones have difficulty with it.

It is unclear what is responsible for the apparent lack of developmental changes here. One possibility which occurred to us is that the structure of the task situation may make for "false positives," that is, correct responses not mediated by role-taking activity. *E* instructs *S* to "see if he can look at" something. But at that moment, *S* *is* already looking at something, that is, the wrong picture. Since instructions generally signal behavior *change*, a number of *S*s might have construed *E*'s words simply as a mandate to change their looking activity, to look at something other than what they are now looking at. Since there are only two pictures available to him, such a construction could automatically lead to the right response. This line of reasoning led us to revise Task IIIC in such a way that a set simply to alter the visual input would not guarantee a correct response.

TASK IIIC (REVISED)

Procedure

The task materials consisted of two 6 × 6 × 6 in. cardboard cubes. Both cubes were identically outfitted with a different colored picture on each of their four vertical faces: a teddy bear, a bird, a chair, and a doll in a cradle. *E* shows one of the cubes to *S* and asks him to name the four pictures, giving help where needed. She then presents the second cube, carefully indicating that it is identical in all respects to the first. "I am going to turn my block around (rotates it at random). Now you turn your block around so that you can see on your block the *same* picture that I am looking at on my block. Be sure to look at the *same* picture on your block that I am looking at on my block." After the child has turned his block, E asks two questions: "What picture are you looking at? What picture do you think I am looking at?"

Results

The responses to this task yielded two sets of data which can be analyzed in combination: (a) S's block placement (b) his answer to the second inquiry question (the answer to the first was for all Ss consistent with block placement, that is, S always said he was looking at the picture he was in fact looking at). Table 29 presents a part of this analysis. The

Table 29
*Number of Subjects Showing Various
Response Patterns on Task IIIC (Revised)*

Response Pattern		Age	
Placement	E's View	3	5
Correct	Correct	1	6
Correct	Incorrect	2	1
Incorrect	Correct	2	0
Incorrect	Incorrect	5	3

first row shows the number of Ss at each of the two age levels who made responses which were completely correct, that is, they turned their block until they saw the same picture E saw on her block and, when asked what E saw, replied correctly. The second and third row show the number of Ss who either rotated the block correctly or verbally predicted E's viewpoint correctly, but not both. It is hard to be sure of just what went into these five responses, but it is suspected that most of them attest to at least some grasp of the task requirements. And finally, the bottom row reports the number of Ss who responded incorrectly on both counts.

The data shown in Table 29 give a somewhat clearer indication of developmental change than did those shown in Table 28. There is also suggestive evidence, not presented in the table, that the revised task, if not the original one, did tap something of an elementary role-taking ability. One would expect, if no factor other than random error were involved, that Ss who erred in block placement would distribute these placements more or less equally across whatever three block faces E was not viewing in each case. Table 29 shows (rows 3 and 4) that a total of

10 Ss made incorrect placements. But of these 10, fully 6 were "ego-centric" placements, that is, the child rotated his cube until he saw the same picture on his cube that he saw on E's (on the opposite side of the cube from the face E was looking at). Similarly, of the 3 Ss who made correct placements but did not predict E's view correctly (row 2), 1 S would make no prediction at all and the other 2 predicted egocentrically.

These results suggest that the visual input from E's block may have interfered with correct responding in some children (as well as consti-tuting, of course, the only available inferential cue for it for all children). Although Ss who gave a less than perfect performance on this task doubt-less did so for a variety of reasons, we believe that one important cause was the tendency to confuse S's own viewpoint vis-à-vis E's block with that of E herself, that is, to respond in terms of one's own role attributes instead of inferring those (different ones) of the other.

TASK IIID

This task was essentially a one-card variation on its predecessor.

Procedure

The task materials consisted solely of one 9 $\times$ 12 in. piece of tagboard with colored pictures of a puppy on one side and a birthday cake on the other. S and E sit facing each other across a small table. "I have a card here that has two pictures on it. On this side (demonstrates) is a little dog, or puppy, and on the other side (turns card over) is a picture of a birthday cake." E then holds the card so that she sees the cake and S sees the puppy. "In this game I am looking at a picture right now. See if you can tell me what picture I am looking at." Should the child try to come around to see, E forbids it.

If S does not give the correct response, E says: "Tell me, what picture is on *this* (S's) side of the card? And what is on *this* (E's) side?" If S cannot answer the latter question, E shows him, and then turns the card back to its initial position. "Now, tell me what picture I am looking at right now."

Results

Table 30 presents the number of Ss at each age level who show each of four response patterns: initially correct; cannot recall or misrecalls the picture on E's side (but does *not* give the egocentric, S-viewpoint re-sponse), and responds correctly as soon as E shows him; gives the ego-centric response initially, then changes to the correct response after E's standard prompt; gives the egocentric response both initially and after

E's prompt. As was the case with Task IIIC, this task appears to have been a relatively easy one even for the younger *S*s, and no very striking age changes emerge. Although we are disinclined to make too much of the fact that the only two *S*s who never managed a correct response were three-year-olds (row 4 in the table), the behavior of these *S*s must have reflected either some kind of serious misconstruction of the *E*'s verbal instructions or else a very profound role-taking incapacity. Both of these *S*s recalled quite well what picture resided on the other side of *E*'s card when asked (they did not have to be shown), and yet persisted in asserting that *E* was looking at the picture that they themselves saw!

Table 30
Number of Subjects Showing Various Response Patterns on Task IIID

Response Pattern	Age			
	3	4	5	6
Correct	7	9	8	8
Forgot, then Correct	0	1	1	2
Egocentric, then Correct	1	0	1	0
Egocentric, then Egocentric	2	0	0	0

TASK IIIE

Procedure

The task materials consisted first of a piece of 11 × 14 in. tagboard, each side of which contained the same three colored pictures in the same spatial positions: an airplane at the top, a teddy bear in the middle, and a clown at the bottom. In addition there were two large pieces of plain cardboard, one of which was hinged in the middle. Both pieces were wider than the tagboard.

E and *S* are seated facing each other across a small table. "This time I have only one card. The pictures are the same on both sides. Here is an airplane, a teddy bear, and a clown, and on the other side they are just the same: an airplane, a teddy bear, and a clown (appropriate card turning and gestures throughout). Here is a piece of cardboard I have folded (the hinged cardboard). First, I will put the cardboard over the top of both sides of the picture." *E* holds the tagboard upright and drops the two halves of the cardboard over it, such that the cardboard sections mask the airplane and the teddy bear, both for her and for *S*, leaving only the clown visible to both. "Now, can you tell me what picture I can see on my side of the card?" *E* records *S*'s response and corrects it if necessary. "This time, I am only going to put the cardboard on my side of the card, and you see if you can tell me what pictures I can see." *E* takes the unhinged piece of cardboard and lowers it on her side until it masks the airplane, leaving teddy bear and clown visible to her. Since the cardboard protrudes on both sides of the tagboard, *S* has clear perceptual cues for inferring exactly what pictures are covered. After the child responds, *E* says: "Now I am going to move the cardboard (drops it further, so that both airplane and teddy bear are now covered). Can you tell me what I see on my side now?"

Results

Table 31 records *Ss*' performance on the two trials of this task. The first three rows are self-explanatory. The fourth row shows the number

Table 31
Number of Subjects Showing Various Response Patterns on Task IIIE

Response Pattern	Age			
	3	4	5	6
Both responses correct	2	7	7	10
One response correct	4	1	2	0
Neither response correct	3[a]	2	1	0
Number of pictures: trial 1 > trial 2	6	1	2	0
Number of pictures: 3 on trial 1 or 2	2[a]	1	2	0
Pretest response incorrect	2[a]	4	3	1

[a]One three-year-old, not included in the data analysis because of presumed incomprehension of instructions, would have had entries in these three cells.

of *Ss* who made either one or two incorrect predictions, the first of which included more objects than the second, thus in perfect ordinal correspondence with the two correct predictions. The fifth row indicates the number of *Ss* who made at least one prima facie egocentric response, that is, a prediction that *E* sees exactly what *S* sees (all three pictures). And finally, the last row shows the number of *Ss* who either predicted erroneously or pleaded ignorance in the pretest and had to be corrected by *E*. Four of these 10 *Ss* subsequently performed correctly on both trials of the test proper (two four-year-olds, one five-year-old, and one six-year-old); one additional *S* (a three-year-old) went on to make only one correct response. Needless to say, a number of other *Ss* negotiated the pretest without help but subsequently failed one or both test trials.

The various row and column entries suggest that performance on this task is strongly age-dependent during the preschool period. As in Task

IIIB, six-year-old performance is errorless, three-year-old performance is quite poor, and that of the middle age groups is intermediate between these. It is worth noting that five Ss in the three younger groups respond in what looks like a purely egocentric fashion (row 5), asserting, in effect, that movements of the card on E's side leave her visual field as unaffected as they do theirs.

Equally interesting is the fact that 9 of the 13 Ss in the second and third rows reduce the number of objects predicted from first to second trial (row 4), rather than either increasing it or leaving it equal. This may reflect a global representation of the effect of changes in card position on E's visual input: that is, these Ss may have an awareness that the card does have a differential effect on their and E's perception, and also that its downward movement progressively restricts her visual field, but may still not know or be unsure about just how to "compute" E's exact perspective from the observed spatial relationship between cardboard and tagboard. The responses of two Ss in particular seemed to support this interpretation. One three-year-old spontaneously told E he thought that moving the cardboard "made it different," but did not know how. And a five-year-old asserted that the initial placement of the card covered teddy bear and clown (correct), plus *one-half* of the airplane! This intermediate level of responding, that is, a general awareness of the role-taking problem coupled with inadequate conceptual skills for its exact solution, is reminiscent of the transitional responses found in Task IIIB and closely analogous to the numerous partial successes observed in Task IC (Chapter 2).

TASK IIIF

This task also purported to measure perceptual role taking, but in the tactual rather than visual mode.

Procedure

The materials comprised only an ordinary pencil with a sharpened point on one end and an eraser on the other. "I am going to hold my hand up like this (E's hand straight up, palm facing the child). Now you hold your hand up, like mine. Now I am going to take this pencil and put it between our hands (E causes the pencil to be suspended in air, horizontally, by gently pressing the eraser end into S's upraised palm and the pointed end into her own). Does it hurt *my* hand?" Regardless of S's response, E then has S feel both ends of the pencil and asks if each one hurts. She then places the pencil in its suspended position again, eraser in the child's palm, point in hers, and asks: "Does it hurt *your* hand? Does it hurt *my* hand?"

Results

It is scarcely credible that a study of such simplicity would founder on the basis of procedural problems, but this seems to be exactly what happened. The results turned out to be utterly chaotic. The "perfect" response pattern on this task was of course to assert, successively, that the pencil hurt *E*'s hand on the first trial; that the point did and the eraser did not hurt *S*'s hand when *S* touched them himself; and that the pencil did not hurt his hand but did hurt *E*'s on the second trial. Only 9 of 40 *S*s followed this pattern: 4, 1, 1, and 3 *S*s at ages 3, 4, 5, and 6, respectively! The other 31 *S*s followed any of some 7 other patterns, some logically consistent and some not.

We are quite sure that the nub of the problem lay in *S*s' definition of, and/or emotional reactions to the concept of "hurt." Many children— more accurate in this respect than we, perhaps—simply denied that the pencil could really be said to "hurt" either *E* or *S*; they tended to substitute terms like "only hurt a little," "tickles," "pricks," as more descriptive. Thus it seems that the procedure never really had a chance to differentiate *S*s on role-taking skill, since our assumptions about the differences between the two perceptual inputs appear not to have been admitted by many of the children.

TASK IIIF (REVISED)

An attempt was made to reduce the apparent ambiguities of Task IIIF, while maintaining its fundamental characteristics.

Procedure

The task materials again consisted of a single object only: a pencillike stick with a very sharp point on one end and a piece of absorbent cotton attached to the other (blunt) end. "In this game we have a little stick. I will put my hand out and you put your hand out." *E*'s and *S*'s hands now rest on the table, palms up. *E* then places the cotten end of the stick on *S*'s palm. "This feels nice and soft, doesn't it?" *E* places the cotton end on her own palm. "It feels nice and soft in my hand, too." *E* repeats the above procedure, placing the soft end first in *S*'s palm, then in her own. "Now, put your hand up like mine. We will put the stick between our hands." The stick is suspended as in Task IIIF, cotton in *S*'s palm and point in *E*'s. "It feels soft in *your* hand, doesn't it? Does it feel soft in *my* hand, too?"

Results

The results here were considerably more straightforward and orderly than those yielded by Task IIIF. Six of the 10 three-year-olds asserted that the stick felt soft in E's hand, too (one of them subsequently changed to a negative answer, however); three of them said it did not feel soft; one refused to join E in holding the stick, and so could not be tested. In contrast, only two of the 10 five-year-olds gave the incorrect positive answer; one of these two kept changing his mind, finally stating that the stick "maybe felt a little bit soft" in E's hand.

ADDITIONAL DATA

All of the data thus far discussed in this book have consisted of children's responses to standardized tasks given to them in a school setting. In 1962, however, after the termination of Studies I, II, and III, we had an opportunity to gather interview data on some of the role-taking behavior which young children spontaneously show in the course of their daily activities at home. The opportunity came about in the following way.

Procedure

William L. Klein, June B. Higgins, and the senior author conducted an interview study (unpublished) of the private, nonsocial—as contrasted with social-communicative—speech behavior of 1- to 6-year-olds. The families under study ($N = 65$) were headed by faculty members at the University of Rochester. Each of us interviewed about one-third of the mothers in these families. In 35 of the 65 interviews, the mother alone served as informant; in the other 30, both father and mother were seen jointly.

Data were gathered in this fashion on a total of 90 children, of which no more than two were drawn from any one family: 15 at each of ages 12–24, 24–36, 36–48, 48–60, 60–72, and 72–84 months.

The interview schedule was made up of 28 items, each item consisting of one or more questions. The entire schedule was mailed to the parents about two weeks prior to the interviewer's visit to their homes, to give them a chance to ponder the questions and to be on the watch for relevant behavior in their children. A number of parents told the interviewer that this preview had in fact been extremely helpful to them, for example, that it led them to notice behavior which could otherwise have gone unnoticed, and would hence not have been reportable during the interview proper. These parents of course constituted a most unrepresentative sample of the population at large, and the child behavior they reported may well have been unrepresentative also. In recompense, however, the interviewers were impressed with the sensitivity and apparent objectivity of their observations, as well as with the clarity with which they communicated them.

One of the 28 items in the schedule had nothing to do with the subject of the study, that is, children's private verbalizations, and was included simply to give us added information about early role taking. That item read as follows:

Does he ever act as though he were unaware that, at any given moment, you may not see what he sees—unaware that you and he may not have exactly the same visual experience at the same instant? For example, he might be in one room and you in another and he says "What's *this*?" or "I can't do *this*." Such statements would perhaps suggest that he were (at least momentarily) unaware of the fact that you and he have different *perspectives* (since you cannot see *"this"* from where you are, you do not know what he is talking about), unaware that *his* immediate view of things is not necessarily *yours*. Do you ever see anything remotely like this in your child? Conversely, do you ever see behavior which clearly indicates that he *is* aware of the difference in perspective, instances where he *does* show this awareness?

Results

Although all parents were requested to scrutinize all 28 items with respect to all children, some of the items obviously did not apply to children as young as 12-24 months. This was judged to be true of the item considered in this volume, and we shall therefore exclude from discussion the few—and probably dubious—reports obtained on this youngest group. The remaining data, those of the 75 2- to 6-year-olds, will be examined in two ways. On the one hand, we will look at them quantitatively, in terms of the number of children at each age level reported as showing this or that behavior pattern. Since what got reported obviously depended in part upon the vicissitudes of the parent's observational skills, memory, response tendencies, etc., whatever age trends may appear in these numbers should not be taken too seriously. Nonetheless, the quantitative aspects do add something to the overall picture and ought to be mentioned. On the other hand, we shall be especially interested in examining the actual responses of individual parents, that is, the qualitative aspects of the data, for anecdotal evidence of how role-taking problems may emerge in everyday social interactions at home, and how young children may cope with them.

The item requests answers to two, nonmutually exclusive questions: Does the child show role-taking failures? Does he show role-taking successes? We scored a response to each of these questions as affirmative, either if the mother gave a valid example of failure or success, or if, unable to recall a concrete example, she was convinced that the behavior in question occurred. Table 32 shows the number of affirmative and non-affirmative answers to each question as a function of age. It can be seen

Table 32
Number of Children Reported as Currently
Showing Role-Taking Failures and Successes

Behavior Reported		Age				
		2	3	4	5	6
Failures	Yes	10	12	10	7	5
	No	5	3	5	8	10
Successes	Yes	1	7	8	7	7
	No	14	8	7	8	8

that 44 of the 75 children were said to evince role-taking failures, most of these observations clustering in the 2- to 4-year groups. Only 30 children were reported as showing positive evidence of role-taking skill, these children comprising about half the subjects in every group but the youngest. There were 10 informants who spontaneously indicated a developmental change from past to present, with role-taking successes tending to replace failures.

Let us examine the reports of failure more closely. Not surprisingly, most of the failures described were quite similar to those given as illustrations in the item statement, that is, indefinite verbal references reminiscent of those made to the blindfolded listener in Task IA (Chapter 3). The following are some examples of this genre of role-taking failure. Note that some of the parents also allude to their own attempts (largely unsuccessful) at correcting the child's egocentrism.

Sometimes, when the family is driving in the car, the child (age 3:2) will suddenly ask, "What was that?" although the "that" is already out of sight. The mother says that she just cannot make the child understand sometimes that she (mother) cannot see the "that" anymore.

When child (6:11) and parent are in different rooms, the child expects the parent to understand her problem—"What's this?" etc. The mother reports that she has said she cannot see the referent over and over again in order to make the child realize the existence of perspective differences.

The mother indicated that she had noticed precisely the examples given in the item. Mother and daughter (3:7) are in different rooms and daughter asks mother to fix "this" or to tell her what "this" is. Mother said she explains that she cannot see the object, but daughter does not grasp what the problem is.

The child (5:0) is said not to be as aware of perspective as her older sister (6:10) is. She will say "What's this?" when the mother is in the next room. When told that the mother cannot see the object, she acts surprised and then comes and shows it.

The child (2:7) is not aware of different perspectives. She expects you to know what she is doing even if you are in another room—expects you to know what she cannot do, why she is crying, etc.

The child (2:4) will, for example, struggle with a drawer in the kitchen and then come to the door and say, "I can't do it." The mother added that she usually knows what the child means, however.

The child (3:0) does engage in the "What's this?" type of failure. The mother added that she thinks there are lots of similar examples, but it is hard to recall specific ones. She said she has the continuous feeling that her daughter lacks this sense of perspective.

The mother recalls a recent instance when she was on the telephone and did not realize that her daughter's (3:11) calls meant that she was on the potty and needed help. "Didn't you *know*?" said the child in an outraged tone.

The mother says that her child (6:6) usually adds the necessary information but does still show instances such as "I can't tie this," said from upstairs. She will also call from the bathroom, "You *know* I need toilet paper!" as if she really thought the mother did know.

There is a possible ambiguity in this category of role-taking failures which some of our interviewees (sic) brought to our attention. It is that at least some of the indefinite references made from the other room (that is, "I can't do this," etc.) may have represented nothing more than convenient verbal formulae for getting the parent to come in and look, help out, etc. There is obviously no way to know, on present evidence, how seriously one ought to take this explanation. It can at least be said, however, that there were other types of behavioral anecdotes—unfortunately fewer in number—to which this alternative explanation could not apply. The most interesting ones recall some of our Study III tasks: the child fails to orient some object, for example, a book, in such a way that the parent can see what he or she is intended to see. Six children were reported as showing this kind of behavior. The following are three of these anecdotes.

When the child (2:1) wants to show the parents something in a book, she holds it so the page still faces her. When she shows them her fingernails, she holds her hands up so the palms, rather than the backs face them.

When the child (3:2) wants the mother to identify a picture in a book, she will hold the book pressed against her face and ask what it is, with the mother obviously unable to see it.

The mother was drawing a statuette of a lion. The child (5:0) could not understand why the mother could not continue drawing it when the child turned it toward herself. The child's six year old sister tried to explain the reason to her.

The data on role-taking successes are in most respects the reciprocal of those on failures. For example, a number of parents indicated that their children have begun to take steps to insure that the other person will be in a position to see what the child is talking about.

The mother laughingly reports that the child (5:6) seems to do something like this (that is, role-taking failures) at least once a day. He may be out in the garden and ask, "What's this on my sunflowers?" with the mother somewhere in the house. She has noticed, however, that more and more he is beginning to switch to, "*Come out* and look at my sunflowers," or, "*Come here* and I'll show you something."

The mother said that her child (2:9) is just now getting the idea that if she is not right near him he has to bring to her what he wants her to see. Before now, she said he didn't realize this and she would tell him that she couldn't see what he was talking about.

If he starts to do it (that is, talk about something the mother cannot see), the child (5:3) will catch himself right away—you can almost see him catch himself. (Example?) "Come here and look at this," etc.

"I used to be able to get away with 'looking' at something she (6:0) wanted to show me from across the room, but now I have to come directly over and look."

The following anecdotes give even more convincing evidence of a beginning role-taking capability in the children concerned.

The child (2:7) walks in front of her brother when he's watching TV and giggles as she does it.

While reading his son (about 3) a story, the latter's head obscures the father's view of the book. When asked what the father is seeing, the child replied, "My head."

While mother and child (4:6) were shelling peas, the child held up a bowl of peas high enough so the mother could not see the contents and said, "See how many peas I've shelled—you *can't* see!" Then he held it down lower and said, "See?"

GENERAL DISCUSSION

Their small scope and "pilot study" character notwithstanding, the investigations reported in this chapter have yielded some cognitive profit. On the one hand, they have served to clarify certain methodological aspects of role-taking assessment, especially with young children. On the other hand, they have led to some tentative ideas regarding the nature of role-taking development during these early years.

As to methodological aspects, we now see, in retrospect, that the tasks used in Study III have certain points of similarity and dissimilarity, an examination of which may illuminate both the interpretation of present results and the planning of future research. They differ, first of all, in the extent to which the task instructions explicitly and unequivocally demand role-taking activity on the child's part. Two tasks from Study I will illustrate this sort of difference. The instructions in Task IC (Chapter 2) are maximally explicit: S is expressly told to predict the visual perspective of O, that is, engage in perceptual role taking. In contrast, those of Task IA (Chapter 3) say nothing about role-taking activity at all. S is instructed only to communicate the game to O; it is left to S himself to infer that a careful reading of O's listener role attributes could provide useful cues in shaping an effective message.

Most of the Study III tasks resemble IC rather than IA on this dimension. In Tasks IIIA (Revised), IIIC, IIIC (Revised), IIID, IIIE, IIIF, and IIIF (Revised) S is explicitly told to discover E's perceptual input: *"You take the picture and show it to me so I can see the man standing on his head,"* in IIIA (Revised); "Now, can you tell me what picture I see on my side of the card?" in IIIE; "Does it feel soft in *my* hand, too?" in IIIF (Revised), and so on.

But this is not true of Tasks IIIA and IIIB. The IIIA instruction simply to show S's favorite picture to E is obviously not in itself a direct request to think about E's perspective and, as we noted in the introduction to Task IIIA (Revised), it may not even be an implicit one for all Ss. This task begins to resemble the others only when and if an S fails to orient the picture correctly on his first try and E gives more explicit instructions ("Show it to me so I can see it as you see it," and after a second failure, "It doesn't look right side up to me; can you show it to me so it does?"). Task IIIB does not expressly ask for role-taking behavior either. S is instructed only to choose a present for O; it remains for him to reason that the gift ought to be a suitable one, and that an estimate of O's needs and wants could determine its suitability. While it is unlikely that the Level A and B responders (Table 27) did much of this kind of estimating when making their choices, it does not necessarily follow that all the Level D responders did, that is, that here-and-now role-taking activity on S's part was a precondition for making appropriate selections. In both Tasks IIIA and IIIB, so it now seems, an S *could* achieve a "correct" response by simply utilizing acquired habits or experiences of one sort or another, for example, a trained-in social response of always handing an object to another in a particular spatial orientation or a recollection of what his mother and father have actually received as gifts in the past. This is not to say that Tasks IIIA and IIIB could in no sense be thought of as "role-taking tasks," but only that there is an uncertain correlation in these tasks between level of performance and the occurrence of role-taking cognitions.

The Study III tasks which do clearly mandate role-taking activity differ among themselves in another respect: the probability that correct responding is achievable by some means other than an accurate assessment of O's perspective. In the case of Tasks IIIC (Revised) and IIIE, this probability is relatively low. In the former, the child must select the correct orientation of the cube from among four possible orientations. In the latter, S must choose from among a still larger number of options: that is, E sees none of the three pictures, some particular one of them, some particular pair of them, or all three of them. In the remaining tasks, the possibilities—or at least the likely ones—are binary: one of two orientations of a picture in IIIA (Revised), one of two pictures in IIIC and IIID, and "Yes" or "No" in IIIF and IIIF (Revised). If a child accurately predicts what E sees on both trials of IIIE, we can say with some confidence that he has demonstrated a certain measure of skill in perceptual role taking. If he happens to say "No" instead of "Yes" on IIIF (Revised), or to hold his card so that he sees one side rather than the other on IIIC, we cannot be so sure.

The moral for future research of what we have been saying is this. If a task is to measure with any precision an individual S's ability to assess another's role attributes, it should have at least these two characteristics. First, the task instructions should as unequivocally as possible convey to S that he should engage in this assessment activity. If the instructions imply such engagement rather than explicitly request it, the interpretation of his subsequent task performance is necessarily obscured, and special research procedures will be needed to distinguish between a role-taking capability per se and related capabilities, for example, that of recognizing that certain nonrole-taking goals demand role-taking means. Second, regardless of whether the role-taking mandate be explicit or implicit, the task should be so structured that S's performance pattern is a faithful reflection of what he has or has not done in the way of covert role taking. Good performance should mean good role taking, and nothing else; poor performance should mean no role taking or poor role taking, and nothing else. Repeated trials and/or numerous response options would thus increase the sensitivity of any role-taking measure. By this standard, IIIC (Revised) ought to be a moderately good task, IIIE a better one, and all the rest decidedly on the insensitive side.

Conclusions about early role-taking development from our data are necessarily tempered by these methodological considerations, in addition to those of small sample size and the small number of tasks investigated. Even uncertain evidence invites speculations, however, and here are ours

—overprinted with a large *caveat emptor*. What skills or knowledges in the realm of perspective taking probably emerge during early childhood, as opposed to those which await middle childhood and adolescence?

The fundamental and most important acquisition must be the budding awareness, no doubt only slowly generalized across a range of interpersonal situations, that there *are* perspective differences—an awareness that they *exist*. What evidence we have, both from Study III and from the interview material, points to the conclusion that many children of the early preschool period are simply unaware of perspective variation as one of life's possibilities. On the other hand, there seems little doubt that most six-year-olds do possess it, subject to certain limitations that we shall shortly describe. The parental interviews, for instance, only rarely yielded reports of a six-year-old acting as if perspective differences were utterly incomprehensible, although there were a number of such anecdotes about younger children. Similarly, the older *S*s responded to the Study III tasks as if what *E* asked of them "made sense," that is, as if they were cognitively mature enough to accept the tacit assumption underlying a role-taking problem. Piaget and Inhelder (1956, ch. 6) also tested young children on perceptual role-taking tasks and concluded that an awareness of the very possibility of perspective differences is not present in force much before $5\frac{1}{2}$–$7\frac{1}{2}$ years.

It is important not to overestimate the late preschooler's capability in this regard, however. There may be at least two limitations on how accessible such awareness is to a child of this age. The first has to do with the content of *O*'s perspective. The recognition of perspective differences is hypothesized as being less probable when the perspectives in question consist of cognitions, motives, feelings, affects, and the like rather than percepts, especially visual percepts. It is quite possible, therefore, that the same five- or six-year-old who can readily grasp the implications of, say, the Task IIIE instructions might be unable to make much sense out of an instruction to predict *O*'s thoughts, attitudes, or feelings about something.[4] Several of the studies reviewed in Chapter 1 would seem to support this hypothesis (for example, Dymond, Hughes, and Raabe, 1952).

The second limitation has already been alluded to in the discussion of implicit versus explicit instructions. It is virtually certain that a

[4]The following is an amusing example of what looks like precocious role-taking behavior of this more mature, "prediction-of-*O*'s-cognitions" variety. A three-year-old boy was out driving with his father. After a time he began squirming and repeatedly asking how far it was to the next gas station. Following the *n*th repetition of the question he paused, studied his father, and said, "I bet you think I have to go wee-wee!"

momentary recognition of perspective differences is much more likely
to occur in a young child when the prediction of O's perspective is the
stated objectives of the task (explicit instructions) than when the stated
objective is some accomplishment, such as the construction of a communicative message, for which role-taking activity is a useful means
(implicit instructions). Our own data (Chapters 3 and 4), as well as those
of others (Piaget, 1926; Krauss and Glucksberg, 1965), indicate that the
typical child in this age group is not likely to be sensitized to the existence of perspective differences when occupied with a task of the latter
kind.

We have suggested, then, that the all-important accomplishment of
the preschool period is a sensitivity to the very fact that differences in
role attributes can obtain, a sensitivity most clearly manifested when the
role attributes concern perceptual input and where the instructions explicitly direct him to predict these attributes. Given this most favorable
of task settings, and assuming that this sensitivity comes into play, what
characteristics of O's perceptual input can he then go on to predict
accurately? It is one thing to know that O's view of things differs from
one's own and quite another to know exactly *what* O perceives. Our evidence suggests that there are at least three, closely interrelated things
which the late preschool child has learned how to do, and further research would no doubt uncover others.

First, he learns how to infer whether a given stimulus is or is not
visible to O, at least where the cues for such inference are strong and
readily noticeable. Dichotomous judgments of this "O-sees-X-or-does-not-
see-X" type were demanded in Task IIIE, and accuracy of judgment was
clearly age dependent across the 3- to 6-year range (Table 31). The $4\frac{1}{2}$
year-old who holds up the bowl so his mother cannot see the contents
(last protocol cited in the Additional Data section) is demonstrating the
same competence—and perhaps also demonstrating that he has only recently attained it.

Second, he learns that when an object is interposed between himself
and O, O will see not what he sees but whatever view is presented on
the opposite side of the object. Tasks IIIC, IIIC (Revised), and IIID
clearly pertain to this acquisition, with IIIF (Revised) perhaps consti-
tuting a tactual-perspective analogue of these. Although we have no evidence on this point, one supposes that the child would also have achieved
the corresponding knowledge for other O placements, for example, O
facing the right or left side of X. Notice that there is no presumption
that a preschool child can *reconstruct* O's perceptual input from what
he *himself* sees, as Task IC demands. What he has acquired is considerably more primitive than that, and consists only of the recognition

that *O* will see *whatever there is to be seen* from *O*'s side. Knowing nothing more than that fact, he could readily solve Tasks IIIC and IIIC (Revised) merely by turning his own duplicate card or cube so that he views *O*'s side, and Task IIID by simply recalling what picture is displayed on *O*'s side of the card.

Finally, he attains the recognition that, when he and *O* are at opposite ends of X and are looking down at it, *O* will see it upside down if he himself sees it right side up and vice versa. The relevant tasks in our study were IIIA and, especially, IIIA (Revised). As with the previous skill, it would probably turn out that children of this age could also manage such tasks if *O* were seated to either side, thus viewing the object in a lying-down position.

It makes intuitive sense that these three would be among the earliest role-taking skills to develop. For one thing, they pertain to *S*'s and *O*'s visual percepts, rather than to more subtle, more "interior" organismic activities. For another, the analysis of *O*'s perspective which they represent is of the most global and undifferentiated sort: *O* sees X or does not; *O* sees this side of X or that side; *O* sees X right side up or upside down. Indeed, it is difficult to think of behaviors which would look like genuine instances of role-taking activity and at the same time require a lower order of cognitive skill then these three do. On the other hand, it would be surprising if these early "role-taking schemas" turned out to be the *only* ones of consequence to emerge during this period. There could thus be two objectives for future research in this area: first, to attempt to establish the developmental timetable for these three schemas, using better testing methods than we have used; second, to try to discover what other acquisitions may be developmentally synchronous with them.

CHAPTER SIX

The Modification of Communicative Behavior

All of the studies so far reported have had the same general form. The child is confronted with some kind of role-taking or communication problem and fulfills his duty as an *S* by giving *E* a single, first-effort solution to that problem. He receives no feedback whatever as to the adequacy of his effort, and in particular is given no opportunity to show whether or not he could use such feedback to improve the quality of subsequent solutions to that or similar problems. Research designs which do incorporate a feedback component would, however, be of more than passing interest to both developmental naturalist and educational psychologist.

The former could reason that children may frequently receive feedback of sorts regarding their everyday role-taking and communicative efforts, and that their ability to profit from it, like their ability to perform prior to it, is a proper and interesting object of developmental-descriptive research. There is, in fact, a very close relationship between what the skilled performer is assumed to do before feedback and following it. In both cases, he tries to use whatever he can infer about the other person as a means to the end at hand (for example, effective communication). Whereas feedback may well sharpen or otherwise modify *S*'s initial inferences, it is unlikely to replace a state of noninference with a state of inference. What the child does in response to feedback ought therefore to be related to what he has done prior to receiving it, and ought similarly to show variations with chronological age. As for the educational psychologist, his concern with feedback effects would follow from any interest he may have in tampering with the "natural" ontogenetic course of skill acquisition in this area, that is, in finding training procedures which could hasten and facilitate that course. It is hard to imagine effective procedures here which would not include knowledge of results as a prominent component.

The purpose of this chapter is to report some research information we have gathered on the child's ability to profit from immediate feedback about the effectiveness of his communicative messages. There were three studies. One (by Jarvis) was a straightforward developmental-descriptive investigation. The other two (by Fry) were motivated by educational-psychological interests, and involved attempts at training fifth-grade children to improve their communication skills by providing feedback.

JARVIS STUDY

Subjects

The Ss were drawn from the suburban school system utilized in Studies I and II. There were 12 children from each of three grades: 6 of each sex from the second grade, 8 girls and 4 boys from the sixth grade, and 7 girls and 5 boys from the ninth grade. All Ss were performing satisfactorily at their grade level, according to teachers' reports, but no IQ or other relevant data were taken on them.

Procedure

The stimulus for S's communications consisted of a 5 × 7 in. card with four simple geometric figures drawn on it in India ink. These figures and their spatial arrangement were virtually identical to Display X of Task IIB (shown in Figure 8, Chapter 4). S's audience (L) was a female undergraduate. E and S entered the testing room together, and E explained that they were going to play a game[1] with L, who would enter shortly. The object of the game was to see how well L could reproduce the four-figure design solely on the basis of S's verbal description of it. It was S's job, therefore, to communicate the appearance of the design as effectively as possible, so that L could succeed in drawing it accurately. L then entered the room and sat down at the opposite end of the table from S. A 12 × 24 in. cardboard screen, mounted on a wooden base and placed between S and L, prevented the latter from seeing the design.

After S had completed his message, and L had pretended to draw something, E went around the table and looked at L's "reproduction." He told her that she had not done a very good job, that she should be able

[1]For the ninth graders, the situation was structured, not as a "game," but as an "experiment" in which S was helping E find out how well L could reproduce a design.

to do better than that, and asked her to listen very carefully while S described the design a second time. Then, going back to S's side of the table, E asked S if he would describe the design once more, this time in such a way that L should be certain to be able to make an exact copy. Regardless of the quality of S's second message, L then drew a reasonable copy of the design, which was praised by E and shown to S before the latter was sent back to his classroom. S's two messages were tape recorded, and subsequently typewritten for purposes of data analysis.

The above procedure was calculated to permit S to experience a *communicative* failure, together with an opportunity to redress it on a second trial, without at the same time experiencing much if any *personal* failure. E's instructions to S and comments to L were meant to imply that the onus for that communicative failure really lay more on L than on S. Regardless of what S himself may have thought about the quality of his message (if he thought about it at all), E seemed to be saying that L had extracted less information out of it than S or E would have been justified in expecting. This displacement of blame in no way changes the negative-feedback character of the situation, of course; S's first communication is still represented to him as objectively inadequate in terms of its prescribed function.

The predictions made in this study were analogous to those made in Study IA (Chapter 3). There is a wholly trivial, main-effect hypothesis which asserts that both first and second messages will "improve," that is, become more informative, as a function of age. The nontrivial hypothesis predicts a message by age interaction: older Ss will improve more, from their first to their second message, than will the younger ones.

Results

Ss' transcribed messages were rated according to a more elaborate version of the scoring system used in Study IIA (Chapter 4). What S said about each of the four elements of the design was scored as shown below on each of five attributes or categories.

Presence

(0) Element not mentioned.

(1) Element mentioned, but either given grossly incorrect name ("rectangle" instead of "triangle") or so poorly described, if not named, that it would not be possible to draw anything resembling the stimulus element from the description.

(2) Element described somewhat more accurately—so that it would be possible to draw it from the description, without any name given to

it. Or, an incorrect, but not grossly so, name given to the element ("rectangle" for square). Or, a description such as "a thing like the moon" for circle and "a box" for square. Less accurate, more projective, descriptions such as "a pile of sand" should be scored 1, not 2.

(3) A correct name given to the element, "triangle, square, circle, Z, (or 'last letter of the alphabet')."

Size

(0) No mention of the size of the element.

(1) Recognition of size as a useful factor in description, but little actual communication of size, either relative or absolute ("a big triangle" or "a medium size square").

(2) Size given relative to some other element(s) for which there is no absolute size given.

(3) An attempt to give the absolute size of the element, but with the dimensions not given accurately (see criteria under 4) or the size given relative to some other element the description of which rates 3 points for size.

(4) Accurate dimensions given: sides of the triangle given a value which lies between $1\frac{1}{2}$–$2\frac{1}{2}$ in.; sides of the square given a value between $\frac{3}{4}$–$1\frac{1}{4}$ in.; circle said to be "the size of a quarter" or given a diameter value between $\frac{3}{4}$–$1\frac{1}{4}$ in.; horizontal bars of Z given a value between $\frac{3}{4}$–$1\frac{1}{4}$ in., and either the diagonal given a value between 1–2 in. or the vertical distance between horizontal bars given a value between $\frac{3}{4}$–$1\frac{1}{4}$ in. In the case of Z, if only the length of the horizontal bars is correctly stated, score 3 points. Score 4 points for an element whose size is given relative to another element which rates 4 points for size.

Position

(0) No mention of position.

(1) Simple indication of direction from another element, without attempt to give distance.

(2) Indication of direction and distance but with distance inaccurately given (see criteria under 3) or distance given only in rough, more qualitative than quantitative terms ("a little ways down").

(3) Indication of direction and distance with distance given accurately. Score 3 points if distance given is from —50 to +50 percent of the actual measured distance.

(4) Indication of direction and distance with distance accurate and enough information given to make the location completely unambiguous.

Also score 4 points for accurate absolute location of an element (square "right in the center of the card" or distances from the edges of the page given for an element).

Color

(0) No mention of the color of the element.

(1) Mention of the color of the element (a black or filled-in square, or an empty circle). Also score 1 point here for reference to quality of lines (dark or heavy line on circle, rough or wavy or jagged lines on the circle or Z).

Other

(0) No additional useful information given.

(1) Score one point for *each* additional piece of useful information, (for example, triangle is isosceles or equilateral; prefatory statements which give some picture of the gestalt, such as, "there are four figures on the page," or "these are all close together on the page)."

Each message can thus be given a subscore for each of these five categories, and also a total score equal to the sum of these. Two judges scored each typewritten message "blind," that is, with all identifying marks removed. The interjudge reliability coefficient was .97.

Table 33 presents the group mean total scores for prefeedback and postfeedback messages, and also the differences between these means.

Table 33
Mean Total Scores per Grade for Prefeedback and Postfeedback Messages

Message	Grade 2	Grade 6	Grade 9
Prefeedback	8.7	17.8	22.1
Postfeedback	9.9	22.3	28.1
Difference	1.2	4.5	6.0

The mean scores for each message show the expected increase as a function of age, most noticeably between second and sixth grade. Of greater interest, of course, is the apparent increase with age in the difference between the prefeedback and postfeedback means. A simple analysis of variance performed on Ss' difference scores showed these group differences to be statistically reliable ($F = 5.42$; $p < .01$; $df = 2,33$). Here again, the increase is most prominent between second and sixth grades. In absolute terms, the prefeedback to postfeedback increase in mean scores for the sixth and ninth graders is approximately four and five times, respectively, that shown by the second graders. In relative terms, the youngest group increase their prefeedback score by about 14 percent, the sixth graders by about 25 percent, and the ninth graders by about 27 percent. These data appear to support the hypothesis that the ability to profit from negative feedback in a communicative situation is a function of age, at least across one portion of the ontogenetic span.

Table 34

Number of Subjects per Grade Giving Some Information of Each Category in Each Message

| | Category and Message (Pretest versus Posttest) | | | | | | | |
| | Presence | | Size | | Position | | Color | |
Grade	Pretest	Posttest	Pretest	Posttest	Pretest	Posttest	Pretest	Posttest
2	12	12	0	1	1	2	1	4
6	12	12	4	6	9	9	9	10
9	12	12	4	7	10	11	9	10

Table 35

Number of Subjects per Grade Whose Category Subscores Increased After Feedback

| | Category | | | |
Grade	Presence	Size	Position	Color
2	6 (3)	1	1	3
6	1	5 (1)	5 (2)	3
9	0	6	8	6

Note. The figures in parentheses represent the number of Ss whose subscores on these categories decreased.

The distribution of the category subscores provides a basis for a more specific characterization of what the three groups tended to communicate to L, before and after negative feedback. Most of the relevant information is presented in Tables 34 and 35 above. Table 34 shows the number of Ss at each grade level who, in each message, gave at least some information relevant to the Presence, Size, Position, and Color categories, that is, whose message received a nonzero score on a given category for at least one of the four elements of the design. Table 35 represents the number of Ss who improved their scores within a given category after feedback. It can be seen from Table 34 that all Ss say something about what the components of the design are (Presence), both before and after feedback. Conversely, only one-third to one-half of even the older Ss think to give any information about the absolute or relative size of these elements. Position and Color are intermediate in frequency, with three-quarters or more of the older Ss making reference to these attributes in both messages.

As for the behavior of individual groups, the typical second grader seems to construe his communicative task as that of simply telling L what depicted objects he sees in front of him (and judging from his mean total score as shown in Table 33, he is able to do this much with fair effectiveness). With few exceptions, Ss in this group seem utterly oblivious to the fact that L needs other sorts of information if she is to make even an approximate reproduction of the design. Upon learning that their initial communication was inadequate for L, some of the second graders do a bit better on their second try. But here again, the most conspicuous improvement seems to take place within the Presence category (6 of 12 Ss), with only minimal change in the others (especially in the most important categories, that is, Size and Position).

The two older groups behave rather similarly on this task, and in a way which seems qualitatively as well as quantitatively different from the behavior of the youngest group. The data on prefeedback performance shown in both Tables 33 and 34 indicate that most Ss in these older groups recognize at the outset that L requires more than a mere enumeration of design elements. Thus, they attempt also to convey some information about the spatial arrangement of the array of elements, about their color, and—less frequently—about their size. After learning that their initial communication did not accomplish its intended purpose, they tend to improve it and, according to Jarvis' scoring procedure, improve it to a greater extent than do the second graders. And here again, they appear to concentrate their efforts within the same three categories—the ones which the younger Ss tend to ignore in both messages. This concentration is most evident in the ninth grade group, where one half or more of the Ss manage to better their score in these categories (Table 35).

Discussion

The major finding of this study was that the younger children improved their communications less following negative feedback than the older ones did. At the beginning of the chapter we speculated that an S's reaction to feedback regarding O's role attributes ought to be closely related to the nature of his prefeedback performance vis-à-vis O. This relationship may be the key to an understanding of Jarvis' results.

Our hypothesis is that it simply never occurred to most of the second graders, either before or after feedback, that L would require information regarding size, position, and color in order to reproduce the design, and that it never occurred to them largely because they failed to represent to themselves in any fashion the process of reproducing it, as experienced from L's vantage point. This being the case, their only avenue of improvement in the second trial lay in the remaining (Presence) category. In contrast, the older Ss tended to make communicative entries in all categories at the outset, and therefore had that many more opportunities for improving their scores. According to this interpretation, therefore, the age differences in communicative improvement after negative feedback were largely due to age differences in the initial disposition or ability to take L's role.

It should be made clear that such an interpretation in no way implies that role-taking skill was the *only* age-dependent variable at work in Ss' performance. For example, we would readily stipulate that the average second grader in our sample could not have specified the size and position relationships of the design with anything like the precision and clarity of the average ninth grader, no matter how aware he might have been of L's need for exact information here. On the other hand, it seems safe to assume that, if he *had* been so aware, he could at least have said *something* which would be scorable in these categories. We simply cannot believe that most second graders, given a self-instruction to communicate information about, say, size and color, would have been intellectually or linguistically incapable of asserting that, for instance, the triangle was "big" and the square "black" (both scored 1 point). The fact that so few of them said anything like this suggests that they lacked such self-instructions initially, that our nonspecific negative feedback failed to engender any, and that the root cause of both was insufficient role-taking activity.

FRY STUDY I

Fry conducted two studies designed to find out whether, and to what extent, children's communicative skills could be improved through a program of communication training. The first study, his doctoral dissertation research (1961), is described below.[2]

Subjects

The project was carried out within the same school system used in Studies I and II. Sixty-four fifth-grade girls were assigned in equal numbers to a control and three experimental groups. California Mental

[2]This study is also summarized in Fry (1966).

Maturity Test scores were available on all Ss, and the four groups were closely matched on IQ means (116.6–118.2) and standard deviations (10.7–11.6). It was decided to use children of a single sex because the training procedure would require considerable interaction among Ss, and it was further decided to make that sex female on the guess that girls might be more task oriented than boys in this particular situation. The choice of fifth graders as Ss was similarly intuitive: based upon our previous research experience, Fry expected children of this age to be mature enough to profit from the kind of training he planned to give them, and at the same time sufficiently undeveloped in role-taking and communication skills to allow for considerable improvement should the training prove effective.

Procedure

Each experimental S participated in five, one-hour training sessions, carried out over a three-week period. In each session, speakers attempted to describe pictures and listeners attempted to identify these pictures on the basis of that description. The three experimental groups were defined on the basis of which of these two activities their members engaged in during the three weeks. Sixteen Ss served only as speakers (S group), 16 Ss served only as listeners (L group), and 16 Ss alternated between the two roles (I—for "Integration"—group). A battery of communication tests was administered twice to these 48 Ss, two weeks or less prior to training (pretest) and two weeks or less following training (posttest). The 16 control (C) Ss also took the pretests and posttests, but received no training or other treatment during the intervening period.[3]

A decision had to be made at the outset as to the composition of the training materials. The utilization of a range of different sorts of communication tasks might lead to a more substantial and generalized improvement in communicative skill. On the other hand, it would then be difficult after the fact to specify the individual contributions of each task to whatever improvement was produced. The decision was made, therefore, to use varied repetitions of a single type of communication problem during the five sessions. If training on this problem produced changes, one could specify fairly precisely what experiences had been responsible for those changes. Likewise, a narrow rather than broad training base would better permit the assessment of generalization and transfer effects, that is, of the amount of pretest to posttest improvement on tasks different from, as well as similar to those used in training. And

[3]These Ss were drawn from a different school than the experimental Ss so that they would not know of the existence of the training program.

finally, there was always the possibility that no changes at all would emerge from such a brief training regimen unless a great deal of repeated practice on some single type of problem were given.

The species of communication problem finally selected was that represented by the *Discrimination* task used in Study IIB (Chapter 4): speaker and listener each possess identical sets of pictures, and the speaker's objective is to describe a particular member of the set in just enough detail to permit the listener to discover which picture is being referred to. In the present study, 68 different sets of pictures were constructed as training materials, and introduced in a fixed order across the five sessions. In general, the pictures within a set increased in number, complexity, and similarity as training progressed, thus making the speaker's communicative task more and more exacting. The pictures themselves were essentially abstract designs composed of combinations of lines, geometric forms, nonsense shapes, etc. Each set possessed some features which were common to all pictures in that series, and also some features which were not. Only information pertaining to the latter was potentially useful to the listener, of course.

Fry trained the Ss in teams of four. At any given moment during a training session two of the Ss in the team occupied the speaker role and the other two the listener role. The actual procedure was as follows. S_1 returns to the training room from an adjoining room, where she has been busy preparing to communicate. As she enters, S_2 departs for the adjoining room, where she will similarly prepare with respect to another set of pictures. S_3 and S_4 are seated together facing a long table. S_1 spreads her set of pictures on the table in front of S_3 and S_4. Then, standing behind them, she delivers her communication, which is recorded on tape. The tape is then played back one or more times and it is at this point that S_3 and S_4 actually begin trying to identify the picture described, with S_1 listening to her own message and observing the listeners' attempts to interpret it. A discussion of the message then ensues among listeners and speaker, in an effort to specify the nature and source of any misinterpretations which may have occurred. The listeners are encouraged to address themselves to three main questions during the discussion. First, was enough information included in the communication to permit S_3 and S_4 to be certain as to which picture had been described? Second, was additional, unnecessary information also given? Third, could the listeners find alternative ways of making the message more effective? Following the discussion, S_2 is summoned from the adjoining room to deliver her message, with some other S leaving to prepare hers. E's role throughout the training was largely nondidactic, although he occasionally stepped in to moderate discussions. His principal functions were to operate the tape recorder, hand out the picture sets, and generally insure that proper procedures were followed. So far as Fry could judge, the Ss really enjoyed the training sessions and were highly motivated throughout.

Team membership was constant (except for an occasional absence) during the five sessions. Eight of the 12 teams were composed of two S and two L children. The remaining four contained only I Ss, who took turns serving as speakers and listeners. Thus, the L children spent all of their time listening (and discussing messages); the S children spent half their time communicating (and discussing messages) and the other half preparing to communicate; and the I children spent one-quarter of their time speaking, one-quarter preparing to speak, and one-half listening.

Three categories of tests made up the pretest and posttest battery: (a) three *Discrimination* tests, similar to those used in training, (b) two *Description* tests, requiring a full rather than critical-feature characterization of whatever is being described, and (c) one *Listening* test. One Discrimination test, one Description test, and the Listening test were group-administered; two Discrimination and one Description test were given individually. Administration time for the six tests was about one hour and 20 minutes.

In each Discrimination test, S was given a set of pictures and told to communicate just enough information (and no more) about some one of these pictures to permit another individual, who also has the whole set before him, to identify it. In the group-administered Discrimination test (A), the listener was imaginary and S wrote her message. In the two individual Discrimination tests (B and C), S's "audience" was a photograph of a man and S delivered her message verbally. The pictures in test A were very similar to those used in Study IIB (Chapter 4). As in that study, several picture elements varied simultaneously from picture to picture, thus allowing several alternative ways to specify the crucial picture uniquely but briefly. Tests B and C were on either side of A on this dimension. Almost all of the elements of the crucial picture required specification in test B if the listener were to be certain of identifying it, whereas only a single element needed description in test C.

The group-administered Description test (D) was virtually identical to that used in Jarvis' study, except that no audience was present and the message was written. That is, S was given only the critical (to-be-discriminated) design from Discrimination test A and told to write a description which would enable someone who had not seen the design to draw a replica of it. The individually administered Description test (test E) consisted of the communication task used in Study IA (Chapter 3). After learning to play the game herself with E as opponent, S was shown a photograph of a blindfolded man (her attention was carefully drawn to his blindfolded condition, as in Study IA) and instructed to tell him how the game was played.

The group-administered Listening test (test F)[4] consisted of a series of stories, reports, etc., which were read aloud to the Ss. Following each passage, a set of multiple-choice questions about its contents were read aloud and the Ss responded in individual answer booklets. The six tests were given to all Ss in the same fixed order on both pretest and posttest: F (Listening, group)—D (Description, group)—A (Discrimination, group)—B (Discrimination, individual)—C (Discrimination, individual) —E (Description, individual). Fry did all the pretesting but only the group-administered posttesting. Individual posttesting was done by a trained person who had had no previous contact with the children and was ignorant of their group membership.

The study was designed to give answers to three questions regarding the nature and effectiveness of Fry's five-hour training program. First, does repeated training and experience on a single type of communication problem lead to improved performance on other problems of this same type? Since the training problems were of the Discrimination variety, this amounts to asking about pretest to posttest changes on the three Discrimination tests A, B, and C. Second, does this training and experience also lead to improved performance on tasks of other types? That is, would what the child learned in these Discrimination tasks transfer or generalize to the Listening test (F) or, of greater interest to us, to the two Description tests (D and E)? And finally, do the differences in training and experience represented by the three experimental treatments result in differences in posttest performance? Does massed experience in listening (L group), for example, lead to relatively greater improvement on the Listening test? And particularly, would the experience of alternating between speaker and listener roles (I group) lead to more communication-skill learning and transfer than would experience in either of these roles alone (S and L groups)?

Results

Ss' pretest and posttest performance was evaluated in a variety of ways. For the Listening test, S's score was simply the total number of questions answered correctly. Performance on the five communication tests was scored on each of the following measures.

Words. The total number of words contained in S's message (number of verbal "tokens").

[4]The instrument used was *Sequential Tests of Educational Progress: Listening, 1957, Form 4a* (first half), published by the Educational Testing Service, Princeton, N. J.

Different Words. The total number of different words in the message (number of verbal "types").

Overall Evaluation. A rating of how effectively a listener could perform his assigned task (for example, in the Discrimination tests, to identify the correct picture) on the basis of S's message. Eleven levels or categories of message adequacy were defined for each test. The rater attempted to assign Ss to categories so as to approximate a normal distribution of entries across the categories.

Useful Information. The number of message segments or units which were judged as satisfying two conditions: (a) the segment described something about which the listener needed information, and (b) the segment was sufficiently well stated to allow the listener to grasp what was being described.

Useless Information. The number of message segments which did not meet both of the above two requirements.[5]

All scoring was done without knowledge of S's group membership. Interjudge reliability was assessed only for the measure which seemed most likely to be unreliable, namely, Overall Evaluation. The reliability coefficients for this measure ranged from .81 to .96, however.

The interdependencies among the five measures were assessed in the following way. Taking as his score entries the pretest to posttest *changes* in score (rather than the pretest or posttest scores themselves), Fry calculated the correlations between each pair of measures for each test separately. He then averaged correlations across the individual tests of each test type, that is, across the three Discrimination tests and across the two Description tests. The resulting two correlation matrices are shown in Table 36. The patterns of correlations for Discrimination tests (lower left in the table) and Description tests (upper right) show what appear to be reasonable similarities and differences. One would expect, for example, that the intercorrelations among Words, Different Words, Overall Evaluation, and Useful Information to be quite high and positive in Descriptive tasks, and this is largely the case. In contrast, only the correlations among Words, Different Words, and Useless Information ought to be relatively high and positive in Discrimination tasks, with the others zero-order or negative, and again, this is roughly true.

The first question Fry wished to pose of his data, it will be recalled, concerned the effects of training on tasks similar to those encountered during training. For each of the three Discrimination tests, he first car-

---

[5]Test E was treated somewhat differently: Words and Different Words were computed as in tests A, B, C, and D; Overall Evaluation was not scored; Useful Information and Useless Information were translated into their (very similar) counterparts Game Information and Inadequate Information, respectively, and were scored on these latter categories exactly as was done in Study IA (Chapter 3).

Table 36

*Mean Correlations among Performance Measures within Each Type
of Communication Test (Discrimination versus Description)
Using Pretest to Posttest Change Scores*

Discrimination Test Measures	Description Test Measures				
	(1)	(2)	(3)	(4)	(5)
(1) Words		.83	.57	.55	.18
(2) Different Words	.91		.54	.52	.25
(3) Overall Evaluation	—.24	—.22		.64	.03
(4) Useful Information	.00	.06	.66		.03
(5) Useless Information	.72	.68	—.45	—.29	

Note. Averaging of correlations was carried out by means of Fisher z conversions.

ried out analyses of variance to test for overall differences between pretest and posttest on each of the various measures. If an *F* ratio for a
given measure proved statistically significant, he then did *t* tests on the
pretest to posttest changes for each of the four groups separately. The
results of these analyses are shown in Table 37. All of the *F* ratios turned

Table 37

*Discrimination Tests: Direction and Significance of
Pretest to Posttest Changes on Each Measure*

Measure	Trends	Discrimination Tests		
		A	B	C
Words	Direction	Decrease	Decrease	Decrease
	Significance Level	< .001	< .01	< .001
	Groups	ILS	LS	ILS
Different Words	Direction	Decrease	Decrease	Decrease
	Significance Level	< .001	< .05	< .001
	Groups	ILS	S	ILS
Overall Evaluation	Direction	Increase	Increase	Increase
	Significance Level	< .001	< .001	< .001
	Groups	ILS	ILC	LS
Useful Information	Direction	Increase	Increase	Increase
	Significance Level	< .001	< .001	< .05
	Groups	ILS	IC	none
Useless Information	Direction	Decrease	Decrease	Decrease
	Significance Level	< .001	< .001	< .001
	Groups	L	ILS	ILS

Note. In the Trends column, "Direction" refers to the mean direction of change from
pretest to posttest, "Significance Level" to the significance level of that change for all
groups combined (*F* ratio), and "Groups" to the particular group or groups whose
change in that direction was significant (*p* < .05) according to *t*-test analysis.

out to be statistically reliable, and the overall pretest to posttest trends on all three tests were perfectly regular: an increase in Overall Evaluation and Useful Information, and a decrease in Words, Different Words, and Useless Information. Moreover, the entries in the Groups rows of the table make it clear that it is the trained rather than control Ss who are largely responsible for these trends. Discrimination test instructions enjoin S to impart only enough information (but no *more* than enough) about the critical picture in the set to permit the listener to distinguish it from the others. The data shown in Table 37 suggest that five hours of experience on tasks of this type did improve the children's ability to operate effectively within these requirements.

Fry also wanted to find out if this experience would lead to improved performance on communication tasks with different requirements. Table 38 is the counterpart of Table 37 for tests D, E, and F. A minor prediction of the study was that the L group would show a significant improvement in listening skill, and this prediction appears to be borne out.

Table 38

Description and Listening Tests: Direction and Significance of Pretest to Posttest Changes on Each Measure

Measures	Trends	Tests		Listening
		Description		
		D	E	F
Words	Direction	Decrease	Decrease	
	Significance Level	$< .01$	$< .05$	
	Groups	I	S	
Different Words	Direction	Decrease	Decrease	
	Significance Level	$< .05$	$< .05$	
	Groups	I	S	
Overall Evaluation	Direction	Increase		Increase
	Significance Level	NS		$< .01$
	Groups	None		LS
Useful Information	Direction	Increase	Increase	
	Significance Level	NS	NS	
	Groups	None	None	
Useless Information	Direction	Decrease	Decrease	
	Significance Level	NS	NS	
	Groups	None	None	

Note. The Trends column is interpreted as in Table 37. Test E was not scored for Overall Evaluation, and hence has no entry in that row. Test F had only a single score, arbitrarily categorized here as "Overall Evaluation."

However, the S group also improved while the I group (which, like the L group, had some experience in critical listening) did not—a pattern of findings which scarcely would have been predicted. The data from tests D and E were of greater interest, but yielded disappointing results. Improved communicative performance on these particular tests would be most unequivocally indexed by significant increases in Overall Evaluation and Useful Information, but no such increases were found. The table shows that the I and S groups produced significantly briefer messages on posttest in tasks D and E, respectively. While this might be interpreted as transfer of training (terseness is important in Discrimination tasks), it remains to be explained why the other experimental groups did not also show the same transfer on these tests. In any case, we are not prepared to claim that an increased terseness coupled with no loss in informativeness (for example, as measured by Useful Information) is necessarily an instance of "communicative improvement." We would conclude instead that Fry's data give no convincing evidence whatever that his training had any beneficial effect on S's ability to deal effectively with Description as opposed to Discrimination tasks.

The final question was whether the different kinds of training received by the three experimental groups led to differences in degree and kind of skill, as reflected in test performance. One can get some sense of whether any systematic differences are likely to obtain by scanning the Groups rows in Tables 37 and 38. A better way is the one adopted by Fry. He first computed the F ratio for the interaction between groups (I, L, S, and C) and testing sessions (pretest versus posttest) for each measure on each test. If an F were significant ($p < .05$), he then tested (t tests) for differences in pretest to posttest change scores among the three experimental groups. A significant t here would indicate that one of a pair of experimental groups had shown a reliably greater change on the test and measure in question than the other had. In general, these analyses turned up little of interest. Only about one-third of the interaction F ratios proved significant, and only about one-third of the t's which these significant F's permitted Fry to compute were significant. Fry had expected, for example, that the I group's more variable training might lead to greater learning and transfer on the five communication tasks. In fact, however, the I group never exceeded either of the other two in pretest to posttest change—not on any measure of any task. The curious pattern of findings on the Listening test (Table 38) was confirmed in the present analysis: while not significantly different from each other, both the L and the S groups showed a significantly greater posttest improvement in score than did the I group. The remaining few significant comparisons show no coherent pattern and (together with those cited above) may reflect nothing more than the capitalization-on-chance process.

Discussion

What, if anything, did Fry's Ss learn from their brief "practicum course" in verbal communication? The data suggest that they may have learned something, but do not clearly indicate its nature and scope. The interpretation which we favor is that they probably learned how to adapt passably well to aspects of the specific genus of communicative problem to which they were repeatedly exposed, and little else. Certain character-istics of their training experience may have been partly responsible for this apparently very narrow and limited set of acquisitions. At the be-ginning of training, Fry noticed, many speakers essentially treated the Discrimination tasks as if they were Description ones, that is, they would attempt to describe a critical picture in its entirety, often ignoring the other pictures in the set. Since the listeners could in fact frequently identify the critical picture from so redundant a message, their post-message criticisms necessarily focussed more on what was said that need not have been than on what should have been said but was not. To say (at least) enough to permit identification was probably not overly dif-ficult for most of these fifth graders on most of the Discrimination train-ing tasks they encountered, and thus the training program may simply have done little or nothing to prepare them for tasks, such as tests D and E, where being able to "say enough" is precisely the central difficulty and where no accurate information about what is being talked about will likely be useless. We think it probable, then, that these Ss may have principally learned how to avoid gross excesses of unnecessary verbiage when communicating in Discrimination-task settings, something which doubtless *would* need some practice and listener feedback for a child to acquire (recall the results of Study IIB, given in Chapter 4). Some of them may have applied (or better, *misapplied*) this newly minted skill to one or both of the Description tasks, although the evidence is am-biguous on this point (see Table 38). It seems most unlikely that they did what Fry hoped they would do, namely, induce from their experi-ence with a single type of communication task a more generic and flexible set of skills and approaches, a set which would serve to sharpen their communicative performance over a wide variety of communication situa-tions.

There was also little evidence that differences in the kind of practice an experimental S received made much difference in what she learned. In retrospect, we wonder if the three exprimental groups really did have three distinct and different patterns of experience. The S group did, after all, listen to the playback of their own messages, and the L group, in criticizing the speakers' messages, effectively played the communicator role. All Ss had an opportunity to see messages arise from communicative instructions plus a datum to communicate about, and all Ss had an opportunity to see how listeners interpreted and acted upon these messages. In short, what the child could have learned in these training sessions was probably not importantly determined by any constraints or opportunities specific to the experimental condition he was in.

FRY STUDY II

Although generally modelled after its predecessor, this study differed from it in several respects. There was only one experimental (that is, training) group. It was most closely patterned after the I group of the previous study, in that all of its members served as both speakers and listeners. There were three types of training task instead of one, and six one-hour training sessions instead of five. Two of the criterion measures were administered three times instead of twice, the third administration constituting a second posttest which was given six months after training was completed. Other differences between the two studies will become apparent in the sections which follow.

Subjects

There were 37 Ss, who constituted the entire fifth grade of a private day school.[6] These children were separated by the school into two classes (class assignment was essentially random). The two classes took some of their academic work together, but had separate home rooms. One class of 19 children (5 boys and 14 girls) constituted the experimental (E) group and the other class of 18 children (5 boys and 13 girls) served as a no-training control (C). Unlike the case in the previous investigation, the control Ss did know that the other class was receiving some sort of extra-curricular experience (and some pleaded with Fry to be included!) What effect, if any, this may have had on the results is of course unknown. The Ss in this study were undoubtedly brighter than those of the preceding one. Their mean IQs (based upon group tests routinely administered by the school) were 129 and 131 for the E and C groups, respectively.

Procedure

As indicated, three types of training tasks were used. First, there was a graded series of Discrimination problems, generally similar to those used in Fry Study I. Second, there was a graded series of Description tasks of the test D variety. In these tasks the speaker is given a line draw-

---

[6]We wish to express our appreciation to the staff and students of Belfield School, Charlottesville, Virginia, for their generous cooperation in the conduct of this study.

ing of one or more objects or geometric designs and describes it to a group of listeners (other Ss). The listeners then attempt to reproduce the figure in a drawing (in test D there were of course, no live listeners and no actual attempts at figure reproduction). The third type of communication problem was reminiscent of the practice (single listener) subtasks of Study IE (Chapter 3). Fry designed a response box containing eight three-position bipolar switches wired in series to a red light. When all eight switches were set into a particular pattern of up and down positions the red light would go on (thus, the patern of switch positions is analogous to the safe combination of Study IE). This pattern could readily be changed by E from trial to trial. Each listener was given a card which indicated only a subset of the eight correct switch positions. The speaker had a list of the entire "combination" and also a copy of each listener's information. He was instructed to deliver a communication which all listeners could hear, but which would permit only the person who holds one particular card to complete the combination. As in the other training tasks, he received immediate postmessage feedback regarding the success of his communicative effort. This task is clearly of the Discrimination rather than Description type; in fact, the onus here against sending excess unneeded information is particularly salient (several listeners may end up with the complete switching pattern).

The experimental group was divided into three teams for training purposes, two composed of six Ss each and one of seven Ss. Team membership was constant (save for an occasional absence) across the six training sessions. The speaker role was rotated during each session among the team members, all Ss serving as listeners when not communicating. Each of the first three sessions introduced a new type of task, and only tasks of that type were worked with during that session. During each of the last three sessions, Fry alternated among the three types in a more or less random fashion. His own role in these sessions was about the same as it had been in the previous study. The general procedure on each trial was also the same: the speaker delivers his message into a tape recorder, the tape is played back one or more times, the listeners attempt to perform on the basis of it, and afterwards discuss and criticize the message with the speaker. The Ss were for the most part spontaneous, verbal, "overprivileged" youngsters who played their assigned roles of speaker, listener, and critic-discussant with little prompting and great enthusiasm. While Fry had of course deliberately planned to be relatively passive and nondidactic during these sessions, he is presently unsure whether these children would have permitted him to be anything else!

The effects of training were assessed by means of three of the tests used

in Fry Study I: Discrimination test A and Description tests D and E.[7]
Tests A, D, and E were administered once during the 10 days preceding
training and a second time during the 10 days after completion of training. Tests A and D (but not E) were given a third time, approximately
six months after training, to 15 of the 19 experimental Ss and to all of
the control Ss.

Results

The tests were scored exactly as in the previous study (see footnote 5
for the special treatment accorded test E). F ratios were then computed
on the interactions between groups (E and C) and testing sessions (pretest versus first posttest, and pretest versus second posttest) for each
measure and test. Table 39 summarizes the outcome of this analysis. Two
comments about the table. First, "decrease" and "increase" indicate the
mean direction of change for the E group alone; in some cases the C group
showed a mean change in the same direction, in some cases it did not.
Second, borderline F ratios (that is, $p < .10$) are indicated because they
give added information regarding the stability over time of pretraining
to posttraining changes.

Tests A and D are the likeliest sources of reliable information about
training effects, since they were readministered in both the immediate
and delayed posttest. As in the previous study, the training regimen appears to have induced a disposition to be relatively terse and to the point
on Discrimination problems, a disposition which still persisted six months
after training. In contrast with the findings of Fry Study I, however,
there is no evidence that the training had any effect on the Overall
Evaluation or Useful Information measures of that test. It appears that
this acquired disposition to be brief was also applied to Description test
D, again with some stability across test occasions. There is no good evidence, however, that the E group acquired any increased competence in
meeting the listener's more important informational needs on tests of
this kind. The significant interaction for Overall Evaluation does not
hold up six months later, and there are no significant interactions for
either set of change scores in the case of the Useful Information measure.
The data on test E—the single index of transfer in this study—are no

[7]The pretest and posttest battery also included four new tests: two in which S had
to tell a listener how to get from one geographical location to another by means of a
map which they both possessed; and two in which S had to diagnose and correct the
inadequacies of someone else's message. Unfortunately, the interjudge reliabilities for
the more important scoring categories on these tests were quite low (.30–.70 range).
Not surprisingly, comparisons between groups on pretest to posttest changes on these
tests yielded little of significance.

Table 39

Significance Levels of Group (E and C) by Testing Session (Pretest versus First Posttest, and Pretest versus Second Posttest) Interaction F Ratios and Direction of E Group Changes on Each Measure

Measures	Trends	Pretest to First Posttest			Pretest to Second Posttest	
		Test A	Test D	Test E	Test A	Test D
Words	Direction	Decrease	Decrease	Decrease	Decrease	Decrease
	Significance Level	< .10	< .10	NS	< .10	< .10
Different Words	Direction	Decrease	Decrease	Decrease	Decrease	Decrease
	Significance Level	< .05	< .05	< .05	< .10	< .05
Overall Evaluation	Direction	Increase	Increase		Increase	Increase
	Significance Level	NS	< .05		NS	NS
Useful Information	Direction	Decrease	Increase	Decrease	Decrease	Increase
	Significance Level	NS	NS	< .10	NS	NS
Useless Information	Direction	Decrease	Decrease	Decrease	Decrease	Decrease
	Significance Level	< .10	NS	NS	< .05	NS

more impressive. While there is reason to suspect that the brevity strategy may also have been inappropriately transferred here, there is no evidence that the experimental Ss had learned anything which was very useful in coping with this test, either (notice that the near-significant interaction for Useful Information reflects a relatively better performance by the *Control* group).

Discussion

The experimental Ss had what appears to have been a somewhat richer and more varied training diet in Fry's second study than in his first. Each S had a chance to operate both as speaker and as listener, and to do so in the context of three communication situations rather than one. And yet the results of this study, too, were in all important respects negative. As before, the experimental evidence failed to show that the children were really much more capable for having participated in the training sessions—that they had acquired any significant amount of communicative prowess in the course of their training.

Why the negative results in these two experiments? One possibility, of course, is that the assessment procedures were at fault. Perhaps the children really did learn something of value from the training sessions in one or both studies, but Fry's criterion measures were either too blunt or too unfocussed to pick it up. While we are far from satisfied with the tests of communicative skill used in these studies (or in our others), we very much doubt if their shortcomings could carry the entire explanatory burden here. Consider the Useful Information measure on test D, for example. The rater reads S's description of the design and simply totals the number of message segments which convey, with reasonable clarity, items of information about the stimulus which the listener would find useful in making an accurate reproduction of this design. We believe that this measure has good credentials as a performance index for Description tasks. It is fairly easy to score in a consistent fashion, and it certainly is a face valid measure of how adequately S has carried out his prescribed function. If the training had in fact improved Ss' ability to perform on Description problems, the improvement would surely have been registered in these Useful Information scores. But there were no significant group differences on this measure: neither in Fry Study I, where the Ss did not have training experience with Description problems, nor in Fry Study II, where they did.

One could multiply instances of this sort, and they all tend to shift one's suspicions from the way the training effects were assessed to the training itself. Fry's retrospections about what actually happened during the training sessions increase these suspicions. It has already been noted that, in the first study, Ss' behavior in the training sessions quickly took a turn which could hardly lead to improved performance on Description-type problems and might even work against it. There is also reason to doubt whether the new training tasks introduced in the second study were fortunate additions. Given the results of Fry Study I, it was probably unwise to crowd the training battery with yet another task of the Discrimination variety (that is, the switch-combination task). Moreover, it was Fry's impression that the children quickly reached a plateau on this task, that is, they early learned to communicate only the portions of the correct combination which the intended listener did not already have. It is doubtful if merely acquiring this simple strategy could have substantially affected their overall communicative competence. The Description tasks might have fared better, given the virtually unlimited performance ceiling characteristic of such problems. But this would be to reckon without a curious and wholly unexpected behavior pattern on the part of these children. The speaker would attempt to describe the design and the listeners would attempt to draw it. Provided only that there were *some* resemblance between original and reproduction, however, both speaker and listeners were frequently satisfied with the speaker's communicative effort. This amounted to a redefinition of the task requirements, of course, and a redefinition which could only serve to dilute whatever pedagogic value the task might otherwise have had.

These observations suggest what may have been a basic inadequacy in the training programs used: insufficient control over the educational inputs to the child. In these two programs E did little more than put children into a situation in which they *might* obtain formative experiences, that is, experiences which could give them new insights into the nature of the communication problem. He did not, however, keep careful track of whether any given child actually *did* obtain such experiences, and above all, almost never intervened in order to make *sure* he did. It was left to the child to extract heuristic value from his own spontaneous activities and those of his teammates, and the indications are that the child was largely unable to do this. It would have been better, perhaps, if Fry had played a more active role during these sessions, calling attention to message inadequacies which the children had ignored or overlooked, persistently attempting to get them to seek new and better approaches to the problem, and so forth. The word "perhaps" is inserted here because we really have no assurance at all that such a revision in program, or any of several others that have occurred to us,[8] would actually succeed where Fry failed. It may turn out that role-taking and communication skills, like some of the cognitive acquisitions described by Piaget (Flavell, 1963, ch. 11), will prove somewhat resistant to short-order shaping in the laboratory or classroom.

[8] One of the authors (Botkin) has recently been attempting to teach role-taking and communication skills to sixth graders by means of programmed instruction. Her research project is not far enough along, however, for us to be able to tell if this approach to training will prove more successful than Fry's.

CHAPTER SEVEN

Retrospect and Prospect

The title of this chapter suggests its major aims: to review the past and to speculate about the future. The first section gives a summary and interpretation of the research described in previous chapters. In the second section, we indicate what may be promising lines of future research inquiry into the nature and genesis of role-taking and communication skills.

RETROSPECT

Theoretical Background

The research strategy and the theoretical conceptions which formed the context for most of our research were outlined in Chapter 1. The primary research objective was to subject an interesting but largely unexplored area of psychological study to what we have termed a *developmental-descriptive analysis*. The intended output of such an analysis would be a fairly detailed, first-approximation picture of what develops and when in the domain of role-taking and communication behavior. The analysis was made by first constructing a crude, working model of the nature and interaction of these activities; then, using the model as a heuristic for identifying a number of more specific, situationally constrained abilities; subsequently devising tasks which seemed likely to tap these abilities and administering them to children of different ages; and finally, drawing upon the results to sketch in the developmental-descriptive picture.

The model defined role-taking activity as the attempted discrimination of another person's role attributes, "discrimination" and "role attributes" taken in a very inclusive sense. In most situations in which an individual engages in role-taking activity, this activity serves as a means for some other end. It may, for example, be instrumental to a full-fledged enactment of the other person's role or to some kind of cooperative or competitive endeavor vis-à-vis the other. A particularly important activity for which it can serve an instrumental function is that of communication. Part of the theoretical section of Chapter 1 was thus devoted to an analysis of two paradigmatic cases of communicative behavior: that which proceeds without benefit of prior or ongoing role-taking activity, and that which is monitored and directed by such activity (see Figures 1 and 2 and their accompanying text). This analysis was offered as a revealing but obviously oversimplified account of the actual processes involved, and some of the more important limitations and qualifications which attend it were also discussed.

Role-Taking and Communication Development

The data from our various studies provided at least some interesting segments of the developmental-descriptive picture we were after. As a prelude to reviewing these studies, however, it would be useful to consider the general question of just what it is that *needs* developing in this area of social-cognitive functioning, given the analysis of this functioning provided by our model. We said that it was typically the case that role-taking activity serves as a means to some end, for example, that of effective communication to another person. The question is, what sorts of things does the individual have to know, or know how to do, in order to achieve any role-taking-mediated end? In our view, there are five major things he has to know:

1. *Existence*—that there *is* such a thing as "perspective," that is, that what you perceive, think, or feel in any given situation need not coincide with what I perceive, think, or feel.

2. *Need*—that an analysis of the other's perspective is called for in this particular situation, that is, that such an analysis would be a useful means to achieving whatever one's goal is here.

3. *Prediction*—how actually to carry out this analysis, that is, possession of the abilities needed to discriminate with accuracy whatever the relevant role attributes are.

4. *Maintenance*—how to maintain in awareness the cognitions yielded by this analysis, assuming them to be in active competition with those which define one's own point of view, during the time in which they are to be applied to the goal behavior.

5. *Application*—how actually to apply these cognitions to the end at hand, for example, how to translate what one knows about the other's listener role attributes into an effective verbal message.

A closer look at each of these hypothetical constituents will call attention to a number of interpretative themes which have run through the preceding chapters.

Existence. The knowledge represented here is of course logically prior to all the rest, and there is every reason to believe that some form of it first emerges during early childhood. It can be characterized as the simple awareness that the other and the self may apprehend the same objects or events differently; it is not defined as including any cognitive mechanisms for discovering what the other's perspective actually consists of. At the present time, next to nothing of interest is known about the acquisition of this fundamental attainment. We have speculated (Chapter 5) that an awareness of perspective differences is an occasional and fragile affair initially, heavily dependent upon direct instigation (for example, explicit instructions to find the other's perspective), and that it may first appear in connection with perceptual as opposed to other role attributes.

Need. A child may well know that perspective differences exist in the world and yet fail to call to mind or act upon this knowledge in all situations where it would be appropriate to do so. Given a communicative task, for example, he may for any of a number of reasons simply fail to take note of a fact which, were his attention called to it, he could readily understand and acknowledge, namely, that the listener's point of view differs from his own. Alternatively, he may spontaneously recognize this fact but fail to realize that it has any implications for his communicative endeavor. The *Need* constituent, then, refers to the following developmental acquisition within the role-taking domain: a growing awareness that certain situations which do not explicitly call for role-taking activity do so implicitly; that certain situations constitute a signal to engage and utilize one's role-taking capabilities.

Prediction. Assuming the child knows all the foregoing, he still faces the considerable problem of actually carrying out the intended analysis of the other person's role attributes. There is obviously a great deal we do not know about how this is done—and also about developmental changes in how it is done. Our working conception has been that role-taking activity usually takes the form of an inferential process of some sort, a process of making guesses about what the pertinent role attributes are in a given situation on the basis of our general knowledge of human behavior, together with whatever specific information we can extract from the immediate situation. The cognitive operations involved in this inferential process are not specific to role-taking activity, but figure in a variety of performances in the intellectual domain. Since these operations themselves enter the repertoire at different points in the developmental timetable, it follows that the nature and quality of the child's role-taking activity will also change with age. We have described aspects of this change in previous chapters (for example, Chapter 2, in discussing the results of Study IB), and will do so later in this one in the course of reviewing specific studies.

Maintenance. As indicated in Chapter 1 and subsequently, cognitive sequences involving role-taking activity are likely to have some of the features of a system in dynamic equilibrium. That is, one's own point of view may function, intermittently or continuously, as an active, spontaneous force which opposes a role-taking analysis and which must somehow be neutralized. The phenomenon categorized here applies both to the genesis of a represented picture of the other's perspective and to its utilization: the picture must be unsullied by one's own perspective in its process of formation, and must remain unsullied whenever one uses it as an information source, for example, in deciding how to phrase the next part of the message. The ability to counter this force, to establish and maintain the necessary barriers between one's own and the other's point of view, is postulated to be another developmental acquisition in this area.

Application. Given a representation of the other's role attributes, at any level of veridicality and stability, there remains the task of "behaving appropriately" in terms of that representation. In some situations involving role-taking activity, knowing how to make the appropriate goal response does not constitute much of a problem. Having represented to himself that the opponent will probably choose the two-nickel cup in Task IB, for instance, even the youngest child in our sample readily understands that this implies removal of the money from that cup on his part, given the rules of the game. Similarly, given a clear and enduring image of what Display 1 looks like to E_2 in Task IC, there should be little difficulty in situating one's block accordingly. The problem of application may loom large in other situations, however, notably in communication tasks. To know that the blindfolded listener needs to be informed about the game materials in Task IA is not necessarily to know how to frame a message which will in fact adequately inform him. As with the *Prediction* component, there are age-dependent skills at work here, and their acquisition may be regarded as at least partly independent of what is involved in role-taking development itself (see Chapter 1).

While this conceptualization is little more than an expanded paraphrase of the analysis presented in Chapter 1, it does bring into better focus some of the problems involved in trying to interpret an individual's performance on tasks in this area. What it asserts is that there is a "successive hurdles" character to the activities which underlie the performance output, the number and nature of the hurdles partly depending upon the specific task situation. If a child produces a poor solution to some problem which entails role-taking activity, it may not be—and often will not be—obvious where the trouble lies. He may have been unaware of perspective differences as one of life's possibilities, or unaware that the present task has an implicit role-taking requirement, or unable to achieve or maintain an adequate representation of the other's perspective, or unable to use the information contained in his representation, or some combination of these. The problem of determining exactly what an individual knows and can do from what he happens to do in response to your testing procedures is of course omnipresent in psychological research. The foregoing is simply a specification of the particular shape the problem assumes in this area. In addition, it is intended to innoculate the reader against overliteral and simplistic interpretations of some assertions we will shortly be making: assertions that this task measures that skill; that children in such-and-such age group acquire this or have not yet acquired that; and the like. While assertions of this ilk about developmental phenomena do indeed convey something which needs to be conveyed, they inevitably and necessarily claim more power for the measuring instrument and more simplicity for the developmental process than obtains for either.

Early Development. There is considerably less research evidence about early acquisitions than about later ones, whether one searches our work or the literature in general. Our data at least suggest that the young preschool child has not yet achieved a firm concept of perspective variation (*Existence*), even in the case of perceptual perspectives. As indicated in Chapter 5, it is possible to devise more sensitive and reliable instruments for assessing a young child's understanding of this concept than we used in our pilot study, and careful research with such instruments would doubtless give a more precise understanding of his capabilities and limitations here.

In contrast, there is strong evidence that the child is likely to have achieved some understanding of perspective variation as an existent by the time he enters school. Once again, however, very little is known about the constraints and qualifications which hold for this understanding. Extrapolating from our work with older children, we would guess that the concept is still quite shaky where cognitive perspectives are concerned, but there is no direct evidence on the matter. The research on older children also implies that the first grader's abilities in the *Need*, *Prediction*, *Maintenance*, and *Application* categories are severely limited, although probably not nil. It implies, for example, that he would be markedly insensitive to the hidden role-taking requirements of communication and other tasks (*Need*). On the other hand, our data suggest the hypothesis that he has acquired some *Prediction* skills of a limited sort in the case of perceptual perspectives, providing that the task structure eliminates the *Need* problem (that is, gives an explicit mandate to analyze the other's point of view). We speculated that, by the end of the preschool era, the child is capable of certain elementary inferences about what the other perceives: for example, that if self and other are looking at opposite sides of an object, the other will see, not what the self sees, but what is presented on the other's side (see Chapter 5). Further investigation could not only check these speculations but might also turn up additional simple skills within the *Prediction* and other categories.

Development in Middle Childhood and Adolescence. This was the age group with which most of our research dealt. The data from these studies abundantly document the generalization that profound and widespread changes in role-taking and communication skills take place during this period. Most of the changes we have identified appear to involve those components of the process which presuppose but go beyond a mere awareness that role attributes vary with people and positions, that is, those components we have schematized under *Need, Prediction, Maintenance,* and *Application.* Our studies amount to an inventory—obviously partial and incomplete—of what the child acquires as regards these components, and the effects these acquisitions have on his solutions to particular social-cognitive problems.

Not surprisingly, the communication data give the clearest evidence for changes in the *Need* category. As he develops, the child becomes increasingly aware of the necessity of paying careful attention to the characteristics of his audience when communicating. This developing sensitivity to the listener becomes especially apparent in situations which present the child with *contrasting* audiences, generally a standard-average listener versus one who is deviant in some way. In Task IA, for example, there was a normal adult listener and a sensorily handicapped (blindfolded) one. There was an increasing tendency with age to take careful note of these differences in listener role attributes and to try to fashion the two messages accordingly. In IIA the situation was different but the principle was the same. A communication which would be adequate for a standard-average listener was already prepared in advance by *E* (in the form of a written fable); *S*'s assignment was then to communicate the same information to a deviant listener, in this case a young child whose cognitive immaturity paralleled the blindfolded adult's sensory handicap in Task IA. Since most children used the written text as a point of departure in fashioning their communications to the young listener, one almost had the impression of "seeing" the older *S* repeatedly attend to his listener role attributes in order to bring each portion of the message into line with his intellectual and linguistic limitations. In IIB there were again two messages concerning the same content addressed to two different listeners, different this time in terms of the use to which they had to put the information received: reproduce a stimulus figure in the one case; merely identify it from among an array of figures in the other. The oldest Ss (eleventh graders) in particular showed by what they said to each listener that they had paid careful attention to these differing listener requirements. In Jarvis' study the two listeners were embodied in the same person: standard-average in the first message; cognitively substandard in the second (postfeedback) message. The results of this study likewise attest to a developing sensitivity to the input needs and capabilities of the audience.

Other studies also point up ontogenetic changes in the *Need* component. A good persuasive message in IIC can be taken as evidence that the child has attained such sensitivity. Indeed, a few of the older Ss in this study went so far as to include the persuasee's reactions to their message in the message itself, as though they were actually engaged in a dialogue with the depicted other. Likewise, an S could scarcely detect the flaws in the Task IIE message without trying to represent its probable stimulus value to someone who, unlike the child, neither knew where he was presently located on the map nor where he was going. The same argument could be made for the child's objective in ID, IE, and a number of other tasks.

The *Prediction* component entered into S's performance on all of our tasks, of course, but the intellectual abilities required for prediction were no doubt quite variable from problem to problem. Good performance on Task IE, for example, appears to presuppose the ability to carry out certain logical operations—operations which are themselves clearly age-dependent. What the child had to do in this task was to reduce a trio of listeners to a single (hypothetical) listener, who then became the communication target. In order to accomplish this, however, the child had to know how to find the logical product and the logical sum of the sets of information which each of the three listeners already possessed. The development of logical abilities must also have played a part elsewhere, for example, in identifying the listener's minimum informational needs in the Discrimination subtask of Study IIB.

Prediction of the other's role attributes in a number of tasks quite clearly entailed some understanding of people, and age changes on these tasks must have reflected advances in this understanding. Good performance on IIA, for instance, presupposes a reasonably accurate assessment of the cognitive-linguistic capacities and limitations of the typical preschool child. Task IIC calls for an estimate of the motivational and attitudinal systems of particular (S's father) and generalized (a male customer) others. Task IB can be construed as measuring S's "theories" regarding the nature of cognitive representation and the symbolic objects it can subsume. Several tasks seem in part to assess what the child knows about the nature of information processing in humans. In the case of ID, for example, it was argued that the young child may not recognize the multivalent, potentially ambiguous quality of visual input, and hence is not in a position to imagine how the naïve other's interpretation of the picture series might differ from his own. In the communication tasks the potential ambiguity resides in verbal rather than visual input, but the problem is similar. The child has to come to the recognition that the listener must *interpret* what gets said, and that a poor message segment is one in which the likelihood of an unintended interpretation is relatively high. In the case of Task IIE, for instance, he must know that there are two possible interpretations of the sentence, "The house you want is the second one on the street," for a listener whose map shows houses on *both* side of the street in question. The ability to recognize such ambiguities, like the ability to impute complicated reasoning to others (Task IB), can be interpreted as reflecting a growing understanding of how human beings function. The data from a variety of studies thus suggest that knowledge of the "person perception" sort burgeons on a number of fronts during middle childhood and adolescence, and that this knowledge manifests itself in increasingly more accurate and complex predictions concerning the role attributes of particular others in particular situations.

The process assigned to the *Maintenance* category were particularly salient in certain of our tasks. In ID, for example, it appeared that much of the child's difficulty in seizing and maintaining the other's perspective must have stemmed from the fact that his own perspective was continually redintegrated in the very act of doing so. The *Prediction* problem in this task was construed as being relatively trivial, providing only that one could keep out predictive intrusions originating in one's own previous interpretation of the pictures (the *Maintenance* component). But for some of the younger Ss at least, "only" doing that posed real difficulties. The problem here and in other tasks was essentially to establish and keep active a clear distinction between the dictates of the task situation and those of impulse or natural inclination, and to obey only the first. The inclination of all Ss in Task IIA, for instance, was undoubtedly to impart the fable in the same form that it was received; nonetheless, many of the older Ss continually tried to suppress this inclination in favor of rewording the difficult passages. In the Discrimination subtask of IIB similarly, the child needed to inhibit tip-of-the-tongue verbal codings in favor of a decidedly unnatural terseness; let *S* forget for a moment the needs of this particular, "deviant" listener, and superfluous verbalizations would hasten to join necessary ones. In the role-enactive narrations of Task IID the child would again need to keep more or less continuously alive a representation of the sort of individual she was portraying, in order to speak as such an individual would speak and to say what such an individual would say. For here also there were countervailing forces in operation: let the child momentarily lose track of the perspective she is simulating and her own role attributes will effect a "drift" or "regression" to a different narrative style. It is not altogether clear how best to conceptualize the abilities ascribed to the *Maintenance* component, for example, in terms of impulse control, conceptual differentiation, or maintenance of attention. It does seem clear, however, that they play a vital role in successful role-taking activity and that, like the other components, they undergo considerable development during middle childhood and adolescence.

The *Application* component is a residual one, essentially defined as that coterie of abilities necessary to get the individual from a solution of the purely role-taking elements of a problem to a solution of whatever elements remain. As already indicated, this remainder may call for real skill, as in most communication tasks, or it may not, as in most "pure" role-taking tasks. While it is obvious that some of these skills must be strongly age-dependent, for example, the verbal and conceptual skills needed for expressing clearly that which prior role-attribute analysis has established as necessary to communicate, they need not all be, as witness the freedom from inhibitions needed to enact a role in the presence of an audience. About all that remains to be said about *Application* skills is that, on the one hand, we were continually attuned to the fact that their contribution to Ss' performance was substantial in a number of tasks and, on the other hand, that they were themselves not the intended object of our developmental research. Whatever the problem setting, our interest was always focussed on the contributions of role-taking activity to problem solution, not on those of other factors.

Before concluding this backward look at our research, a few words about the relationship between the behavior we saw and what one would expect to see in real life situations. Our tasks were of course calculated to emphasize age differences in performance, with these differences interpreted as demonstrating a wide gap in capability or competence in this area between the young preschooler and the near-adult. Would naturalistic observations of children "in the wild" give the same sense of gap, the same sense of extensive developmental movement?

We doubt it. It would rather seem to be the case that the child will typically set his enterprises in rough correspondence with his capabilities, to make what he tries to do accord reasonably well with what he can do. Communication behavior provides a good example of what we mean here. There is no reason to suppose that the young child would in every-day interchanges *look* as inferior to his elders in communicative skill as our studies show him to be, for the very good reason that the communicative tasks he poses for himself are typically much simpler than those which his elders undertake. It does not follow from our developmental analysis, in other words, that he perforce must fail to accomplish his communicative ends much more frequently and dramatically than the older child does, because the ends themselves do not remain constant across age. In a sense, this observation points to one of the scientific motives for turning from the naturalistic study of children to experimental interventions which test and probe for underlying competencies. It is simply a fact that children are not masochistic enough to be forever aiming at targets which their intellectual weaponry cannot reach.

Having said all this, however, there may still be the interesting question of developmental variation in the gap between target and weaponry. It could be—and this is pure speculation—that there are particular periods in ontogenesis in which the gap typically widens, perhaps with a quickening in development as its consequence. When children first enter school, for example, they may suddenly face new and more distant targets, targets which are teacher-selected rather than self-selected, and this may stimulate the creation of new and better weaponry. Bruner (1959) once suggested that the ontogenetic succession of thought structures described by Piaget may in part reflect developmental responses to the tasks and pressures successively imposed on the growing child by his society. It would be interesting if this same "challenge-response" model were found to fit role-taking and communication development.

PROSPECT

Our research endeavor, like any other, can count itself successful to the extent that it accomplishes two things. First, it should offer at least tentative answers to the specific questions it has chosen to ask; and second, it should clarify the area of inquiry in such a way as to suggest additional questions and problems for future research. We have already had our say regarding interpretations of our data and now wish to conclude chapter and book with some speculations about what remains to be done.

The research possibilities that we presently envisage are quite diverse, but can roughly be sorted into two broad categories. We could first of all continue along the road we have chosen in the present investigation. A developmental-descriptive account of what gets acquired in this area is far from complete, to say the least, and there are a number of interesting questions here which remain to be asked and answered. Alternatively, we could opt for a more causal-analytic approach, searching for revealing relationships among role-taking and related skills, and between these skills and other variables. We shall first take up some of the possibilities afforded by a causal-analytic approach.

Causal-Analytic Questions

Correlations among Tasks. One class of causal-analytic questions would take as its data intercorrelations among tasks assumed to call for role-taking activity. Such a correlational approach could derive from at least two rather different conceptual orientations. On the one hand, there is the factor-analytic orientation, in which an attempt is made to delineate the skill structure of a domain. There is of course much to be discovered about the nature and pattern of correlations among tasks purporting to measure role-taking activity, and in particular, about the number and kinds of independent skills ("factors") which mediate performance on these various tasks. While we confess to some skepticism regarding the usefulness of factor-analytic approaches to the analysis of psychological structure, a systematic and carefully run investigation of this sort might suggest useful revisions of our current conceptions in this area.

There is another motivation for correlational analysis which we find more interesting, however. One begins with a theoretical analysis of some psychological process or behavior not ordinarily construed in role-taking terms, and from this analysis emerges with the hypothesis that role-taking activity does in fact serve such and such a mediating function there. The hypothesis is then tested by attempting to find out if S's role-taking skill, estimated as accurately as present technology allows, will predict (that is, correlate with) his performance on some suitable test of the process or behavior so analyzed. Confirmation of the hypothesis serves two purposes. It advances by that much our understanding of the structure of the process or behavior in question, and it strengthens by that much a theory which argues for the importance and ubiquitousness of role-taking activity in human affairs.

One could make a plausible case, for instance, for the notion that role-taking ability is involved in skillful listening as well as skillful communicating. The ability to interpret correctly an inadequate message may be mediated in part by shrewd conjectures about the "speaker role attributes" of the communicator and what these might imply about the message; such conjectures would surely qualify as role-taking activity. Mothers often try to do this when listening to their young children, and some are better at it than others. An experimental verification of this hypothesis would add to our understanding of listening and role-taking activity alike.

There are other questions of this type which experimental ingenuity might permit us to answer. Is the ability to devise effective persuasive messages correlated with the ability to diagnose, as persuasive rather than simply informative, the messages of others? It would seem that skills of the role-taking genre could as readily mediate the latter as the former. How about other social and cognitive behaviors in the extralaboratory life of the child and adult? In our discussion of Study IB (Chapter 2) we argued that emerging role-taking skills may "support"—in the necessary but not sufficient sense—new and different forms of social behavior as the child grows. We would here append the view that his attained skill level may also define his readiness for certain educational experiences. It is not inconceivable, for instance, that an analysis in role-taking terms of what is needed to grasp important principles in political science, history, sociology, economics, and other fields could lead to intelligent suggestions regarding the content and timing of instruction in those fields. The work of Fry (Chapter 6) touched on the possibility of putting role-taking skill into the curriculum. We are here speculating about the extent to which it is already there in disguise, and about how its diagnosis could be turned to educational profit.

Variables Associated with Role-Taking Skills. If we know how well an individual performs on role-taking tasks, what else of interest can we predict about him? Assuming individual differences in this domain of skills, with what other variables are they reliably associated? First a word about the justification for the assumption itself. We were repeatedly struck with the wide variation in skill level to be found in even small samples of children at any given age. It can now be taken as a fact that at least the developmental *rate* of skill acquisition in this area is enormously variable from child to child. How about the asymptotic level of these developmental curves—that is, do the individual differences in rate of growth find their parallel in stable ability differences at the adult level? It would be astonishing if this were not the case, and one is hardly tempted to do studies simply to demonstrate it. Such studies would in any case be redundant, given research data of the sort recently gathered by Robert Hess and his associates at the University of Chicago (Hess and Shipman, 1965). The Ss were Negro mothers and their four-year-old children, drawn from different social classes. The mothers were taught simple tasks by the *E*s and then asked to teach them to their children. One of the tasks was to sort a number of toys by color and by function. A skeptic has only to scan the interchanges between mother and child cited in the paper to be convinced that individual differences in adult communicative ability can be very wide indeed. Here is how one of the mothers dealt with the communicative problem:

> "All right, Susan, this board is the place where we put the little toys; first of all you're supposed to learn how to place them according to color. Can you do that? The things that are all the same color you put in one section; in the second section you put another group of colors, and in the third section you put the last group of colors. Can you do that? Or would you like to see me do it first?"
> "I want to do it." (p. 881)

Compare this with the following excerpt.

> "I've got some chairs and cars, do you want to play the game?"
> (No response)
> "O.K. What's this?"
> "A wagon?"
> "Hm?"
> "A wagon?"
> "This is not a wagon. What's this?" (p. 882)

The authors indicate that the conversation continued in this vein for several more pages. We were struck by how similar this mother's communicative performance is to those of our less talented second graders in Study IA.

Schatzman and Strauss (1955) also found striking variations in adult communicative behavior correlated with differences in social status. They interviewed the survivors of a tornado and recorded their accounts of the experience. Lower-class informants were characterized in terms like this:

> . . . displayed a relative insensitivity to disparities in perspective . . . seldom anticipates responses to his communication and seems to feel little need to explain particular features of his account . . . much surnaming of persons without clear referents . . . seldom qualifies an utterance, presumably because he takes for granted that his perceptions represent reality and are shared by all who were present (p. 331).

This description of communicative behavior, too, gives us a *déja vu* experience.

We can be assured, then, that individuals at any age level will show considerable variation in role-taking and communication skill, and it would be desirable to find out with what this variation is correlated. The associated variables of greatest interest are of two types: those which can be categorized as manifestations, derivatives, expressions, or outcomes of this skill variation (consequents); those which contribute to or are partly responsible for it (antecedents). We have already mentioned the first type in the preceding section, in suggesting that role-taking skill may contribute to listening ability, readiness for certain school content, etc., and there are doubtless many other consequents of equal interest. (Does role-taking prowess also enter as an independent variable into things like leadership and popularity, marital adjustment, or child-rearing skills?)[1]

The identification of antecedent variables is of especial importance because it could contribute to our understanding of the conditions and constraints which govern developmental rate and asymptotic level. We should like to know just what qualities or characteristics of the individual and of his environment during the formative years contribute to or impede the attainment of these skills.

As to the individual, there are a number of candidate variables. We would suppose that the vague trait we identify and measure under the label "general intelligence" could play a considerable role. More interesting, perhaps, would be a finding that the individual's cognitive style facilitates or inhibits these acquisitions. High field-independence (for example, Witkin, 1964), for instance, may facilitate the sustained differentiation between one's own and the other's points of view which we have termed *Maintenance;* high field-dependence may interfere with this differentiation. Likewise, a generalized disposition to reflect and ponder alternatives before acting (Kagan et al., 1964) may also contribute to skill development here. A recent finding by Neale (1966) hints at this possibility. He found that perceptual role-taking performance in emotionally disturbed, aggressive children was inferior to that of normal controls at each of four age levels; whatever other difficulties may beset them, these disturbed children would surely qualify as "nonreflective" in cognitive mode.

A more obvious implication of Neale's study, however, is that there may be personality characteristics which importantly influence the de-

[1]Some beginning evidence on correlations between role taking and other variables has come to our attention since this chapter was written. There are now data suggesting that performance on role-taking tasks does in fact covary significantly with (independently assessed) performance on communication tasks, both in children (Cowan, 1966) and in adults (Feffer and Suchotliff, 1966; Phillips and Feffer, 1966). Swinson (1966) has also obtained significant correlations between Feffer's role-taking test and several of Piaget's concrete operational tasks (for example, conservation of quantity), with age, grade and IQ partialled out. And finally, Rothenberg (1967) has reported small but statistically reliable associations between social sensitivity and several measures of intelligence and interpersonal adjustment.

velopment and use of role-taking and communication abilities. We would be intrigued to find out whether children with high dependent and affiliative needs, for instance, are especially precocious in acquiring these abilities. On the one hand, skill in communicating with and predicting the role attributes of others would seem to be a useful instrument in satisfying these needs; on the other hand, the needs themselves serve to put the child in frequent interactive contact with others, presumably a necessary condition for the acquisition of this kind of skill. There is added interest in testing hypotheses of this sort because the outcome is not foreordained. It might be, for example, that there is an egocentric component in a dependence-on-others orientation which effectively counteracts the formative influence just mentioned.

On the environmental side, the aim is to identify those circumstances and conditions which provide (or preclude) opportunities for the growth of these skills. Social interaction patterns in the child's home would naturally come to mind as a major setting for learning opportunities. Parents undoubtedly vary a great deal in the extent to which they implicitly or explicitly call the child's attention to perspective differences, to the importance of communicative clarity, and other relevant matters. The mothers in the Hess and Shipman (1966) sample appear to show this sort of variation to a very marked degree, and it would be interesting to find out what effects their widely disparate styles of verbal interaction with their children are having on the latter's role-taking and communication development.

We can imagine certain specific socialization practices which might be developmentally formative. A mother who persistently tries to induce her child to recode inadequate messages (even when she understands or can guess what the child is trying to say) may be engaging in such a practice, especially if she at the same time helps the child to understand the specific nature or source of the inadequacy; for example, his mouth is too full, his speech is too rapid and excited, or he has failed to indicate the subject of his discourse. No doubt there are more and less skillful ways of carrying out this kind of informal communication training, and its effectiveness would also probably interact with the kind of child one is dealing with. We would further expect that the parent who repeatedly invites the child to make inferences about the thoughts and feelings of others—either directly or by example—is helping to shape the child's role-taking skills. There is a somewhat more fanciful hypothesis we have entertained with regard to the genesis of persuasive abilities: parents who tend to grant the child's requests only on condition that he justify his case by means of rational argument are unwittingly serving the development of this type of communication skill (in contrast, say, to parents who are unmoved by argument or are too readily susceptible to nonargumentative forms of persuasion). Here the rewards for skillful persuasion are immediate and unambiguous—the child gets what he wants.

Certain kinds of interactions with other children may also be developmentally formative. We suspect, for example, that the child who has a sibling at least two or three years younger than himself may have better than average opportunities to stretch his role-taking and communicative capabilities. It will often be to his own advantage to read the younger child's role attributes accurately for purposes of both informative and persuasive communication. This hypothesis, especially, would be easy to test empirically. Piaget (1928) long ago argued that social interaction, especially among peers, provides the crucial setting for the development of role-taking and related cognitive skills. While in general agreement with this thesis, we would want to emphasize the possible heuristic value of interchanges with certain nonpeers: with parents and other tutor-socializers on the one hand, and with younger children on the other.

A careful search for the crucial social-interactional antecedents of role-taking and communication skills would obviously be a well-motivated venture on purely basic-research grounds. In addition, however, it might make a contribution to what has so far proved a most troublesome applied research problem (Chapter 6), namely, how to facilitate their acquisition in the laboratory or classroom.

Developmental-Descriptive Questions

There is similarly no dearth of researchable questions in this area for an investigator whose tastes run to developmental-descriptive rather than causal-analytic work. We shall simply indicate a few of the possibilities which we personally would favor investigating.

Role-Taking Studies. It needs reiterating that almost nothing is yet known about the early genesis of role-taking skills; Study III was a pilot study, nothing more. As indicated earlier, however, there are now testing procedures available which would allow a rather precise and systematic assessment of the young child's ability to estimate perceptual perspectives. We ourselves would also be interested in devising procedures for tapping into the very beginning of the developmental process, that is, the young child's initial awareness of what a perspective is (the *Existence* component). How might this be done? Supposing the young child and an adult are seated in different positions vis-à-vis some display such that the adult sees an object which is not *visible* from where the child sits, although we have previously insured that he *knows* it is there. If physical conditions were suitably arranged, questions of the form, "What is this?"

(point toward object locus) and, "What does he (the adult) see?" become semantically equivalent, the uniquely correct answer to both being an identification of the object in question. We would predict, however, that there exists an early stage of development during which these questions are *not* equivalent for the child: while he can answer the first one easily and correctly, the second may give him trouble because it makes reference to a subjective experience or perceptual act rather than to the external, concrete referent of that experience or act. Although at home since infancy with the world of everyday objects, in or out of his sight, he has not yet become attuned to the perceptual actions by which he gains access to them. He knows about objects, but not about perceptions of objects; in the present case, he knows what is there, but not the (equivalent) content of the other's perception. If we could demonstrate the existence of such a stage and locate its age of termination, we would argue that a crucial first step in role-taking development had been experimentally diagnosed.

As for later developments, one understudied process is clearly that of role enactment. It has occurred to us that puppetry might offer experimental possibilities here. Many children of our acquaintance have at one time or another enjoyed staging impromptu puppet shows, one mitten-type puppet on each hand. Even a medium-grade performance under these conditions is no mean intellectual feat. At the very least, the puppeteer is required to make frequent and abrupt shifts between role enactments, all the while keeping each one consistent with the overall situation, stable in character, and distinct from and complementary to the other role. Casual observation suggests, not surprisingly, that most young children seem to manage all this quite poorly. Roles remain relatively undifferentiated, interchanges tend to consist largely of repetitive and stereotyped motor and verbal gestures (frequently aggressive in tone), and so on. For all its commonplace character, this particular form of play activity appears to be a far richer vehicle for studying the development of role-enactment skills than Task IID was, and might be profitably exploited in the service of developmental-descriptive research. One would like to find out, for example, which of these subskills tends to emerge earlier and which later, and also exactly what forms of preskill activity they replace.

Another line of investigation has Task IB as its point of departure. The diagram shown in Figure 4 (Chapter 2) depicts the first three terms in an infinitely-extendable series of role-taking cognitions. It is obvious to an adult that having begun a cognitive chain, such as, "He thinks that I think that he thinks . . . ," one could in principle continue forever. Moreover, the typical adult would know precisely *how* to extend the chain from any given point; that is, he would possess an operative grasp of the simple recursive rules which generate it. We suspect that his ability to understand and apply such rules in this instance is partly facilitated by the knowledge he has acquired about the nature of inter-personal cognition. Chains of this kind have a psychological validity for him; he has long known that human thinking can have this "wheels within wheels" character, where one person's thought can become the object of another (or the same) person's thought, and so on ad infinitum. He knows, in other words, that recursiveness *is* a potential characteristic of this sort of thinking, and hence he quickly catches on to the kind of series one is commencing in saying, "He thinks that, etc."

We expect that the young child would not "catch on" so readily, in part because he has not yet acquired this supporting competence in role-taking matters. It is not that recursive rules would necessarily give him trouble in any and all situations. We could imagine, for instance, that he is already familiar with the recursive properties of certain sorts of events, and would therefore need only to access that familiarity from memory storage in the same way that the adult presumably does in the case of, "He thinks, etc."

We might get some empirical evidence on these matters in the following way. An attempt would be made to assess the comparative difficulty of two problems which demand the induction of recursive rules. In one the child might be shown, say, a "recursive picture" of a man holding a picture of a man holding a picture of a man holding . . . , and tested for his ability to grasp the principle of the picture's construction, to recognize that only artistic and visual limitations keep the series from being extended indefinitely. In the other the child is similarly tested on a role-taking series of the kind we have been discussing. We would in any event be curious about the age at which the latter problem becomes easily solved, and about the partial solutions and semi-insights which may precede an adult-level understanding. We would also be curious, in addition, to see whether the first problem is systematically easier than the second. If it were, it would suggest that the difficulties experienced with series like, "He thinks, etc." do not reside solely in the fact that these series entail recursive rules. This line of inquiry would of course also open up further possibilities for causal-analytic studies, for example, to find out if insight into the recursive nature of such cognitions is correlated with performance on other role-taking tasks.

Communication Studies. Even less is known about early communicative skills than about early role-taking ones. Study of preschool communication behavior should at the very least provide additional—and perhaps clearer—data on the sorts of immature communicative forms which we encountered in our younger school-age Ss. A more important justification for such study, however, would be the possibility of identifying forms which even our youngest Ss had entirely outgrown, and hence of contributing something new to the developmental-descriptive picture.

Gestural communication is another area which would repay close study. We expect that young children have difficulties here exactly analogous to those they encounter in verbal communication. Tasks based on the familiar game of charades might be useful vehicles for developmental research on gestural communication. We could, for example, look for revealing ontogenetic changes in the way the child attempts to portray for an audience, via gesture alone, some commonplace action or familiar animal. We suspect that the young child would pay more attention to whether his gestures satisfied him as adequate expressive-iconic symbols for the object or event in question than to the representational processes they might plausibly elicit in his audience; we would likely see, in other words, the gestural equivalent of the coding-for-self-alone strategy which so often seems to characterize the young child's verbal messages.

An alternative approach would be to adapt Task IIE for gestures instead of words. Here is one of several possible ways it might be done. The child is told that he is about to witness a gestural communication of some message in company with another individual (an experimental confederate); the child knows what the message is to be, but the confederate supposedly does not. After part or all of the gestural sequence has been shown, the confederate makes a plausible but erroneous interpretation and the child is to suggest reasons why the confederate might have made that particular inference from the gestural evidence. As in Task ID, the gestures become "polarized" in meaning for the child by virtue of his knowing beforehand what the message is to be, and his problem in this task is to "unpolarize" them—to see and continue to see them through the eyes of the naïve, uncoached confederate. Developmental changes here would, in other words, be interpreted as reflecting acquisitions within the *Maintenance* component.

Jarvis' study was our only attempt to investigate developmental changes in the child's response to listener feedback regarding the success of his message. Moreover, the feedback employed had specific features which distinguish it from other varieties commonly encountered in everyday communication situations. The feedback was negative rather than positive; verbal rather than gestural; salient rather than minimal; and once-occurring rather than repeatedly occurring during the ongoing message. It might be worthwhile to look for developmental changes in the effects of other types of feedback; that is, feedback showing other combinations of the above-mentioned attributes. We would be interested, for example, in studying age differences in the child's sensitivity to minimal gestural evidence regarding the adequacy of his communication—to the listener's puzzled frown or slight head shakings at this point in the message, to his yes-I-understand-all-that-let's-get-on-with-it head noddings and facial expressions of impatience at some other point in the message, and so forth. Responses to such cues figure prominently in the behavior of a highly skilled communicator, but we know nothing whatever about their ontogenesis.

There was likewise only a single investigation of age changes in persuasive communication (Study IIC), and this important form of social behavior surely deserves more intensive study. In our discussion of Study IIC in Chapter 4 we suggested an approach which, as with the gestural communication study just proposed, would constitute a variation on the Task IIE method. The child is first presented with a specific persuasion problem: this individual wishes to persuade that individual to do thus and so. Information is given about persuasion-relevant characteristics of the individuals concerned and of the setting in which the persuasive attempt is to be made. The child's task is not to compose a persuasive message, as it was in Study IIC, but to evaluate already-prepared messages or components of messages. He would be asked to choose among or rank order sets of alternative persuasive arguments in terms of their predicted effectiveness in this particular context, and also to justify his choices or rankings. Rationalized judgments of this sort would be obtained across a variety of problems, problems involving different persuaders, persuasees, persuasive objectives, and settings. We would expect to find an increasing preference with age for more subtle and roundabout techniques for manipulating the listener's behavior, and also more variation in favored techniques to deal with problems—recall the results of our studies of informative communication where the role attributes of the listener were made to vary. We think that studies like this could give a richer and more valid picture of what develops and when than could studies like IIC, where so much depends upon the child's ability to devise and execute persuasion strategies "on his feet."

Final Comments

We have described a number of causal-analytic and developmental-descriptive research problems which strike us as worthy of investigation, and have also made general suggestions as to how some of them might be investigated. The various lines of inquiry proposed serve to enrich—to further extend and further differentiate—the research domain implied by "role-taking development" and "communicative development." They serve to indicate how many research questions, and how many different *kinds* of research questions, are available for the asking here. It now remains only to be pointed out that the domain is still not completely specified by adding together what we have done and what we have just said ought to be done.

In the case of "role-taking development," there remains the whole conceptual space populated by whatever is meant by "empathy" and "sympathy," that is, role-taking activities (often passing into role-enactment activities) which bear on the emotional attributes of the other and which usually entail affective responses in the self. There is likewise a space involving the as yet cloudy linkages between what we have construed as role taking and the referents of such terms as "imitation," "internalization," "introjection," "identification," and "projection." One could no doubt add spaces by reading Tagiuri and Petrullo (1958) and current journals which report research in personality and social psychology.

The same argument is at least as valid in the case of "communicative development." There are whole aspects of this development about which almost no one has even raised questions. The linguistic anthropologist Dell Hymes is one of the few exceptions, and he here indicates some of the relevant variables.

The end result of verbal development is a child who can produce utterances characterized not only by grammaticalness, but also by appropriateness. Put otherwise, the child not only knows the grammatical rules of its language, but also its speaking rules or some portion of them. Its conduct shows some knowledge of expectations as to when speech is obligatory, when proscribed, when informative as an act by virtue of being optional. It shows some knowledge of a system of speaking, a system characterized partly by the fact that not all theoretically possible combinations of such various factors of speech events as senders and addressors, receivers and addressees, channels, settings, codes and subcodes, topics, message-forms can appropriately co-occur. It shows some knowledge of the hierarchy of functions which may characterize speech generally, or speech events particularly, in its society. And such knowledge is necessary, for of course it is not enough for the child to be able to produce any grammatical utterance. It would have to remain speechless if it could not decide which grammatical utterance here and now, if it could not connect utterances with situations (1964, p. 110).

It is clear that the ability to inform or persuade forms a part of Hymes' "end result of verbal development," but only a part; there remains much more that gets developed, and hence much more for psychologists to study the development of.

Bibliography

Abelson, R. P., & Lesser, G. S. The measurement of persuasibility in children. In C. I. Hovland & I. L. Janis (Eds.), *Personality and persuasibility*. New Haven: Yale Univer. Press, 1959. Pp. 141-166. (a)

Abelson, R. P., & Lesser, G. S. A developmental theory of persuasibility. In C. I. Hovland & I. L. Janis (Eds.), *Personality and persuasibility*. New Haven: Yale Univer. Press, 1959. Pp. 167-186. (b)

Ausubel, D. P., Schiff, H. M., & Gasser, E. B. A preliminary study of developmental trends in socioempathy: accuracy of perception of own and others' sociometric status. *Child Develpm.*, 1952, **23**, 111-128.

Bruner, J. S. Inhelder and Piaget's *The growth of logical thinking*. I A psychologist's viewpoint. *Brit. J. Psychol.*, 1959, **50**, 363-370.

Bruner, J. S., Goodnow, J. J., & Austin, G. A. *A study of thinking*. New York: Wiley, 1956.

Burns, N., & Cavey, L. Age differences in empathic ability among children. *Canad. J. Psychol.*, 1957, **11**, 227-230.

Cameron, N. Experimental analysis of schizophrenic thinking. In J. S. Kasanin (Ed.), *Language and thought in schizophrenia*. Berkeley: Univer. Calif. Press, 1954. Pp. 50-62.

Cowan, P. A. Cognitive egocentrism and social interaction in children. Paper read at Amer. Psychol. Ass., New York, September, 1966.

Cronbach, L. J. Processes affecting scores on "understanding of others" and "assumed similarity." *Psychol. Bull.*, 1955, **52**, 177-193.

Cronbach, L. J. Proposals leading to analytic treatment of social perception scores. In R. Tagiuri & L. Petrullo (Eds.), *Person perception and interpersonal behavior*. Stanford: Stanford Univer. Press, 1958. Pp. 353-379.

Dymond, R. F., Hughes, A. S., & Raabe, V. L. Measurable changes in empathy with age. *J. consult. Psychol.*, 1952, **16**, 202-206.

Elkind, D. Piaget's conceptions of right and left: Piaget replication study IV. *J. genet. Psychol.*, 1961, **99**, 269-276.

Elkind, D. Children's conceptualizations of brother and sister: Piaget replication study V. *J. genet. Psychol.*, 1962, **100**, 129-136.

Ervin, S. M., & Miller, W. R. Language development. In H. W. Stevenson et al. (Eds.), *Child psychology: 62nd yearbook of the National Society for the Study of Education*. Chicago: Univer. of Chicago Press, 1963. Pp. 108-143.

Feffer, M. H. The cognitive implications of role taking behavior. *J. Pers.*, 1959, **27**, 152-168.

Feffer, M. H., & Gourevitch, V. Cognitive aspects of role-taking in children. *J. Pers.*, 1960, 28, 383-396.

Feffer, M., & Suchotliff, L. Decentering implications of social interaction. *J. Pers. soc. Psychol.*, 1966, 4, 415-422.

Flavell, J. H. *The developmental psychology of Jean Piaget.* Princeton, N. J.: Van Nostrand, 1963.

Fry, C. L. The effects of training in communication and role perception on the communicative abilities of children. Unpublished doctoral dissertation, Univer. of Rochester, 1961.

Fry, C. L. Training children to communicate to listeners. *Child Develpm.*, 1966, 37, 675-685.

Gage, N. L., & Cronbach, L. J. Conceptual and methodological problems in interpersonal perception. *Psychol. Rev.*, 1955, 62, 411-422.

Gage, N. L., Leavitt, G. S., & Stone, G. C. The intermediary key in the analysis of interpersonal perception. *Psychol. Bull.*, 1956, 53, 258-266.

Gates, G. S. An experimental study of the growth of social perception. *J. educ. Psychol.*, 1923, 14, 449-462.

Gollin, E. S. Forming impressions of personality. *J. Pers.*, 1954, 23, 65-76.

Gollin, E. S. Organizational characteristics of social judgment: a developmental investigation. *J. Pers.*, 1958, 26, 139-154.

Gough, H. G. A sociological theory of psychotherapy. *Amer. J. Sociol.*, 1948, 53, 359-366.

Hartley, E. L., & Hartley, R. E. *Fundamentals of social psychology.* New York: Knopf, 1955.

Harvey, O. J., Hunt, D. E., & Schroder, H. M. *Conceptual systems and personality organization.* New York: Wiley, 1961.

Hess, R. D., & Shipman, V. C. Early experience and the socialization of cognitive modes in children. *Child Develpm.*, 1966, 36, 869-886.

Hovland, C. I., Janis, I. S., & Kelley, H. H. *Communication and persuasion: psychological studies of opinion change.* New Haven: Yale Univer. Press, 1953.

Hovland, C. I., et al. *The order of presentation in persuasion.* New Haven: Yale Univer. Press, 1957.

Hovland, C. I., et al. *Personality and persuasibility.* New Haven: Yale Univer. Press, 1959.

Hymes, D. Formal discussion: In U. Bellugi & R. Brown (Eds.), The acquisition of language. *Monogr. Soc. Res. Child Develpm.*, 1964, 29 (1), 107-112.

Kagan, J., Rosman, B. L., Day, D., Albert, J., & Phillips, W. Information processing in the child: significance of analytic and reflective attitudes. *Psychol. Monogr.*, 1964, 78, No. 1. (Whole No. 578)

Kaplan, E. An experimental study on inner speech as contrasted with external speech. Unpublished MA thesis, Clark Univer., 1952.

Kraus, R. M., & Glucksberg, S. Some aspects of verbal communication in children. Paper read at Amer. Psychol. Ass., Chicago, September, 1965.

Leavitt, H. J., & Mueller, R. A. H. Some effects of feedback on communication. *Hum. Relat.*, 1951, 4, 401-410.

Lovell, K. A follow-up of some aspects of the work of Piaget and Inhelder on the child's conception of space. *Brit. J. educ. Psychol.*, 1959, **29**, 107-117.

Maccoby, E. E. Role-taking in childhood and its consequences for social learning. *Child Develpm.*, 1959, **30**, 239-252.

McCarthy, D. Language development in children. In L. Carmichael (Ed.), *Manual of child psychology*. (2nd ed.) New York: Wiley, 1954. Pp. 492-630.

Maclay, H., & Newman, S. Two variables affecting the message in communication. In D. K. Wilner (Ed.), *Decisions, values and groups*. New York: Pergamon, 1960. Pp. 218-229.

Mead, G. H. Language and the development of the self. In T. M. Newcomb & E. L. Hartley (Eds.), *Readings in social psychology*. New York: Henry Holt, 1947. Pp. 179-189.

Milgram, N. Cognitive and empathic factors in role-taking by schizophrenic and brain damaged patients. *J. abnorm. soc. Psychol.*, 1960, **60**, 219-224.

Milgram, N., & Goodglass, H. Role style versus cognitive maturation in word associations of adults and children. *J. Pers.*, 1961, **29**, 81-93.

Moore, O. K. Problem solving and the perception of persons. In R. Tagiuri & L. Petrullo (Eds.), *Person perception and interpersonal behavior*. Stanford: Stanford Univer. Press, 1958. Pp. 131-150.

Murphy, L. B. *Social behavior and child personality: an exploratory study of some roots of sympathy*. New York: Columbia Univer. Press, 1937.

Neale, J. M. Egocentrism in institutionalized and noninstitutionalized children. *Child Develpm.*, 1966, **37**, 97-101.

Newcomb, T. M. An approach to a theory of communicative acts. *Psychol. Rev.*, 1953, **60**, 393-404.

Phillips, T., & Feffer, M. The use of an experimental confederate in password interaction: a preliminary report. Unpublished paper, 1966.

Piaget, J. *The language and thought of the child*. New York: Harcourt, Brace, 1926.

Piaget, J. *Judgment and reasoning in the child*. New York: Harcourt, Brace, 1928.

Piaget, J. Comments on Vygotsky's critical remarks concerning *The Language and Thought of the Child*, and *Judgment and Reasoning in the Child*. Attachment to L. S. Vygotsky, *Thought and language*. Cambridge, Mass. and New York: M.I.T. Press and Wiley, 1962.

Piaget, J., & Inhelder, B. *The child's conception of space*. London: Routledge and Kegan Paul, 1956.

Piaget, J., & Inhelder, B. *La genèse des structures logiques élémentaires: classifications et sériations*. Geneva: Delachaux et Niestlé, 1959.

Ratner, S. C., Darling, M. L., & Jackman, C. The effect of the listener on spoken communication. Paper read at Amer. Psychol. Ass., New York, August, 1957.

Rothenberg, B. B. Children's ability to comprehend adults' feelings and motives. Paper read at Soc. Res. Child Develpm. Meetings, New York, March, 1967.

Ruesch, J., & Bateson, G. *Communication: the social matrix of psychiatry*. New York: Norton, 1951.

Sarbin, T. R. Role theory. In G. Lindzey (Ed.), *Handbook of social psychology.* Vol. 1. Cambridge, Mass.: Addison-Wesley, 1954. Pp. 223-258.

Schatzman, R., & Strauss, A. Social class and modes of communication. *Amer. J. Sociol.,* 1955, **60,** 329-338.

Skinner, B. F. *Verbal behavior.* New York: Appleton Century, 1958.

Smith, M. Communicative behavior. *Psychol. Rev.,* 1946, **53,** 294-301.

Strunk, O. Empathy: a review of theory and research. *Psychol. Newsletter,* 1957, **9,** 47-57.

Sullivan, H. S. *The interpersonal theory of psychiatry.* New York: Norton, 1953.

Sullivan, H. S. The language of schizophrenia. In J. S. Kasanin (Ed.), *Language and thought in schizophrenia.* Berkeley: Univer. Calif. Press, 1954. Pp. 4-15.

Swinson, M. E. The development of cognitive skills and role-taking. *Dissert. Abstr.,* 1966, **26** (7), 4082.

Taft, R. The ability to judge people. *Psychol. Bull.,* 1955, **52,** 1-23.

Tagiuri, R., & Petrullo, L. (Eds.) *Person perception and interpersonal behavior.* Stanford: Stanford Univer. Press, 1958.

Vygotsky, L. S. *Thought and language.* Cambridge, Mass. and New York: M.I.T. Press and Wiley, 1962.

Wallach, M. A. Research on children's thinking In H. W. Stevenson et al. (Eds.), *Child psychology: 62nd yearbook of the National Society for the Study of Education.* Chicago: Univer. of Chicago Press, 1963. Pp. 236-276.

Walton, W. E. Emphatic responses in children. *Psychol. Monogr.,* 1936, 48, No. 1. (Whole No. 213)

Werner, H., & Kaplan, B. *Symbol formation: an organismic-developmental approach to language and the expression of thought.* New York: Wiley, 1963.

Witkin, H. A. Origins of cognitive style. In C. Scheerer (Ed.), *Cognition: theory, research, promise.* New York: Harper, 1964. Pp. 172-205.

Wolfe, R. The role of conceptual systems in cognitive functioning at varying levels of age and intelligence. *J. Pers.,* 1963, **31,** 108-123.

Zajonc, R. B. The process of cognitive tuning in communication. *J. abnorm. soc. Psychol.,* 1960, **61,** 159-167.

Zimmerman, C., & Bauer, R. A. The effect of an audience upon what is remembered. *Publ. opin. Quart.,* 1956, **20,** 238-248.

Author Index

Subject Index

Accuracy, as criterion of role prediction, 27-29

Activity, as dimension in role taking, 27-29, 30
measured by task IB, 44

Additions, in simplifying recodings, 125

Adult role taking, 23-29; *see also* Role-taking skills

Advantage to others, argument of, 143

Age, and adequacy of communication, 154, 158-159
and communication skills, 39-41, 82, 94, 101, 128, 129, 132, 154
and multi-listener communication, 106, 112, 116
and perceptual role taking, 144
and persuasiveness, 139
and prediction of preferences, 165
and role enactment, 147, 151-154, 210
and role-taking skills, 30, 31, 32, 34, 35
and spatial perception, 64-68
and use of causal connectives, 74
and use of feedback, 184, 186, 189, 190, 225-226
and variety of verbal content, 93
see also Early childhood; Middle childhood and adolescence

Antecedent-consequent attack, 3

Application, 208
described, 210
in early childhood, 211
in middle childhood, 215

Argument, as evidence of role-taking skill, 54

Arguments, number of, related to age, 140

Audiences, effect of on communication, 36-39
multi-listener, 103

Auditory stimuli, and role taking, 35

Behavioral audacity, in role enactment, 148, 149, 151

Causal-analytic questions, 217-222
correlations among tasks, 217
variables associated with role-taking skills, 218

Cognitive style, and role-taking skill, 220

Collective monologue, 39

Communicating situations, 105
relative difficulty of, 113
in Task IE, 107

Communication skills, adult, 36-39
effective, defined, 129
effects of training, 196, 200
egocentric, 8
expressed in gestures, 225
informative, 9, 135
inhibition of, 134, 200, 202
lack of, 101
means of studying, 3, 4, 208
nature and development of, 4-12, 208
nonegocentric, 9
persuasive, 10, 135
questions related to research of, 224
and recoding, 10
and role-attribute discrimination, 11-12
studies of in middle childhood, 82-122, 123-129
theory of, 12-23
variation with age, 94

Concept, in tests of role-taking ability, 32

Conjunctive concepts, 120

Connectives, use of causal, 74-75

Context of role-attribute discrimination, 6-8
Sarbin on, 6

Correlational analysis, factorial, 217
of other psychological behavior, 217

Covert activity in role taking, 7, 23